Introduction
to
Gerontology

Introduction to Gerontology

ARTHUR N. SCHWARTZ

and

JAMES A. PETERSON

Ethel Percy Andrus Gerontology Center
University of Southern California

Holt, Rinehart and Winston

New York   Chicago   San Francisco   Dallas
Montreal   Toronto   London   Sydney

PHOTO CREDITS: Hal Smith, pages 20, 63, 69, 14, 121, 141, 145, 152, 157, 159, 182, 187, 200, 210, 230, 251, 267, 285; Arthur N. Schwartz, pages 9, 36, 97, 167, 225, 246, 283; Andrus Gerontology Center, pages 262, 284; John King, page 31; American Forest Industries, page 85; *Survival Handbook for Children of Aging Parents* (Chicago: Follett), page 115

Library of Congress Cataloging in Publication Data

Schwartz, Arthur N
   Introduction to gerontology.

   Bibliographies:
   Includes indexes.
   1. Gerontology. I. Peterson, James Alfred, joint author. II. Title. [DNIM: 1. Geriatrics. WT100.3 S399i]
HQ1061.S347   362.6'042   78-21890
ISBN 0-93-019506-3

Foreword

When the University of Southern California first formed an organizing committee in 1964 to develop a comprehensive program of research and education about aging, there were barely a half-dozen institutions in the country that had pioneered the field and could serve as models. Research in the field was sparse and training almost nonexistent. Since then the field has grown exponentially. Today over fifteen hundred institutions of higher learning have courses in aging. Gerontology has become a major focus of a great many schools. Because of this the need for textbooks that can integrate the findings of the various disciplines in both introductory and advanced treatments has become imperative. *Introduction to Gerontology* has just such a purpose as its goal.

No single text can adequately treat in depth all of the research or all the programs for aging that are now available. The authors have wisely included after each section a selection of further readings that have been carefully chosen to enable students to read more comprehensively about various aspects of aging. The book has some valuable emphasis such as its review of various theoretical frameworks in the field; its summary of the findings of the last White House Conference; its unique chapter on religion and aging. The book tries to stimulate the thinking of students by listing basic issues raised in each chapter about the subject matter. Students are thus introduced to the growing edges of thinking about our graying population.

Doctors Peterson and Schwartz are long-term members of the gerontology team at the Andrus Gerontology Center at the University of Southern California. They bring a special dimension to the Center and to this book in that they are both scientists and therapists. Thus they have added case studies and humane insight to their discussions of theoretical and research issues. It is essential that gerontologists develop increasing insight into the many facets of aging, but it is equally important that the focus is always on the aging of individual persons. This book tries to maintain that essential balance between accurate reporting and awareness of persons, so that the uniqueness of the older person is not lost in statistics. On the other hand, generalizations from statistics enable us to deal more adequately with the individual.

Legislative programs, new research findings, and political changes are making an impact in the field of gerontology every day. It is interesting that changes in the Social Security law and the age of retirement came about just as this text was completed, an illustration of how important it is for any teacher to up-date his or her materials month by month. For writers this means that books on gerontology must be constantly brought up-to-date; for instructors it means a creative use of new research reports, changes in government programs and policies, and economic indices if they are to deal adequately with their field.

This text is a "first" in that it is the first book specially designed and written to provide a general introduction to the field of gerontology. The authors have accomplished this remarkably well and as a "plus" have succeeded in producing a substantive, information-packed text that is eminently readable. It will fill a gap in the gerontological literature.

JAMES E. BIRREN
Director and Dean
Andrus Gerontology Center
The University of Southern California

Preface

This volume is an introduction to the major issues and concepts pertinent to the study of the aging process—gerontology. Gerontology is a broad field of study that concerns itself with every aspect of human functioning in the later years of life. It is to be distinguished from *geriatrics,* the term commonly used to denote that special branch of medicine devoted to the study of the diseases of old age.

Many students in the process of developing a professional identification, as well as those who have already identified themselves professionally in such areas as nursing, mental health, physical and occupational therapy, nutrition, social work, and the like, now wish to apply their particular interests and skills in the field of gerontology. Many policy makers and service providers, such as business, governmental, and agency persons and volunteers as well, must make decisions and provide services now. Such persons must carry out their functions and responsibilities from a base of knowledge and accurate information rather than from stereotypes and myths about the aged and the aging process. It is to this diverse group of persons who wish to get a good start in the field that *Introduction to Gerontology* is directed.

Our purpose is to provide a fair and reasonably well-balanced overview of gerontology. We have placed a greater emphasis on the pragmatic application of gerontological knowledge to the problems of the aged than to theoretical and academic approaches. This special concentration on practical applications and on the practitioner that permeates the book is not intended to minimize the reader's interest in research. Quite the contrary, our primary goal is to present information about aging so as to underscore its heuristic value to those who work with aging in a direct, clinical fashion as well as those who develop research studies based on theoretical models. Because it impinges on every aspect of human living and behavior, gerontology must attend to many different kinds of information. Traditionally, the study of aging has been divided into discrete categories and topics. Such an approach is almost impossible to avoid, and this text is, in general, organized in this way. For pragmatic reasons, however, we have felt it necessary to arrange all such bits and pieces into some sensible and meaningful themes in order to enable the reader to get a "handle" on aging. The subject of death and dying, for example, is discussed in several chapters other than the chapter so titled simply because this subject, like others, must be considered in several contexts.

We make no claim to presenting the *facts* about aging completely without bias. For one, we hold that the study of aging should ultimately help improve the lives of people in their later years. For another, we believe that the maintenance of competent living and the enhancement of self-esteem for each individual are issues of paramount importance in the field of aging. Finally, we believe that the study of gerontology is not a fixed or static body of "facts" or findings; rather, it is a dynamic, complex field which must, like medicine or psychology, continuously relate itself to the ever-changing, dynamic variables characteristic of the field.

A book such as this, stemming from a point of view, cannot, therefore, presume to be all things to all people. We have tried to keep in mind that the purpose of *Introduction to Gerontology* is precisely what the title indicates: to introduce the reader to the salient issues, research, problems, and current service approaches to gerontology. We hope it will provide the "generalist" in the field with what he or she needs and wants to know, and leave to the specialist a range of choices for further detailed exploration and study.

A.N.S. / J.N.P.

Contents

PART III / PHYSIOLOGY AND PSYCHOLOGY

PART IV / THE DISCIPLINE OF GERONTOLOGY

CHAPTER 11 / GERONTOLOGY: A NEW SCIENCE?   257

CHAPTER 12 / GERONTOLOGY: ITS CONTRIBUTIONS AND PROSPECTS   275

Introduction
to
Gerontology

Frames
of
Reference

CHAPTER 1

Some Perspectives on Aging

I like Spring, but it is too young
I like Summer, but it is too proud
So I like best of all Autumn

Because its leaves are a little yellow
Its tone mellower
Its colors richer

And it is tinged a little with sorrow
Its golden richness speaks
    not of the innocence of spring
    nor of the power of summer

But of the mellowness and kindly wisdom
    of approaching age

It knows the limitations of life
    and is content.

LIN YUTANG

As a first formal introduction to gerontology, this chapter presents a number of frames of reference. This introduction is intended to help the student gain at the outset some sense of the "size and shape" of the field of gerontology. Other material presents a variety of concepts and issues involved in the study of aging.

Aging can be viewed from a broad, historical perspective, or from the individual, personal experience, which provides much of the richness of aging data. Still other perspectives grow out of the study of a variety of specific, separate, yet interrelated issues. This chapter helps the student identify and examine such perspectives.

Eventually the student will find it useful—indeed, necessary, we believe—to evolve his own individual "handle" on aging. This chapter will help him begin that process.

The following case is an edited version of a recent interview with an elderly woman which took place in a park located near the center of a large city. Even though this woman need not be considered "typical" of the elderly in our country, this interview nicely sets forth and illustrates many of the personal concerns of aged persons in our society. It also touches on a number of major issues to which gerontology devotes considerable attention. Some of these issues will be specified further along in the chapter.

AN INDIVIDUAL PERSPECTIVE ON AGING:
THE PERSONAL EXPERIENCE

Mrs. B. is a widow in her mid-seventies, residing near central city in a congested urban environment. She is a small woman with thinning gray/white hair, clean, neatly groomed though plainly dressed. She displays a few pieces of bright jewelry on her gnarled, blue-veined hands and arms. She lives in a tiny, shabby house embedded in a complex of run-down apartments and converted hotels, nearby a city park. That small greenbelt serves as a "living room" for her and her peers. She goes there to visit with acquaintances who happen by, to get a breath of fresh air, and to watch the comings and goings of ducks in the pond and people in the park.

Her first reaction when approached was to wave off the interviewer with her hands, saying "No, no!" while shaking her head. After some explanations were offered she was drawn into conversation which she then engaged in with obvious interest and enthusiasm. At the conclusion of the conversation she complimented the interviewer for not having accepted her initial brush-off. "You have to ease in with older people" was her wry comment.

Mrs. B.'s husband died six years ago. The months following his death were the most difficult time for her. The couple had no children, a fact she insists she has no regrets about. After her husband's death, several neighbors she had known for years also died within a short period of time. She has no deep or intimate relationships now and talked about periodic bouts of loneliness and severe depression. She says a close relationship with others is now impossible for her.

"You can't really trust old people," she says. "They'll be friends with you for a while and then they'll turn on you—or leave you." Yet, at another point in the conversation, she confessed that she wished she had a group of friends.

She has kin but has lost track of them. Anyway, she doesn't see relatives as a resource in old age because "you only cause friction if you move in."

She considers her health as good as that of anyone else her age because she "gets around pretty good." She believes if she got really sick she would have to hire a nurse or someone else to come in. The more frightening prospect for her is that if it were a prolonged illness she might be compelled to dispose of her belongings and move into a nursing home.

She says her life has been "just fine" until recently. She has plenty of energy and goes to dances for entertainment, but only if someone will take her. She still would like to go to "musical events" but is apprehensive about public transportation: It "costs so much," it's "confusing," and she's afraid "something might happen." She does her own marketing and visits a local bank to deposit her Social Security check, but finds these excursions emotionally draining and physically exhausting. Some of her acquaintances tell her she can get "help from the community," but she's not clear how this works or where or how to inquire.

A few months ago she caught the flu and she still feels the effects. Her appetite dropped off; even now she is not eating well. Also, "it's a lot of bother cooking for yourself," she says. She hasn't seen a physician but she plans to do so "soon." She says, "You can't go into old age gracefully. One day you feel just fine and the next day you'll be feeling bad."

She owns her home in a run-down, deteriorating, high-crime neighborhood. People frequently tell her how dangerous it is but she still insists she isn't afraid to live alone. "If they want to come in and kill me, it's all right with me." So far she feels financially secure and doesn't have to "rely on anyone for anything." She planned and saved for her "retirement," and thinks all young people should do the same. But she is worried about the possibility of having to give up her house "sometime, because of the taxes."

Mrs. B. says the old men in the park and at the dances are "just looking for someone to take care of them." She says this in a tone more of disappointment than disgust. "They can be a burden on a woman," she explains. She seems very positive in her insistence that she would never marry again—even a very rich man.

WHENCE OUR INTEREST IN AGING?
HISTORICAL PERSPECTIVE

Mrs. B.'s individual point of view as shown by the interview is an intriguing one. It is equally fascinating to compare her experience with the aging experience of others. The recurring pattern and unending cycle of human birth, maturing, and death continues to generate a seemingly endless source of fascination and curiosity. Human interest in every detail of the constantly evolving, unfolding drama of human existence is as old as human history.

Prior to this century certain individuals anticipated the systematic and scientific study of aging as we know it today. Francis Bacon, Francis Galton, and Benjamin Franklin are counted among the early writers and investigators in the field of aging. A Belgian scientist, Lambert Quételet (1796–1874), was one of the first to apply the concept of measures of central tendency in his inquiries into aging and birth and death rates in the early 1800s.

But primarily it was the advent of the twentieth century that marked the beginning of systematic studies of aging. In 1908 two significant books appeared, Minto's *The Problems of Age, Growth, and Death,* and Metchnikoff's *The Prolongation of Life.* These were followed by two widely cited classics in gerontology, G. Stanley Hall's *Senescence, the Second Half of Life* in 1922, and E. V. Cowdry's *Problems of Aging* in 1939. Hall, a specialist in child and adolescent psychology, was president of Clark University when he wrote *Senescence,* a monograph that grew out of his own concern about his anticipated retirement. Cowdry (according to O. Kaplan, now completing a definitive history of gerontology) is considered by some to be the "founding father" of modern gerontology. This judgment is based on Cowdry's seminal volume, his early recognition of the interdisciplinary nature of gerontology, his synthesizing skills in bringing together a variety of interests in this field, and the significant contribution of his organizational work, particularly in establishing the International Association of Gerontology (IAG).

Following these pioneering beginnings, the truly scientific study of aging seems to have begun to burgeon by the late 1930s through the 1940s. The study of aging began to attract national attention and support through a series of crucial, well-timed conferences. Particularly instrumental in this regard was the Josiah Macy Foundation, whose interest and activities led to the convening of a scientific meeting at Woods Hole, Massachusetts, in 1937, sponsored by the National Research Council and the Union of American Biological Societies. In the following year the National Research Council's committee on the biological processes of aging sponsored another conference.

The mobilizing of national conferences gained momentum during 1940–41. Such influential groups as the American Orthopsychiatric Association, the Medical Clinics of North America, the American Chemical Society, the Public Health Service, and the National Institutes of Health (NIH) sponsored conferences on topics related to aging. The issues ranged from aging as a public health problem, industrial aspects of aging workers, and intellectual changes with age, to such issues as mental health and psychotherapy for those in the later years of life. Many of the early concerns about aging raised in those days anticipated some of the contemporary issues in gerontology.

Pursuit of scientific inquiry into these questions about aging was interrupted by the involvement of the United States in World War II from 1941 to 1945. Following these war years, the resurgence of activity by gerontologists of every description was earmarked by the founding of the Gerontological Society of America, Inc., in 1945, with headquarters in Washington, D.C.

The National Advisory Committee was appointed in 1940, and it developed a unit on gerontology within the National Institutes of Health. This led to legislation that culminated in the establishment of the National Institute on Aging (NIA). Legislation authorizing this unit was signed into law in 1974. Robert Butler, a psychiatrist and gerontologist, became its first director in 1976.

The worldwide scope of the scientific study of aging was signaled by the organization of the International Association of Gerontology (IAG) in 1948. Its organizational meeting was held in Liège, Belgium. Gerontologists representing a variety of disciplines and gerontological interests throughout the world have attended subsequent triennial meetings of the International Congress in such diverse locations as London, St. Louis, Copenhagen, Washington, D.C., Vienna, Kiev (Russia), and Jerusalem.

A growing momentum for the scientific study of aging as well as increasing worldwide attention to professional planning and practice (delivery of services) has developed in the field of aging. There is a continuing debate as to whether or not gerontology has reached the stage of development where it might be recognized as a unique and formal discipline in its own right, as is the case with psychology, biology, astronomy, medicine, theology, and law.

Primary funding for interdisciplinary research and training comes from federal sources such as the National Institutes of Health (NIH), the Administration on Aging (AoA), National Institutes of Mental Health (NIMH) from the newer National Institute on Aging (NIA), from state agencies and departments of aging, and from private foundations such as the American Association of Retired Persons/National Retired Teachers Association (AARP/NRTA), now comprising almost 11 million members.

From the beginning, the name of the game has been survival. Until recently, relatively few individuals survived beyond what we now consider the middle years. Early seers like Cicero (Copley, 1967) recorded observations about the characteristics of the old but indicate that the average life span during early recorded history barely exceeded twenty years. Perhaps that is why old age, this relatively little studied phase of the life cycle, became the object of so much superstitious thinking.

The Trobriand Islanders and the Sinu of Japan believed the secret of long life among their forebears lay in their ancestors' ability to shed their skin like snakes. This same notion of rejuvenation as the secret of long life is embedded in the more familiar accounts of the Spanish explorer Ponce de León's legendary search for the "fountain of youth," primarily in that territory now known as Florida.

This yearning for longer life has dominated the fantasies and searching of people in all ages. People will travel great distances in the hope of discovering some special climate or a chemical that might prove to be the key to long life. Dr. Paul Niehaus in Switzerland has attracted people from all over the world who come to try his injections of ground-up, homogenized sheep embryos. If those fail, they may travel to Rumania where Dr. Ana Aslan offers to all comers an elixir called Gerovital, which promises to retard the aging process. Long life is so precious that pseudo- and quasi-scientific prescriptions lure hundreds of thousands of men and women into spending millions of dollars on dubious nostrums and treatments.

Until less than a half century ago, mystical, magical, and superstitious approaches to aging dominated much thinking about aging and long life. Those who did survive into their seventies and eighties were usually heralded as wise and enjoyed special status. As the natural purveyors of family, clan, or tribal history and wisdom, they lived relatively good lives, as well off as many elderly today, if not better. In the United States, with the gradual transition to and emphasis upon industrialization, urbanization, individual productivity, "progress," and youth, many long-livers, especially those who became infirm and destitute, were sent off to the "poor farm," and a poor answer for them it was.

MODERN GERONTOLOGY

In the twentieth century an entirely new phenomenon has appeared. Since 1900 the segment of the population sixty-five years old or older has increased much more rapidly than the rest of the population in the United States. In 1900 approximately 3 million Americans were sixty-five or older. Today, approximately 23 million (one out of every ten Americans) are sixty-five or older (seven times as many as in 1900). The number and proportion of those seventy-five or older has increased even more dramatically. Four out of every ten older persons, or approximately 8 million, are over seventy-five. The percentage of increase for different cohorts* between 1960 and 1970, for instance, is as follows:

*The use of the word "cohort" in gerontology refers to those members of a group born at approximately the same time.

TABLE 1–1. PERCENTAGE OF INCREASE FOR
DIFFERENT COHORTS

Age Group	Increase
Under 45	11.5
45–64	15.9
65+	21.1
65–74	13.0
75+	37.1

SOURCE: Weg (1977).

Today there are approximately 1.6 million people eighty-five years or older in the United States. These figures are cited to show the marked increase in the number of persons surviving into the seventh, eighth, and ninth decades of life in recent years.

These figures also indicate a major source of impetus for the current and growing interest in old age in the United States. Clearly, we are an aging society and we want to know why and how this is so, what it means to us now, how it will affect our society tomorrow, and what we should be doing about it.

This book is intended to introduce the reader to the field of inquiry and practice that addresses itself precisely to such questions, namely, the field of study and practice called gerontology. Professionals in the

As more people live longer, society's younger members are discovering that their elders have much of value to offer.

field distinguish between gerontology, the branch of knowledge dealing with the study of aging in general, and geriatrics, the branch of
medicine with specific concern about the diseases of old age. The word
"senescence" means simply "to grow old" and is used to refer to normal aging.

Nearly everyone acknowledges some difficulty in defining "old."
Bernard Baruch, in his eighties, when asked who he would call old,
is said to have remarked, "Anyone who is fifteen years older than I
am." Without question, definitions of "old" are influenced by the age
of the individual responding. Professional gerontologists, especially
those engaged in research, are inclined to refer, at least for purposes of
discussion, to biological age, psychological age, and social age.

Chronological age (elapsed time since birth) still serves, however, as
the most commonly used index of age. With the increasing familiarity
with long-livers in other societies (such as the Abkhazians in the Rus-
sian Caucasus, who are reputed to live to 115 and beyond), gerontologists are now beginning to speak of the "young-old" and the "old-old"
(Schmidt, 1975). The young-old are considered to be those roughly
between sixty and seventy-five; the old-old, those over seventy-five.
Some gerontologists believe the old-old have certain special characteristics related to their longevity.

GERONTOLOGICAL ISSUES AS A FRAME OF REFERENCE

History is replete with philosophical references to age. The existential experience of aging is highly colored by personal expectation and
attitude. Some of the fundamental issues to which scientists studying
aging and to which service providers must address themselves grow
out of theoretical speculations and hunches. Many other issues derive
from patterns of life circumstances and practical experiences such as
those described in the interview with Mrs. B. reported at the beginning
of the chapter. It will become evident as you proceed that the study of
aging is very pragmatic and will lead inevitably to practical conclusions and outcomes.

The following listing of issues is not exhaustive. It will, however,
indicate to the student some of the major "discovered territory" and
some of the current directions gerontology is taking.

1. *Health maintenance, nutrition (diet), and exercise:* What is the
desirable balance between health and other high-priority needs of the
aged? How is health care to be paid for and how is cost affected by
concepts of treatment, cure, and prevention? How is "health" to be

defined and what are significant contributions to physical well-being in old age?

2. *Family and marital relations:* What are the particular and unique problems faced by elderly parents of mature children? What are the marital difficulties and what are the obstacles to sensual and sexual satisfactions for the old? To what extent are age/generation differences responsible for family conflicts?

3. *Personality variables and adaptive coping mechanisms:* What are the significant changes that occur in later life and to what extent are these affected by physical or social factors? How stable are personality, intelligence factors, and learning ability throughout the life span? Are there different dimensions of stress in old age? What kinds of adaptation and coping strategies do the elderly use?

4. *Behavioral and cognitive competence:* Are there appropriate norms for competence in old age? What is the special significance of memory lapses and confusion? Is senile behavior a fact or an artifact, and are behaviors associated with brain damage reversible? Is compensation for losses an effective intervention?

5. *Migration and mobility:* How are the life satisfactions and morale of the aged affected by a mobile society? To what extent are the quality and cost of services to the elderly affected by transportation factors? What impact does migration have upon housing, education, health services, and family and friendship networks with respect to the aged?

6. *Attitudes, religious beliefs, and norms (expectations):* Are the expectations of the aged different from or similar to those of other age groups? How important are religion and its practice to the elderly? Do we have adequate relevant norms for old age or are these yet to be established? Are these positive or negative norms?

7. *Environmental planning, design, and impact:* Which environmental factors affect the aging process and how can these be measured? What should be the priorities when considering prosthetic environmental design versus cost? Should the environment be designed to "fit" the elderly or the elderly helped to fit the environment?

8. *Dying, bereavement, and grief:* What kinds of services and care do the dying need? How do we help the elderly deal with bereavement and grief? What problems arise from the preponderance of elderly widows, and what are their special needs? What emotional supports are needed for the dying and their families, and who should be trained to provide this?

9. *Economics and the elderly, work and productivity:* Is the traditional practice of retirement an anachronism? Are there alternative definitions of productivity more appropriate for the aged? How does inflation affect the elderly, and should they be given greater opportunities for work? Do work opportunities exploit the elderly?

10. *Public policy, planning, and administration:* Which decision makers most affect the lives of the elderly? How are policy decisions affecting the old made and implemented? On what basis is planning done, and what must administrators and service providers know to run effective and relevant programs for the elderly?

11. *Housing, congregate living, and long-term care:* How do individual preferences and life-style affect congregate living? What are the social implications and consequences of housing design and location for the elderly? Is long-term care truly a first alternative or a last resort? What congregate living models are most appropriate and relevant to elderly persons?

12. *Legal protection, crime, and safety:* How do the aged become special victims of crime? Are there special legal services needed by the old, and how are these to be provided? How much "protection" do the elderly need? When and where is advocacy for the old appropriate and who should provide it?

We recognize that other terms and formulations can be (and often are) used to denote these as well as other relevant issues in gerontology. Possible additions, for example, might include such important and pressing issues as education and training in gerontology, the appropriate utilization of the communications media to represent and serve the needs of the aged, the role of the expressive arts with respect to aging, and funding resources for research, practice, and information exchange on aging.

RESEARCH PERSPECTIVES

A prime source of vitality in the field of gerontology lies in the rich variety of its research and training programs. The broad spectrum of current research includes programs of inquiry into such matters as genetic determinants, cellular changes with age, attitude and role-status changes, methodological strategies, ecospace design, curricula development, and short-term training in mental health services. In other words, gerontology generates research, both pure and applied, about the kinds of issues indicated above.

A substantial proportion of all such research on aging has traditionally been and continues to be based in university settings. Yet the universities' involvement with aging has been and still is surprisingly limited when one considers the possibilities. Eight years ago Brackbill (1971) surveyed university training programs that offer four-year graduate training/research opportunities in gerontology. This survey identified barely a dozen universities that offered substantial gerontological content in their curricula. More recently the Storandt committee (1977) received 191 replies to a survey sent to 238 departments of psychology (80 percent). The results of this survey indicate that psychology has a long way to go before it can be said to be fully involved with the total life span. Of these responses, only sixteen claimed substantial academic programming in gerontology; eleven have new, developing, or proposed programs. The track record of other disciplines like law, medicine, and theology is little better.

Yet on balance it should be noted that gerontology is making an impact upon the educational system generally, as we shall discuss in the next chapter. At present more than 1,240 universities, colleges, and community colleges across the nation now report at least some course offering or program on the subject of aging (Sprouse, 1976).

Dissemination of information in aging research and practice is vital to the growth of gerontology. The Gerontological Society was founded to encourage the scientific study of and professional practice in gerontology. It is dedicated to the free exchange of such knowledge through its scientific meetings and through two official publications, *The Journal of Gerontology* and *The Gerontologist.* To facilitate dissemination of information, the society is organized into four special interest sections: Biological Sciences, Clinical Medicine, Behavioral and Social Sciences, and Social Research, Planning and Practice.

AGING AS AN INDIVIDUAL EXPERIENCE

When we take a demographic or like perspective on aging, we are dealing with aging as a group phenomenon. However, a great many events, some unique in terms of personal history, contribute to the individual's aging process, thus making that person's experience of aging very subjective and different from anyone else's. What gerontologists deal with is not simply the fact of growing older; rather, it is a matter of getting older in a special, unique way.

This is not to say that common features with regard to the experience do not exist among individuals. They do, indeed. Some gerontologists have attempted to cast elements of the aging process and experience in a conceptual frame that might serve as or lead to a universally accepted theory of aging. Unfortunately, no such widely agreed-upon definition or theory of aging currently exists. There is wide agreement that aging must be understood as a *process.* What makes arriving at a consensus so difficult is that aging is a complex, multidimensional process. In other words, we do not have any simple rationale as to what "causes" aging. The aging process occurs over time. Nevertheless, chronological age in itself does not explain or identify all components or elements of the process. We would, therefore, like to introduce at this point some additional perspectives on aging that, while age-related, are not specifically defined by chronological age.

LIFE-SPAN DEVELOPMENTAL PERSPECTIVE

The study of aging is complicated because aging is a multidimensional process. The life-span developmental approach attempts to take this into account. This approach seeks to give proper status and weight to a large number of interrelated factors while emphasizing the developmental theme along a longitudinal continuum. This frame of reference for the study of aging is based on the premise that human behavior evolves gradually from a diffuse, global pattern (at birth) toward greater differentiation until a peak is reached as we mature. Studies of aging that utilize this perspective focus on growth and development as a continuing process. They find that the peak period is pushed farther and farther along the chronological time span.

Among the elements that can be identified within this broad frame of reference are genetic determinants, biomedical and psychological factors, variations in life-style and attitudes, and learned abilities (including coping strategies). All of these are understood to combine in unique fashion to make up the ingredients embedded in what we call the developmental life cycle. These patterns of life-cycle events are shaped, in turn, by a variety of environmental factors, which include economic and cultural social forces.

THE DECREMENTAL MODEL OF AGING

Among the several existing aging models, the decremental (decline) model of aging appears to be the one subject to the most severe criticism. This model states that aging is inevitably associated with increasing mental and physical losses. There are at least two reasons for criticism. First, the decremental model tends to present a rather grim, in some respects a hopeless, view of aging. Second, this approach is usually seen to rely too heavily on inconclusive and, in some instances, inappropriate data, as is evident from extensive work done on intelligence and learning capacity in senescence (Schaie, 1975).

Another source of weakness in the irreversible decremental model (which includes purely biological theories) lies in the contradiction inherent in the great amount of variability characteristic of human aging. If functional decline is intrinsic to (that is, the built-in *result* of) old age, then logically it must occur universally, uniformly, and without exception in old age. Obviously, that is not the case. Functional decrement does not show up in all people of the same age, or even within a ten- or twenty-year range.

Unquestionably, genetic determinants have a role in setting limits and influencing patterns along which each of us ages. In spite of the respectable correlations between the longevity of parents and children, as an example of the role of heredity, genetic research has yet to clarify what the limits are and to what degree it influences the aging process.

THE BIOMEDICAL FRAME OF REFERENCE

"Aging is an infinitely eliminable variable," Birren (1959) has written. That is to say, many outcomes and events are initially attributed to the aging process itself until a different "causality" has been identified. At that point aging is eliminated as the causal variable. And so on with each new discovery.

A number of biomedical researchers have attempted to establish theories of aging based upon "causal" physiological data. Great caution in evaluating such formulations must be observed because of the temptation to be seduced into biological reductionism—the tendency to reduce complex events involved in the total experience of human aging to the level of mere biological processes. To do that can be just as misleading in the effort to understand aging as would be dissecting a flower, laying its several parts out side by side, and then looking for the "nature" or the beauty of the flower. The following paragraphs present a sample of biomedical formulations, which may be explored further in the references and suggested readings at the end of the chapter, among others.

One such theory of aging (pretty much outdated) might be labeled the "reservoir" theory (Curtis, 1966). It derives from the notion that each individual begins life with a limited amount of energy or vitality. The faster this energy is expended, the more quickly it is "used up" and the reservoir drained. An interesting parallel to this concept is the belief on the part of many men (once widely accepted) that too much or too vigorous sexual activity early in life will use up sexual vitality, "drain the reservoir," and leave one depleted in the later years. Another version is the notion of "exhaustion" of energy over time, analogous to the winding down of a watch spring.

Another theory closely allied to the above and still apparently enjoying some credence is a "wear-and-tear" theory of aging (Shock, 1977). By proposing an analogy between the human organism and a piece of machinery, this view holds that the parts of the body, like a machine, eventually wear out and thus the body breaks down. Like all arguments from analogy, this theory is deficient because it fails to account for the many exceptions to the rule. It also fails to take into account that many organ systems of the body, unlike mechanical systems, can repair themselves and can compensate for specific tissue loss or dysfunction.

Another interesting frame of reference, the "waste product" theory (Shock, 1977), contends that accumulations of the body's waste products account for the phenomenon of aging. Chemical wastes do, in fact, collect and do affect some body tissues. But there is little scientific evidence that under ordinary conditions this interferes with function in any significant manner or "causes" aging.

The "auto-immunity" or mutation theory (Makinodan, 1977) proposes that, with increasing age, mutations induce some body cells to produce protein to which the body responds. Not "recognizing" these "foreign" substances, the body proceeds to produce antibodies and through them an immunizing reaction to its own products. Walford (1969) cites evidence in support of this process by describing how the longevity of lab animals that were underfed during the early course of their lives was greatly increased. The organs that subsequently produce antibodies showed the greatest weight reduction. Undernutrition, especially in the earlier years of the organism's life, has an immuno-suppressing effect, according to Walford.

The special feature of this theory is that when mutations occur in DNA (genetic material that controls cell functioning), subsequent cell division perpetuates the mutations. According to the theory, as the number of mutated cells grows, organs made up of these changed cells become increasingly less efficient and dysfunctional and thus account for biological aging.

Although this formulation offers a promising line of research, geneticists are still cautious about fully embracing the explanation. They continue to investigate findings that point to only a minimum reduction in life expectancy in cases where mutations have occurred many times over.

The so-called error theory (Shock, 1977) is a broader and more complex variation on the mutation theory. Whereas the mutation theory deals particularly with the cumulative effects of mutations in DNA material, the "error" approach addresses itself to the cumulative effects of "mistakes" in a range of body processes, such as RNA synthesis, enzymic reactions, and protein synthesis, to name a few. Genetic and molecular "errors" can be brought about by literally scores of causes. Investigative strategies must therefore be geared to long-range programs of research if the role of these physiological mechanisms in the aging process is to be fully understood.

LIFE STAGES AS A FRAME OF REFERENCE

At quite a different conceptual level, the aging process has been described as an orderly series of stages through which each individual progresses. Organizing life experience has considerable popular appeal ("Oh, he's just going through a stage" is a familiar enough statement made with reference to children, adolescents, middle-agers, and the old).

Stages are usually defined as periods in life in which various roles are played out, periods to which are assigned "tasks" that must be accomplished. These tasks comprise the criteria embedded in successive developmental life themes. And most important, stages are linked to particular periods of chronological age.

Charlotte Buhler and her students developed a system of life stages from biographical and autobiographical material gathered during the 1930s in Vienna. They were interested in relating the course of life to biological development, as Freud (to a limited degree) had done.

Based upon some four hundred sources of biographical material, Buhler and her associates developed the following schema (1935):

Age Stage (approximate)	Developmental Theme or Task
0–15	Early growth in the home; prior to self-determination
15–25	Unfolding of sexual capabilities; testing of self-determination of life goals
25–45	Stable growth; crystallization of self-determined life goals
45–65	Phasing out of reproductive capacity; self-review and assessment of life goals
65 and beyond	Biological decline; continuation of life-satisfying activities or return to need-satisfying orientations of childhood

While Buhler's perspective places a useful emphasis on the individual process of goal setting for life, basically this formulation fails to emphasize the full potential for expansion and growth in the later years. It is a view that can be characterized as an expansion, culmination, and contraction life-cycle process.

Raymond Kuhlen (1968) has elaborated this theme by paying less attention to life stages as such and by emphasizing motivational factors within life-cycle events. He has proposed that motives change the life course because certain needs (such as the need for achievement, power, self-actualization, creativity) have been fulfilled and because of interim changes in social position. Yet he does concur in the notion that there is a "shift from active, direct gratifications . . . to gratifications obtained in a more indirect and vicarious fashion" in the latter half of life. He, too, thus subscribes to an expansion-contraction lifespan developmental view.

Erik Erikson (1963) developed his well-known scheme of life stages out of his clinical impressions and on the basis of Freudian and Jungian psychology. Erikson's contribution consists in his set of descriptions of "eight ages" of man as a series of crucial turning points from birth to death. Each stage represents a "crisis" as part of a developmental task, which crisis must be mastered before the individual moves on to the next sequential stage of life. Success or failure in the later developmental tasks depends, according to this view, upon having come to grips with and mastered the earlier crises.

Stage	*Task*
1. Oral/sensory	Trust vs. Basic Mistrust: testing of relationships, development of confidence
2. Muscular/anal	Autonomy vs. Shame and Doubt: learning to hold on and to let go
3. Locomotor/genital	Initiative vs. Guilt: developing assertiveness, rivalry, morality
4. Latency	Industry vs. Inferiority: developing task orientation, personal competence
5. Puberty/adolescence	Identity vs. Role Confusion: to find one's role in life as a sexual, productive, responsible adult with consistent attitudes about self
6. Young adulthood	Intimacy vs. Isolation: flowering of "genitality," mutuality with others
7. Adulthood	Generativity vs. Stagnation: expansion of ego interests, assuming adulthood responsibilities
8. Maturity/old age	Integrity vs. Despair: emotional integration, making sense of one's life

As can be seen, the major emphasis in this schema is put on the childhood stages of life, with relatively scant attention to the later years.

This particular mode of conceptualizing the life cycle has demonstrated widespread appeal. All such formulations of life "stages," as already pointed out, lean heavily upon chronological age as their overall criterion. Some developmental psychologists are critical of the stages approach because of this. The contrary argument is that time elapsed since birth is not of itself a very useful variable but rather a dimension for recording events (Bijou, 1968). Time as a gross indicator of physical maturation, or of cumulative interactions with the environment, or both, does nothing to advance a workable analysis of behavior and development. Patterns of behavior, in this view, are attributed to an age or stage in life, and thereby birthdays are given magical qualities.

COPING-RESPONSE FRAMES OF REFERENCE

The theories—or better, the frames of reference—touched upon so far exhibit at least one common view of aging: a bipolar growth-decline or expansion-contraction life-cycle theme. The perspectives cited in the following theories tend to give in varying degrees greater weight to adaptive processes in the later years.

The Disengagement Theory

In 1961, Cumming and Henry described a process that was held to be a basic characteristic of senescence. They report data that they interpret in the form of the disengagement theory of aging. In this view, contrary to the traditional notion that society tends unilaterally to isolate or reject the old, individuals in the later years themselves begin to limit their activities and literally begin to disengage themselves from the mainstream of life in preparation for the end and in response to a lower level of energy. Accordingly this process, as if by tacit agreement, is carried out in mutual fashion both by the elderly and by society.

The disengagement theory has serious limitations in accounting for much behavior in old age.

The Activity Theory

In sharp contrast to the disengagement theory stands the so-called activity theory. This formulation, developed by Robert Havighurst, was based on the same series of studies (Kansas City studies, undertaken by the Human Life Development group at the University of Chicago) that gave rise to the disengagement theory. The contention is

An older person's self-esteem is enhanced when emotional interdependence between generations is accepted.

that even though some reduction in levels of activity is to be expected in old age, the most successful agers are those who maintain the highest possible degree of involvement and activity, particularly physical activity.

Social interaction, ego investment in social roles, and change in role activity were the major aspects of behavior measured in developing this perspective. "Life satisfaction" is thus an important dimension of the activity theory. The older individual is considered to experience a high degree of emotional well-being (life satisfaction) if he (a) takes pleasure from activities of daily life; (b) views his life as meaningful and is accepting of life circumstances; (c) believes he has successfully achieved his major goals; (d) has a positive self-image; and (e) ordinarily maintains happy and optimistic attitudes and moods (Havighurst et al., 1968). At least several of these criteria are usually to be found in descriptions of those persons characterized as "successful agers." Lack of such characteristics appears to correlate highly with poor adjustment to aging.

PERSON/ENVIRONMENT TRANSACTIONAL PERSPECTIVES

The foregoing frames of reference allude to or imply the moderating effects of environmental factors upon life-cycle events. A more detailed examination of these formulations indicates their focus is primarily on physiological and/or psychological factors. Just how and to what extent external environmental variables influence the aging process is not consistently identified or clarified. Moreover, all these approaches, almost without exception, tend to place major emphasis on the incremental-decremental (growth-decline) model of life span development, although this is not so marked among the activity theorists.

The person/environment transactional view (Schwartz, 1974), on the other hand, places great emphasis upon the interaction between and mutual influencing of the individual and his or her environment. It further tends to underscore potential continuous and expanding growth and development even throughout the later years.

Within this transactional frame of reference, positive self-regard (self-esteem) is viewed as the psychological foundation that provides the basis for competence throughout the life span. Multiple losses (or decrements) accumulating through the middle and later years are seen as working against the maintenance of self-esteem. According to this notion, then, successful aging depends on structuring or modifying the environment in such ways as to compensate the elderly for losses—physical, social, economic, psychological. Given appropriate compensation, the senescent individual can continue to function quite effectively and with great satisfaction. This frame of reference proposes that the aging process itself as well as services to the aged be assessed on the basis of what does—or does not—contribute to and enhance self-esteem. Whatever in the way of services to the elderly, for example, is inhibiting of or contrary to the maintenance of self-esteem needs to be modified or eliminated altogether.

Experimental work by Aloia (1973), Schwartz and Proppe (1969), Seligman (1973), Lawton (1974), and Moos (1975) lends empirical support to such an approach to the aging process.

Rather than incremental/decremental steps or stages of life, this way of characterizing the life cycle is cast in terms of a continuous, dynamic process of adaptation and growth. In contrast to the decremental model, this view holds that the aging process consists of coexistent elements of decline and renewal, given the compensations for loss required for continued competence throughout the life span. An essential psychodynamic aspect of the person/environmental transactional view is that life-cycle events are as much influenced by current situational events and by goal-oriented problem solving, resolution of conflict, and maintenance of self-esteem factors as they are by biomedical-genetic variables.

THE DEVELOPMENTAL CYCLE LOOKED AT AS AGE OR GENERATIONAL DIFFERENCES

The phrase "generation gap," insofar as it indicates differences between generations with respect to values, attitudes, life-styles, and performance, points up an important caution that students of gerontology must exercise when assessing research data. Care must be taken to distinguish between *age* differences and *generational* (cohort—that is, persons born at approximately the same time) differences.

Most aging research is cross-sectional research. In cross-sectional research the investigator has identified samples of persons representing two or more age groups, say, a sample of thirty-year-olds and a sample of seventy-year-olds. The groups are measured for a selected variable or series of variables that the investigator wishes to study. Such variables may be life satisfaction, response time on a specific task, attitude toward retirement, and so on. The measured differences between groups (assuming the measures are valid and reliable) are presumed to represent age differences.

Such a procedure seems straightforward enough, but it does present problems peculiar to aging research. Every student of gerontology, whether researcher, practitioner, or administrator, needs to be fully cognizant of these problems.

The major difficulty regarding such differences is that the results of such comparisons may be reflecting generational rather than age values. Following an individual or group of individuals across twenty or thirty years (longitudinal studies) and taking repeated measures on selected variables may show differences occurring at subsequent points in time. One can, with a high degree of confidence, claim these as *age* differences (assuming all other variables are controlled) because they occur in the same individual(s) as a function of time.

A seventy-nine-year-old tested today was born sometime during 1900. His life experiences include growing up before the advent of television and jet air travel, in a largely rural era within the context of the extended family, with less opportunity or inducement for education beyond the eighth grade, and living through a traumatic period of severe economic depression and two world wars. Such an individual belongs to a cohort (generation) significantly different experientially from the younger member of the same research project who was born thirty years later. Differences, measured in that way, therefore, may be as much attributable to different life experiences and a different socio-cultural environment as to the mere passage of time (chronological age).

The student of gerontology must, therefore, view such findings with a critical eye. He must be prepared to question which are age and which are generational differences. Without doubt there is interaction between the two, but for researcher and service provider, both of whom wish to understand aging, it is important to distinguish between the two sets of variables.

There is general agreement that the longitudinal strategy of investigation of aging is to be preferred. Unfortunately, it is usually the less practical mode of the two. Longitudinal research requires the kind of long-range commitment few researchers are prepared to make. For one thing, many find their research interests changing over time. Then, too, such long-range research increases the possibility of interruption: subjects themselves can lose interest in participating and drop out, or move away, or die. Finally, longitudinal research is usually very expensive and many funding agencies are reluctant to commit themselves to long-range projects.

A more practical solution to this dilemma is to begin with a cross-sectional sample and to follow the sample by using limited longitudinal sequences for a predetermined length of time, following the model developed by several leading gerontological researchers (Baltes, 1968; Schaie & Strother, 1968). As the example illustrated in Table 1–2 shows, one may compare measures of any given variable (such as medical problems or life satisfaction variables) with the age variable of seventy-year-olds (born in 1905) at different time sequences (following across row A: at 1975, 1985, 1995). This represents a typical longitudinal approach and provides information on age changes, since the repeatedly measured subjects were born at about the same time. Reading Table 1-2 down columns (1), (2), and (3), you see illustrated a typical representation of the cross-sectional approach to measurement of a given variable. A comparison of differences between subjects in column (1), for example, may well be reflecting generational rather than age differences. The varying year of birth (YOB) for subjects in any of the columns will reflect the different cultural and physical experiences and events of this mixed group of cohorts which contribute to differences in measurement (testing) outcomes.

Schaie (1965) has argued for a sophisticated statistical methodology that is intended to separate age and generational (cohort) effects. By utilizing measurements in both directions (across rows and down columns, Table 1–2) a cross-sequential method will derive cohort differ-

TABLE 1–2.   EXAMPLE OF CROSS-SEQUENTIAL METHOD

Year of Birth (YOB)	(1) 1975	(2) 1985	(3) 1995
(A) 1905	70	80	90
(B) 1915	60	70	80
(C) 1935	40	50	60
(D) 1955	20	30	40

SOURCE: Adapted from Kimmel (1974).

ences at each test point (cross-sectional) and yet follow the subjects across time so as to be able to compare each sample with others of the same age at different periods of time.

SUMMARY

Recorded history has always made at least passing reference to long-livers and has given us examples from earliest times from those who have speculated about the phenomenon. In less complex societies, the elder most often earned a special place by virtue of his having survived beyond the norm. Special wisdom was usually attributed to him; generally, he enjoyed a well-defined, useful social role.

Longevity has generally remained the object of great curiosity. Although "magical" and superstitious explanations of longevity were typical of prescientific times, a residue of such thinking remains embedded in popular notions among us even today.

The dramatic increase in the rate and incidence of longevity since the turn of this century, particularly within the past four decades, has confronted us with a striking new phenomenon. The increasingly large number of those surviving into the later years of life has had a powerful impact upon all strata and practically every aspect of societal structure and values. Not least is the special attention now paid to the needs and concerns of a burgeoning population of people over sixty.

Regrettably, the state of the art in gerontology is such that no simple, universally accepted definition of aging is yet available. We do understand that aging is a multidimensional process. Gerontology routinely goes beyond the length of time since birth (chronological age) as an index and now deals with biological age, social age, psychological age, and the like.

Although lacking an overall, inclusive theory of aging as yet, there are a number of perspectives suggested from which the student can begin to look at the vast amount of gerontological information now available. For several reasons many current perspectives tend to reflect negative aspects of the aging process and thus tend to lead to rather pessimistic conclusions. On the other hand, a strong case can be made for more positive perspectives leading to more hopeful, optimistic conclusions. The following chapters present an overview of material from which the student can begin to develop his or her own perspectives.

Research in aging, as well as our own understanding of the aging process, is complicated by the confounding of age and generation differences. Effectively separating out these two effects constitutes one of the major and primary challenges to both the researcher and provider of direct services to the elderly.

REFERENCES

Aloia, A. J. "Relationships between Perceived Privacy Options, Self-esteem, and Internal Control among Aged People." Doctoral diss., California School of Professional Psychology, Los Angeles, 1973.

Baltes, P. "Longitudinal and Cross-sectional Sequences in the Study of Age and Generational Effects," *Human Development*, 1968, 11:3.

Bijou, S. "Ages, Stages, and the Naturalization of Human Development," *American Psychologist*, 1968, 23:6.

Birren, J. E. (ed.). *Handbook of Aging and the Individual*. Chicago: The University of Chicago Press, 1959.

Brackbill, Y. (ed.). Division of Developmental Psychology (Div. 7) *Newsletter*, American Psychological Association, Winter 1971.

Buhler, C. "The Curve of Life as Studied in Biographies," *Journal of Applied Psychology*, 1935, 19.

Copley, F. *On Old Age*. Ann Arbor: University of Michigan Press, 1967.

Cumming, E., and W. Henry. *Growing Old: The Process of Disengagement*. New York: Basic Books, 1961.

Curtis, H. *Biological Mechanisms of Aging*. Springfield, Ill.: Charles C Thomas, 1966.

Erikson, E. *Childhood and Society*. 2d ed. New York: Norton, 1963.

Havighurst, R., B. Neugarten, and S. Tobin. "Disengagement and Patterns of Aging." In B. Neugarten (ed.), *Middle Age and Aging: A Reader in Social Psychology*. Chicago: The University of Chicago Press, 1968.

Kimmel, D. *Adulthood and Aging*. New York: Wiley, 1974.

Kuhlen, R. H. "Developmental Changes in Motivation during the Adult Years." In B. Neugarten (ed.), *Middle Age and Aging: A Reader in Social Psychology*. Chicago: The University of Chicago Press, 1968.

Lawton, M. P. "Coping Behavior and the Environment of Older People." In A. Schwartz and I. Mensh (eds.), *Professional Obligations and Approaches to the Aged*. Springfield, Ill.: Charles C Thomas, 1974.

Makinodan, T. "Immunity and Aging." In C. Finch and L. Hayflick (eds.), *Handbook of the Biology of Aging.* New York: Van Nostrand Reinhold, 1977.

Moos, R. "Evaluating and Changing Community Settings." Address to the American Psychological Association, Chicago. Stanford University and VA Hospital, Palo Alto, Calif., 1975.

Schaie, K. W. "Age Changes in Adult Intelligence." In D. Woodruff and J. Birren (eds.), *Aging: Scientific Perspectives and Social Issues.* New York: Van Nostrand, 1975.

Schaie, K. W., and C. R. Strother. "A Cross-sequential Study of Age Changes in Cognitive Behavior," *Psychological Bulletin,* 1968, 70.

Schaie, K. W. "A General Model for the Study of Developmental Problems," *Psychological Bulletin,* 1965, 64:2.

Schmidt, M. "Interviewing the 'Old-Old'," *The Gerontologist,* December 1975, 15:6.

Shock, N. "Biological Theories of Aging." In J. Birren and K. W. Schaie (eds.), *Handbook of the Psychology of Aging.* New York: Van Nostrand Reinhold, 1977.

Schwartz, A. "A Transactional View of the Aging Process." In A. Schwartz and I. Mensh (eds.), *Professional Obligations and Approaches to the Aged.* Springfield, Ill.; Charles C. Thomas, 1974.

Schwartz, A. and H. Proppe. "Perception of Privacy among Institutionalized Aged." Proceedings of the 77th Annual Convention of the American Psychological Association, Washington, D.C., 1969.

Seligman, M. "Fall into Helplessness," *Psychology Today,* June 1973.

Sprouse, B. (ed.). *National Directory of Educational Programs in Gerontology,* Office of Human Development, Administration on Aging, Department of Health, Education and Welfare, Washington, D.C., 1976.

Storandt, M. "Graduate Education in Gerontological Psychology: Results of a Survey," *Educational Gerontology,* 1977, 2.

Walford, R. *The Immunologic Theory of Aging.* Baltimore: Williams and Wilkins, 1969.

Weg, R. B. "The Old: Who, What, Where, How?" Mimeographed report. E. P. Andrus Gerontology Center, University of Southern California, Los Angeles, 1977.

FOR FURTHER READING

Beauvoir, S. de. *The Coming of Age.* New York: Putnam, 1973.

Binstock, R., and E. Shanas (eds.). *Handbook of Aging and the Social Sciences.* New York: Van Nostrand Reinhold, 1976.

Butler, R. *Why Survive? Being Old in America.* New York: Harper & Row, 1975.

Kalish, R. *Late Adulthood: Perspectives on Human Development.* Monterey, Calif.: Brooks/Cole, 1975.

Newman, B., and P. Newman. *Development Through Life.* Homewood, Ill.: Dorsey, 1975.

Puner, M. *To the Good Long Life: What We Know About Growing Old.* New York: Universe Books, 1974.

Ryder, N. B. "The Cohort as a Concept in the Study of Social Change," *American Sociological Review,* 1965, 30.

Sarton, M. *As We Are Now.* New York: Norton, 1973.

Scott-Maxwell, F. *The Measure of My Days.* New York: Knopf, 1968.

CHAPTER 2

Demographics and Aging

Grecian ladies counted their age from their marriage, not their birth.

HOMER

I'm 65 . . . but if there were 15 months in every year I'd only be 48.

JAMES THURBER

It is now appropriate for us to ask, "Who and where are the aged in our society?" Answers to this question will provide yet another important frame of reference for the student of gerontology. The chapter begins with two contrasting sets of circumstances pointing up, again, the individual experience of aging, and move from them to broader and more general demographic considerations.

The chapter introduces the student to some general characteristics of the aged population as a whole, indicating particular variations and trends within the aged population, and its statistical place within the general population. This will also help the student gain some appreciation and understanding of factors (such as migration, birth and death rates) that in subtle—and sometimes not so subtle—ways affect the economic, social, health, legal, educational, and other circumstances of life of the population, with particular reference to the elderly. It will lead the student to consider some of the ways in which the composition of a population contributes to population dynamics.

The following two brief "case" descriptions are in essence true but with details changed. They are used here to introduce the questions relevant to the discussion that follows.

Mrs. R.G.B. is a sixty-three-year-old black female. On October 17, 1975, she was stricken with and almost died of a massive stroke (diagnosis was left hemisphere cerebrovascular accident and hypertension). She was paralyzed on her right side and could no longer articulate words so as to be understood.

Mrs. B. was admitted to a general hospital on the above date and remained there until October 20, 1975. On that date she was transferred to a rehabilitation facility, where she received physical and occupational therapy for a period of three months. By this time, she had learned to walk falteringly with the aid of a four-pronged cane and was sent home. About six months later she was readmitted to the hospital for kidney surgery. Because of her generally weakened condition, she was subsequently transferred to a nursing home, where she has lived until the present.

The hospital's medical evaluation: Mrs. B. will never walk or talk again. She appears to understand most communications but seems unable to communicate verbally. Her attention span is short and she becomes confused easily. If she does learn to speak it will probably only be to say a word or two here or there.

Her husband's evaluation: Her facial expressions have remained normal, and communication is best accomplished by this means. She recognizes and remembers faces. She becomes easily agitated if approached from her right (paralyzed) side. Nor will she let one touch the right side without coaxing. Cries rather easily but seems to be in good humor most of the time

Our second case is Mr. C.M.F., a seventy-year-old Caucasian male. In June 1973, he retired after many years as a successful attorney practicing in Chicago. By August of that year he and his sixty-six-year-old wife sold their suburban home and fulfilled a longtime dream by moving to Southern California. They had no children and had sufficient income from investments to be financially comfortable. They found a suitable apartment not far from the ocean.

In spite of their involvement with a number of community activities and a growing circle of new acquaintances, Mr. F. found himself restless and dissatisfied. He knew what he didn't want to do (he didn't want to continue along the lines of his prior career) but seemed to have much more difficulty in focusing on what he *would* like to do. The answer came through some consultations with a counselor.

Mr. F. had always been a skillful "Mr. Fixit." He enjoyed and was good at repairing small appliances, clocks, bicycles, and the like. With some encouragement he turned their spare bedroom into a small workshop, passed the word among friends and neighbors of the service he offered, and is now happily able to occupy all his spare time with as much business as he chooses. And he finds that this second career provides a welcome supplement to his income.

These cases suggest any number of pertinent questions and issues which include, but are not limited to:

1. Can either of these two older persons as briefly described be said to be "typical" aged?

2. Do they represent extreme cases, or are both atypical?

3. If we anticipate increasing numbers of elderly like Mrs. B. and Mr. F., will we require a whole new network of social services to meet their special needs and concerns?

4. Who will provide the services and financial support for the increasing number of elderly? Shall it be the younger members of society in general or should it be an individual family and kin responsibility?

5. What will happen to basic social institutions—religious, educational, legal, economic, health—with the graying of America?

6. How will the aging picture in America look twenty, thirty, or forty years from now?

7. Which factors are most likely to affect that future picture: economics, health care, politics, changed attitudes?

For even partial answers to such questions we must look mainly to demography. The kinds of issues indicated above show why demographic data—that is, the study or science of population dynamics—have become so important to policymakers, planners, and providers of services in gerontology.

DEMOGRAPHY: THE STUDY OF GROUPS

Demography deals statistically with changes in large, broad population groups rather than with individual case studies. Demography does not provide for individual variations. It can characterize populations in terms of percentages, means, medians, and modes. On this basis it can "project" into the future (assuming all things remain equal). It cannot truly—nor does it claim to—predict the future. Demographic projections, therefore, as with all statistics, must be read with some caution. They tell us what *could be,* not what *will be.*

Students of gerontology are primarily concerned with populations of persons sixty-five years or older. Even though, as pointed out earlier,

The elderly are constituent members of the total population. Demography helps us understand better how the aged "fit" into the population, how they affect it, and, in turn, how they are affected by it.

chronological age (namely sixty-five plus) is not a precise index of the aging process, it is nevertheless a useful and widely utilized cutoff point to identify "aging" in populations.

Given such cautions, we can use demography as an important frame of reference in our effort to understand aging and its implications for us.

CHANGING TRENDS IN LIFE EXPECTANCY

Human life expectancy historically has undergone a phenomenal shift from the time of the ancient Greeks to the present. Then (about 1000 BC) average life expectancy at birth was about 20 years; in 1970 it was 70.9 years; today life expectancy approximates 73 years. Much of this increase has taken place largely within the past half-dozen decades or so. Table 2–1 shows the remarkable increase in life expectancy since the turn of this century.[1]

A careful reading of this table makes four important facts evident. There has been a singular increase in life expectancy (at birth) from ancient to modern times. Assuming life expectancy in the year 1000 BC to have been approximately 20 years, the increase in expectancy to

[1]This "spurt" of increase parallels the sudden increase in the number of working scientists. It is estimated that 80 percent of all scientists who have ever lived are alive today.

Table 2–1.   LIFE EXPECTANCY AT BIRTH FOR
THE UNITED STATES°

				WHITE			BLACK AND OTHER		
Year	Total	Male	Female	Total	Male	Female	Total	Male	Female
1975	72.5	68.7	76.5	73.2	69.4	77.2	67.9	63.6	72.3
1974	71.9	68.1	75.8	72.7	68.9	76.6	67.0	62.9	71.3
1973	71.3	67.6	75.3	72.2	68.4	76.1	65.9	61.9	70.1
1972	71.1	67.4	75.1	72.0	68.3	75.9	65.6	61.5	69.9
1971	71.1	67.4	75.0	72.0	68.3	75.8	65.6	61.6	69.7
1970	70.8	67.1	74.6	71.7	68.1	75.4	64.6	60.5	68.4
1960	69.7	66.6	73.1	70.6	67.4	74.1	63.6	61.1	66.3
1950	68.2	65.6	71.1	69.1	66.5	72.2	60.8	59.1	62.9
1940	62.9	60.8	65.2	64.2	62.1	66.6	53.1	51.5	54.9
1930	59.7	58.1	61.6	61.4	59.7	63.5	48.1	47.3	49.2
1920	54.1	53.6	54.6	54.9	54.4	55.6	45.3	45.5	45.2
1910	50.0	48.4	51.8	50.3	48.6	52.0	35.6	33.8	37.5
1900	47.3	46.3	48.3	47.6	46.6	48.7	33.0	32.5	33.5

°Prior to 1960 excludes Alaska and Hawaii; prior to 1930 for death-registration states
only.
Note: The 1977 figures, while most recent, are based on sample surveys and thus are to
be viewed as somewhat more "soft" data than the 1971 census data.
SOURCES:US Bureau of Census (1977); US Bureau of Census (1975); US Bureau of
Census (1960).

1975 is about 52.5 years. Of that total, approximately 25 years (or 48
percent) represents the increase since 1900.

A second important fact is that the largest increment occurred between 1900 and 1940 (15.6 years), in contrast to the increase in expectancy between 1940 and 1975 (9.6 years). Thus the *rate* of increased life
expectancy appears to have decreased considerably within the past
three and a half decades.

A third important fact seen in Table 2–1 is the striking discrepancy
between Caucasian life expectancy at birth and that of minority
groups. At the turn of the century white males could expect to live
(actuarily speaking) 46.6 years, black males 32.5 years, white females
48.7, and black females about 33.5. The *increase* in life expectancy
from 1900 to 1975 is greater for minority groups than for Caucasians.

A fourth important observation to be made from these figures is that
for the first time in the history of our nation, the average life expectancy (at birth) of nonwhite females surpassed that of white males by
1970. This "crossover" effect, which actually occurred in 1967, signi-
fies the actuarial advantage that females have over males. Note that in
1900 the average life expectancy of all females was two years higher
than for all males. By 1975, women could expect to live almost eight
years longer than men. These data emphatically point out the relative

advantage that women have over men in average life expectancy at birth, an advantage that continues to increase (Cutler & Harootyan, 1975).

Some of the improvement in life expectancy, especially during the last century, may be attributed in some measure to the success of medicine in overcoming the usual childhood killers, particularly with respect to contagious and acute disease. Of greater significance as determinants of health have been improvements in sanitation procedures and techniques, better nutrition, and birth control (McKeown, 1978). Thus more persons are enabled to survive past childhood and middle age into the later years of life.

The present level of life expectancy at birth in the United States is also reflected in a number of other countries, as can be readily seen in Table 2–2.

TABLE 2–2.   LIFE EXPECTANCY AT BIRTH FOR SELECTED COUNTRIES

| Date* | Country | YEARS | |
		Male	Female
1973	Austria	67.4	74.7
1965–1967	Canada	68.7	75.2
1970–1971	Denmark	70.7	75.9
1966–1970	Finland	65.9	73.6
1971	France	68.5	76.1
1970–1972	Fed. Rep. Germany	67.4	73.8
1966–1970	Iceland	70.7	76.3
1972	Israel	70.1	72.8
1972	Japan	70.5	75.9
1972	Netherlands	70.8	76.8
1971–1972	Norway	71.2	77.4
1972	Sweden	71.9	77.4
1968–1969	USSR	65.0	74.0
1968–1970	United Kingdom	67.8	73.8
1972	United States	67.4	75.1

*Latest available figures.
SOURCE: United Nations (1975).

What should be noted here about the selected countries (of Table 2–2) is that they represent so-called developed, industrialized societies. The picture is somewhat different when we examine the figures in Table 2–3, which includes a selection of countries representing so-called third world or less developed, less industrialized societies.

TABLE 2-3.   LIFE EXPECTANCY AT BIRTH, BY SEX AND POPULA-
TION—AGE 65 AND OVER FOR VARIOUS COUNTRIES AND YEARS

Country	Year	LIFE EXPECTANCY AT BIRTH		POPULATION AGE 65 AND OVER	
		Male	Female	Number (in thousands)	Percent of Total
North America					
United States	1970	67.0	75.0	20,101	9.9
Canada	1971	68.8	75.2	1,744	8.1
Haiti	1972 (est.)	—44.5—		157	3.1
Mexico	1970	61.0	63.7	1,791	3.7
South America					
Argentina	1972 (est.)	64.1	70.2	1,805	7.5
Brazil	1970	—60.7—		4,760	5.1 (age 60 +)
Venezuela	1970 (est.)	—63.8—		252	2.4
Asia					
China	1970 (est.)	—50.0—		—	—
Japan	1970	69.1	74.3	7,330	7.1
Iran	1971 (est.)	—50.0—		940	3.1
Syria	1970 (est.)	—52.8—		193	3.2
USSR	1970	65.0	74.0	28,514	11.8
Europe					
Austria	1970	66.6	73.7	1,047	14.2
Denmark	1969	70.8	75.7	590	12.1
France	1968	68.6	76.1	6,662	13.4
Hungary	1970	66.3	72.0	1,178	11.4
Netherlands	1971 (est.)	71.0	76.7	1,353	10.3
Sweden	1970	71.7	76.5	1,109	13.7
United Kingdom	1971	68.8	75.1	6,397	13.1
Africa					
Ethiopia	1968 (est.)	—38.5—		2,811	11.9 (age 45 +)
Ghana	1970	—46.0—		311	3.6
Kenya	1969	46.9	51.2	391	3.6
South Africa	1970	—49.0—		870	4.1
Uganda	1969	—47.5—		365	3.8
Zambia	1970	—43.5—		135	4.0 (age 60+)

SOURCE: United Nations (1973).

Here we see that the life expectancy in most African countries, for
example, is more like that of our own country at the turn of the century.
Furthermore, not only is the absolute number of elderly in countries
like Haiti, Mexico, Brazil, and Venezuela much smaller, but also the

FIGURE 2–1.   GOMPERTZ PLOT. MORTALITY RATE AS A FUNCTION
OF AGE, UNITED STATES, 1939–41

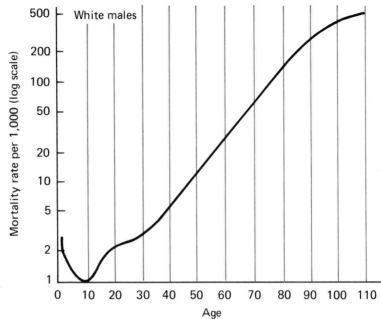

SOURCE: B. L. Strehler, "Dynamic Theories of Aging," in N. W. Schock, ed., *Aging—
Some Social and Biological Aspects* (Washington, D.C.: Association for the Advance-
ment of Science, 1960), p. 286.

elderly represent a much smaller proportion of the population (3.1, 3.7,
5.1, and 2.4 percent respectively) in those societies.

   Another aspect to life expectancy deserves attention. Life expectancy
for humans, as with other species, clearly is related to age. A Swedish
statistician by the name of Gompertz is credited with developing (in
1825) a mathematical formulation showing the exponential increase in
the probability of death with increasing age. In other words, he demonstrated the increasing risk of death with increasing age, a probability
statement (the Gompertz curve) that can be applied with remarkable
accuracy to such diverse entities as humans, horses, and glassware.

   With this in mind, it is instructive to compare life expectancy at birth
and at age sixty-five, as shown in Table 2–4.

   This set of figures leads to an interesting conclusion. Although, as
already pointed out, there has been a dramatic increase in life expectancy at birth since 1900, life expectancy at age sixty-five has increased
only slightly from 1900 to 1970. What this implies is that we may be
seeing not so much an extension of the human life span as a greater

TABLE 2–4. AVERAGE LIFE EXPECTANCY AT BIRTH AND AT AGE 65 IN THE UNITED STATES, FOR VARIOUS YEARS, 1900–70

Age	1900	1939	1949	1955	1959	1970
At birth	47.3	63.7	68.0	69.6	69.9	70.9
At age 65	11.9	12.8	13.8	14.2	14.4	15.2

SOURCE: United States Public Health Service, National Center for Health Statistics (1974).

fulfillment of the possibility of survival to the longevity limits of our species. The reservation implicit in such a statement is that, given the present level of scientific knowledge, we cannot know with absolute certainty what those limits (if any) are for humans.

These life expectancy data are averages of the aging of individuals within a general population. They refer not to individuals but to total populations. What has already been referred to is a parallel demographic measure, namely, the probability of survival from one age category to another, which is known as *age-specific survival rate* (Cutler & Harootyan, 1975). These probabilities of survival at different ages are also averages derived from a given population (for example, the seventy-five plus population). Both these measures of aging, life expectancy and survival rates, are largely a function of changes in mortality (death) rates within a population. Such information helps us understand the age composition of a given population.

Women tend to outlive men. Being single requires elderly women to overcome loneliness and reach out for companionship.

PROPORTION OF AGED IN A POPULATION

Both the absolute (total) number and the proportion (percentage of the general population) of aged in the United States have been increasing in dramatic fashion. Demographers expect this trend, based on past experience, to continue but at a much more modest rate.

TABLE 2–5.   POPULATION AGE 65 AND OVER IN THE UNITED STATES FOR EACH DECENNIAL YEAR, WITH PROJECTIONS TO 2020:1900–2020

| | I | | II | |
| | POPULATION AGE 65 AND OVER | | PERCENT INCREASE FROM PRECEDING DECADE | |
Year	(1.) Number (in thousands)	(2.) Percent of Total Population	(1.) Age 65 and Over	(2.) Total Population
1900	3,099	4.1	—	—
1910	3,986	4.3	28.6	21.0
1920	4,929	4.7	23.7	14.9
1930	6,705	5.4	36.0	16.1
1940	9,031	6.8	34.7	7.3
1950	12,397	8.2	37.3	14.5
1960	16,679	9.2	34.5	18.5
1970	20,177	9.9	21.0	13.3
Projections:		Series B[b] Series E[b]		Series B[b] Series E[b]
1980	24,051[a]	10.2 10.6	19.2	15.6 11.2
1990	27,768[a]	10.0 11.0	15.5	17.7 10.4
2000	28,842[a]	8.9 10.6	3.9	15.7 7.8
2010	30,940	8.1 10.6	7.3	18.3 7.2
2020	40,261	9.1 13.1	30.1	17.3 5.7

[a]Revised data from United States Bureau of the Census. *Current Population Reports,* Series P-25, No. 493, "Projections of the Population of the United States, by Age and Sex: 1972-2020" (December 1972).
[b]Assumptions of completed fertility (average number of births per woman upon completion of childbearing years):
Series B: 3.10 (high-fertility assumption).
Series E: 2.10 (low-fertility assumption, which mirrors present replacement level trend in the United States).
SOURCE: US Bureau of the Census (Nov. 1971; Dec. 1967).

Table 2–5 shows the total number of those sixty-five and over within the general population and their proportional relation to the general population. By way of comparison, the table also shows the percentage of increase of persons sixty-five and over along with the percentage of increase of the total population for each succeeding decade from 1900, with projections to the year 2020.

Table 2–5 also shows the proportion of persons sixty-five and over to the total population in 1900 was 4.1 percent, representing slightly more than 3 million elderly. In contrast, the proportion in 1970 of those sixty-five and over was almost 10 percent, representing somewhat in excess of 20 million elderly. By 1970 the proportion of older persons was greater than 10.5 percent, comprising almost 23 million people age 65 and over.

An analysis of the figures in Table 2–5 shows a small but steady rise not only in total numbers of older persons—column (1) under I—but also in the proportion of elderly to the total population, moving from 4.1 to 9.9 percent, in column (2), I. But while the numbers and proportions show a steady rate of growth, this is not true when we look at the percent of increase by decades in column (2) under II. There was smaller proportionate increase in the 1930s (7.3 percent). The next two decades showed a much larger increase, followed by a smaller increase in the 1960s (13.3 percent).

Two basic factors contribute to these changes, of course: mortality (death) and fertility (birth) rates. When fewer survive into later life (as during an economic depression) the proportion of the elderly goes down. During a "baby boom" (as, for example, following World War II), the percentage of elderly can also decrease. Balancing this may be a period (like the present period of replacement level fertility) when the proportion of elderly goes up. We shall return to this issue shortly.

Another way to demonstrate this change in proportion of aged in the population is to use the common age-sex population pyramid, which shows a profile of the population by age and sex. Figure 2–2 shows these distributions at three time periods (1900, 1940, 1970). The distribution for males and females within each time frame is based on five-year increments up to seventy-five years.

In 1900 when fertility (birth) and mortality (death) rates were relatively high (32 births and 17 deaths per 1,000 population), the population pyramid looks much like a triangle. The shape of the graph undergoes marked change at time B (1940), reflecting the effects of lower birth rates during the great economic depression of the post-World War I years. Further effects of changing birth rates are seen in the pyramid at time C (1970). In this latter graph, the marked increase of the seventy-five and over age group should be noticed, especially with respect to the greater proportion of surviving women.

WHAT ARE THE IMPLICATIONS?

These data should begin to make clear how useful a tool demography is for describing and assessing the age composition of a population. These data show us the increasing probabilities of surviving into

Figure 2-2. AGE-SEX POPULATION PYRAMIDS FOR THE UNITED STATES: 1900, 1940, 1970

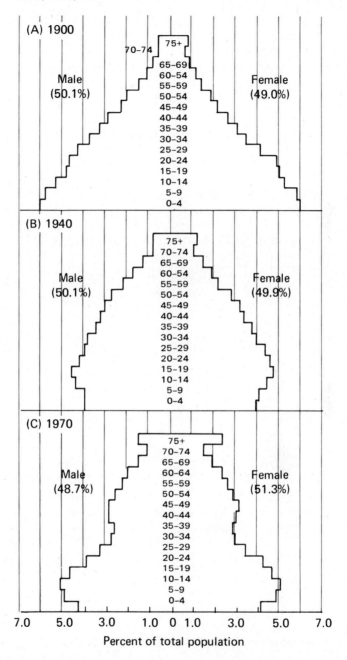

SOURCE: US Bureau of the Census. *Census of Population: Characteristics of the Population,* 1940, 1970.

the later years of life and that this probability is greater for females than for males, greater for Caucasians than for blacks and other minority groups.

Mortality rates, of course, are a primary factor. Every day approximately 5,000 Americans turn sixty-five.* Every day approximately 3,600 Americans sixty-five and over die. The net increase is about 1,400 per day, or more than 500,000 per year. In 1976 the total population in America was 220.3 million; of these approximately 10.4 percent (more than 22 million) were sixty-five years or older. Even more striking is the fact that today there are more than 30 million people sixty years or older. This is called the graying of America. As of mid-1976 the total population was 214.7 million resident in the United States (median age 29.0).

TABLE 2–6.   DISTRIBUTION OF POPULATION 65 AND OLDER

65–69	8,251,000
70–74	5,913,000
75–79	4,051,000
80–85	2,724,000
85+	1,066,000
100+	7,000
	Total 22,012,000

SOURCE: Weg (1977). Note that these are US Census Bureau figures and are considered to be slightly inflated.

TABLE 2–7.   FEMALE/MALE RATIOS

Age Group	1950	1960	1970	Mid-1975
25–44	100.6	100.5	100.5	—
45–64	99.8	104.5	109.1	—
65+	111.5	120.7	138.5	144
65–74	107.5	114.9	128.8	130
75+	120.9	133.1	156.2	171
85+	—	—	200+	200+

SOURCE: Weg (1977).

Throughout most of the life span women outnumber men. More male babies are born than female babies (106 males for every 100 females). But male death rates are higher beginning at birth (including *in utero*), so that by approximately age twenty and thereafter women increasingly outnumber men. This disproportion becomes more dra-

*The following figures are taken from mimeographed material prepared in 1977 by Ruth Weg, Ph.D., Andrus Gerontology Center, University of Southern California, Los Angeles.

matic with increasing age (see Table 2–7) and across time. While the
ratio of approximately two to one (females to males) in the later years is
a dramatic statistic, it can only begin to suggest the dimensions of the
personal struggles, problems, and stresses encompassed in the fact that
after age fifty-five there are some 1.7 million widowers compared to 8
million widows. Given the strong tradition of women marrying men
older than themselves, what are the implications of this for love and
marriage in the later years? What has gerontology to say regarding such
important issues as intimacy and sexual activity and life satisfaction in
the light of the growing number of widowed/single women in late life?
What are the implications here regarding socialization, work, housing,
and similar issues? These issues are discussed in the following chapters.

One factor that may in time affect present demographic projections
relative to male-female longevity is the emerging and broadening role
of women in the competitive and stressful job market. Encouraged by
the feminist movement, women in increasing numbers are entering
occupations traditionally held to be male domains. It is interesting to
speculate (we have few studies) that this growing trend may expose
more women to certain situational stresses which in turn may increase
their susceptibility, for example, to cardiovascular disease. Again, it
has been estimated that up to 50 percent of the difference is due to
higher rates of cigarette consumption by males. Yet female consumption has increased relative to male during the last twenty years. This
also may have some effect. Most important, each year shows that the
female advantage in longevity at birth gets greater, but at a decreasing
rate of increase during the last eight to ten years.

What are the implications of this graying of America and these dif-
ferentials as far as researchers and service providers are concerned?
Demographers project that if mortality, fertility, and migration rates
hold constant, by the turn of the next century the United States should
expect to count a total of 29–33 million older Americans. By the year
2030 we should also expect almost 50 percent of our population to be
forty years of age or older. For service providers, especially, this means
that approximately one out of every three potential "clients" will not
be seventeen or twenty-five or thirty-nine years of age, but is likely to
be fifty-five or seventy-two or eighty. Are young persons now in their
midtwenties, presently socialized into one or another professional role,
being prepared to meet the challenge that will face them less than
twenty-five years hence?

ETHNICITY AND AGING

If it may be said that the aged in our society generally have received
less than their share of many kinds of goods and services, then it would

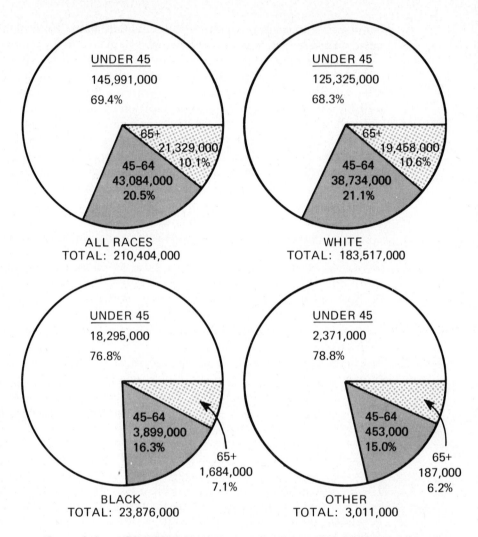

Figure 2-3.   AGE DISTRIBUTION BY RACIAL AND ETHNIC ORIGINS

be accurate to say that historically the minority aged have been virtually invisible to the larger society. Figure 2–3 shows the distribution of
the population of blacks and minority groups in relation to whites.

As Figure 2–3 graphically illustrates, the age-specific proportions
within the several ethnic groups is remarkably similar, although it is
apparent that nonblack minority groups constitute a somewhat younger population than whites (6.2 percent as compared to 10.6 percent are
sixty-five and over). But the total number of minority elderly is much
smaller than that of white elderly. What gerontology has begun to
discover is that the disparity in numbers is reflected in the paucity of

services of many kinds (physical care, mental health, housing, education,) and so on provided minority aged.

TABLE 2–8.   SIZE OF ETHNIC GROUPS, 1970

Race	Population	Percentage of Total Population	Elderly as Percentage of Population
Total	203,211,926	100.00	9.89
Chinese	435,062	0.21	6.22
Japanese	591,290	0.29	8.02
Filipino	343,060	0.17	6.31
Samoan	35,000	0.02	NA
Mexican American	5,023,000	2.47	8.44
American Indian	792,730	0.39	5.74
Black	22,580,289	11.11	7.03

SOURCE: US Bureau of the Census (1973).

As Table 2–8 shows, many minority aged other than black elderly live in our society. Yet much about these aged persons is relatively unknown. These, too, represent a great challenge to gerontologists, researchers, and service providers alike. Are there sufficient numbers of service providers who can speak the language of the foreign-born elderly? Is planning of programs for these minority elderly designed to preserve the ethnic and cultural integrity of these aged persons? Will our society support the maintenance of these elderly within their family units, which has been the unique feature of minority life-style with respect to their elderly? And what role can professional gerontologists play in this?

WHERE ARE THEY?

Demographic data are a tool by which the age composition of a population is described and assessed. These data lend validity to a systematic analysis of the fluidity and dynamics of population age changes.

Frequently, mortality (death) rates are assumed to be the main determining, if not the sole, factor in understanding the "age" of a population. Birth rates and migration (change of residence), however, are factors equally important to a clear understanding of the dynamics of population age changes. As Cutler and Harootyan (1975) have pointed out, one individual can contribute only once to mortality rates. But a single individual can migrate one or more times and thus contribute repeatedly to variations in the composition of subpopulations. By the same token, one woman can give birth to more than one child and thus contribute to the variability of population estimates with respect to fertility rates.

TABLE 2–9.   SELECTED STATE DATA ON POPULATION AGE 65 AND OVER, 1970

		Number Age 65 and Over
A.	1. New York	1,954,427
	2. California	1,800,977
	3. Pennsylvania	1,272,126
	4. Illinois	1,093,654
	5. Ohio	997,694
		Percent Age 65 and Over
B.	1. Florida	14.5
	2. Iowa	12.4
	3. Nebraska	12.4
	4. Arkansas	12.3
	5. South Dakota	12.1
	6. California	9.0
		Percent Increase in Older Population Over a Ten-Year Period
C.	1. Arizona	79.0
	2. Florida	78.2
	3. Nevada	70.4
	4. Hawaii	51.3
	5. New Mexico	37.7
	6. California	30.9

SOURCE: US Bureau of the Census (1971).

Table 2–9 indicates the differential concentration of elderly within the United States.

Such data can be accurately evaluated only in the light of the three basic demographic variables: change rates within these subpopulations in terms of the relationship among mortality, fertility, and migration. These interlocking factors will offer important clues also to service providers and planners as to how many are likely to survive to old age, what proportion of the population they will constitute, and where they are likely to be located.

As of 1977, California and New York reversed positions for states with the largest number of older persons (2,056,000 and 2,030,000 respectively). The three most populous states (California, New York, Pennsylvania) account for just over one-quarter of all our older people. Add the number of older people living in Florida, Illinois, Ohio, Texas, and Michigan to those living in the above-mentioned three, and these eight states account for 50 percent of the nation's elderly. Actually, more than 90 percent of those over sixty-five are concentrated in just thirty states (Weg, 1977).

Such patterns of geographic distribution, concentrations of elderly, and anticipated changes have profound implications for planners of nationwide programs as well as local designers of service programs. It is clear from C. in Table 2–9, for instance, that the high rate of increase of those sixty-five and over in these states reflects the attractiveness of areas with warmer climates and milder winters for a great many older persons. At the same time, this pattern of migration of older persons has a high probability of reflecting further disruption of family and established friendships because of geographical distance.

The urban/rural distribution is also very much affected by patterns of migration of both young and old. Generally, older people, like the rest of the population, are more than 70 percent urban. Within urban areas, more older people are likely to be located within the central city sectors while the under-sixty-five are more likely to be found residing in suburban areas. Older people who reside in nonurban areas mostly live in small towns rather than on farms, although overall the rural population tends to show a prevalence of older persons. Black and other nonwhite older persons tend, to a greater extent than white, to live in urban rather than rural areas (Weg, 1977).

THE IMPACT OF DEMOGRAPHIC CHANGES

These striking changes in the age composition of our population over the past four or five decades has had, and continues to have, marked impact upon the structure and values of our society. Our nation is compelled to cope with issues that it has never before had to face. The impact is felt in many sectors of society.

Impact upon the Political System (Public Policy)

One consequence is the increasing pressures brought to bear for reformulation of public policy, new legislation to meet the needs of the elderly, and new categories of direct services to the aged. They have become much less passive and through organizational strength have learned to be more militantly articulate. Consider, for example, the political and advocacy activities of the almost 12 million members of the American Association of Retired Persons/National Retired Teachers Association alone. Add to this a number of organizations such as the National Council of the Aging (NCOA) and the National Council of Senior Citizens, as well as the militant advocacy of Maggie Kuhn and her Gray Panthers. These and other organizations of elderly have had direct impact upon the whole health-care delivery system regarding definitions of health, delivery of health services, and how these should be financed (Medicare/Medicaid). They have also provided enormous influence in eliminating or liberalizing limits of mandatory unemployment—that is, retirement.

In spite of the fact that the institutionalized aged represent less than 5 percent of those over sixty-five, the enormous amounts of money, literally billions, invested in Medicare and Medicaid programs have had an impact of substantial proportions upon our medical delivery system, not all of it good. It is now a matter of public record and growing public concern that such large sums of money, although intended to underwrite medical services for the aged, when poured into the system with deficient accountability controls, tempt some physicians, some clinics, and some laboratories to misuse and misappropriate these public funds. Whether these problems will be solved by stricter controls, better accountability on the part of user and service provider, and/or a national health insurance program, or by some other means, remains to be seen. The point here is that the dramatic increase in the numbers of survivors into late maturity has produced these troublesome problems.

The inevitable modification of mandatory retirement restrictions (i.e., the recent change in federal law prohibiting mandatory retirement under seventy years) is the result of a political process. This change comes as no surprise to those who are aware of the political activities (lobbying, voting, and so on) of activist, militant groups of elderly. For the same reasons we will continue to see further reforms relating to private pensions and Social Security, such as tying Social Security benefits to cost-of-living increases (see discussions of Social Security factors in chapters 3, 4, and 6).

Impact upon the Educational System

Our educational system also reflects these demographic changes. Not only are there more older people among us, but more of them are expressing their rising expectations regarding their adult educational needs; more are going back to school. There is also the growing need for training in gerontology. Schools of every description at the professional, preprofessional, community college, and high school levels are awakening to the need for offering scientists, researchers, service providers (both professional and paraprofessional), clergy, teachers, and administrators more gerontologically enriched curricula.

At the same time school systems at the primary and advanced levels, which were geared to anticipate the "baby boom" of the late forties, fifties and early sixties, are beginning to experience a receding from the high crest of enrollments. This is especially evident at the university level. In some areas, school systems have been forced to dismiss teachers, to retrench on existing curriculum offerings, to close entire schools. One aspect of the graying of America and the enrollment crunch in our educational systems is the increasing determination and imaginative effort shown by educators in attempting to encourage elderly citizens to return to school. This has also focused attention on the necessity of sensitizing classroom instructors to the special needs, apprehensions, and inhibitions of the many elderly people who are moving into an academic setting. It has focused attention on the need for training understanding counselors of the elderly within the educational system, and the necessity for school administrators to reduce the barriers between reentry into school and the special physical, intellectual, and emotional needs of elderly enrollees.

Impact upon the Legal System

Nor has our system of jurisprudence been able to avoid the impact of the changes in age composition. Increasing attention is being focused upon legal advocacy for the aged, consumer protection, legal counseling, and the effects of crimes that particularly affect the elderly (e.g., mugging, rape, fraud). A federally funded National Senior Citizens' Law Center now serves as a clearinghouse of legal service to the elderly. A national Bicentennial Conference on Justice and Older Americans took place in Portland, Oregon, in September of 1976. This conference was designed as a major effort to synthesize the research and programs attendant to the legal system, the criminal justice system, and older adults.

Over the past two years moves have been made to establish legal service developers in all fifty states and US territories. These offices, in practically every instance associated with state offices or departments of aging, are to serve as focal points for the expansion of legal programs for older persons as well as to provide certain free legal services. Given the large array of legal services required, this may be viewed as too modest an effort. But it does reflect the impact of changes in demography in America.

Impact upon the Economic System

Some of the most profound effects are felt within our economic system. The traditional American economic way of life is increasingly affected by such issues as the legitimacy and utility of forced retirement. Such issues as encouraging second or third careers, the reentry of older women into the work force, "parallel" careers, a reexamination and possibly redefinition of the concept of individual productivity, and such pensions issues as vested interest and portability have become matters of public debate.

Related to this, Social Security provides at least a minimum income for the retired worker. Employers and employees pay into a fund out of which the retired worker draws income following retirement. When initially put into operation in the 1930s, experience with this system appeared to be consonant with the actuarial data upon which it was based—that is to say, most workers did not live (and thus did not draw funds) much beyond the retirement age of sixty-five. Social Security was able to maintain fiscal soundness. The ensuing decades have brought a rise in the standard of living accompanied by staggering inflationary increases and, in some sectors, a lowering of retirement age. In recent years, it has become apparent that longer-living individuals, by drawing on Social Security funds for more extended periods than originally anticipated, appear to be threatening the fiscal stability of the program.

THE CONCEPT OF THE "DEPENDENCY RATIO"

Moving from an earlier economic situation wherein the vast majority of workers "supported" the relatively few retired, as graphically illustrated by the broad-based triangle on the left below, we have entered an economic era in which a larger number of retirees become more economically dependent upon a smaller number of wage earners, as indicated in the triangle on the right. We might ask whether increased shares or benefits of the Social Security system become greater than contributed shares. In effect, the younger wage earners are paying their

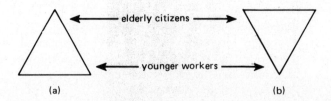

(a)   (b)

Social Security contributions to those who are currently receiving benefits.

One method by which demographers describe this effect upon our economic system is a formula known as the dependency ratio. This is arrived at arithmetically by dividing the "dependent" (retired) population by the number of active wage earners (conventionally defined as the age group eighteen to sixty-four). Of major interest in the dependency ratio is how it changes over time, and to what extent such a commonly used index represents the economic status of pensioners.

TABLE 2–10.   OLD-AGE DEPENDENCY RATIOS FOR THE
UNITED STATES: 1930-2050

1930	1940	1950	1960	1970	2000	2020	2050
.097	.118	.133	.167	.177	.177	.213	.257

Dependency ratio = 65+/18–64.
SOURCE: Years 1930–40 from US Bureau of the Census (1942), Table 8, p. 26; years 1950 –70 from US Bureau of the Census (1972), Table 37, p. 32; year 2000 based on Series E projections from Brotman (1973), p. 3; years 2020 and 2050 based on Series E and Series W projections respectively, prepared by Dr. David M. Heer, Population Research Laboratory, University of Southern California, February 1974.

The old-age dependency ratio (65+ / 18–64) does not imply that every person over sixty-five is dependent economically and that everyone between eighteen and sixty-four is working and financially independent. But for purposes of making gross population analyses, these age groupings are conventionally used.

Note that by the turn of the century (2000) the expected increase in the dependency ratio does not occur because the increased number of the old is offset by the baby boom of the forties and fifties. A lower birth rate such as we are experiencing now, however, will likely mean a relatively smaller work force during the first decades of the new century, which again increases the dependency ratios between 2000 and 2050. One should keep in mind that this statistic is sensitive to *changes* in work status in the population. Thus, if present trends to eliminate mandatory retirement rules are successful, or if the age limits are substantially extended, and if more and more older persons remain in the work force in informal as well as formal ways, the projected dependency ratios for the decades after 2000 will require revision.

SUMMARY

This chapter has attempted to answer the question, "Who are the aged and where are they?" In so doing, it has briefly described how demography, the science of population dynamics, focuses not on individuals but on the composition of broad population groups. Demographic projections tell us, therefore, not what will be but what could be.

In order to do this, demography relies heavily upon birth rates, death rates, and migration rates. These show us how life expectancy has changed remarkably, especially since the turn of this century. Life expectancy has increased dramatically for Caucasian females, for Caucasians over non-Caucasians, and more in the developed, industrialized countries in contrast to many of the third world, underdeveloped countries.

Life expectancy at birth has increased dramatically; life expectancy at age sixty-five has increased only slightly. Thus we see an increase not only in the total number but also the proportion of elderly in our society. This also means a disproportionate number of women surviving into later life. There are fewer numbers of minority elderly, who have consequently been overlooked, in large measure, with respect to age-specific services.

A large proportion of elderly (about one-quarter) are located in our three most populous states. The greatest shifts within the past decade have been to states with warmer climates and milder winters. Nonetheless, most elderly are still located in urban areas.

These demographic changes have had tremendous impact upon our country along a number of dimensions: public policy, education, health care, and legal systems; and, of course, the economical system. Demography measures the latter changes by the age dependency ratio.

REFERENCES

Cutler, N., and R. Harootyan. "Demography of the Aged." In D. Woodruff and J. Birren (eds.), *Aging: Scientific Perspectives and Social Issues.* New York: D. Van Nostrand, 1975.

Brotman, Herbert B. "Projections of the Population to the Year 2000." Statistical Memo No. 25, Administration on Aging, June 1973.

Gompertz Plot. In J. Hendricks and C. Hendricks, *Aging and Mass Society.* Cambridge, Mass.: Winthrop Publishers, 1977.

McKeown, T. "Determinants of Health," *Human Nature,* 1978, 1:4.

United Nations. *Demographic Yearbook, 1972.* New York: United Nations, 1973.

United Nations. *Statistical Yearbook, 1974.* 26th ed. New York: United Nations, 1975.

US Bureau of the Census. *Census of Population: 1970 General Population Characteristics, Selected States and United States.* Washington, D.C.: Government Printing Office, 1971.

US Bureau of the Census, *Current Population Reports,* Series P-25, No. 470, "Projections of the Population of the United States by Age and Sex: 1970–2020," November 1971; Series P-25, No. 38, "Projections of the Population of the United States by Age, Sex, and Color to 1990, with Extensions of Population by Age and Sex to 2015," December 1967.

US Bureau of the Census. *U.S. Census of Population, 1940. Characteristics of the Population.* Washington, D.C.: Government Printing Office, 1942.

US Bureau of the Census. *Historical Statistics of the United States, Colonial Times to 1957.* Washington, D.C.: Government Printing Office, 1960.

US Bureau of the Census. *Statistical Abstract of the United States,* 93d, 96th, and 98th eds. Washington, D.C.: Government Printing Office, 1972, 1975, and 1977 respectively.

US Bureau of the Census, Subject Reports. *Japanese, Chinese, and Filipinos in the United States* PC(2)-1G; *American Indians* PC(2)-IF; *Persons of Spanish Origin* PC(2)-1C; *Negro Population* PC(2)-1B. Washington, D.C.: Government Printing Office, 1973.

US Public Health Service. National Center for Health Statistics. *Vital Statistics of the United States: 1970.* Vol. II: *Mortality.* Washington, D.C.: Government Printing Office, 1974.

FOR FURTHER READING

Brotman, H. "Analytical and Summary Reference Tables: The Older Population Estimates for 1975 Projecting through 2000." Prepared for the National Institute on Aging, January 1976.

Brotman, H. "Life Expectancy: Comparison of National Levels in 1900 and 1974 and Variations in State Levels, 1969–71," *The Gerontologist,* 1977, 17:1.

Coale, A. J. "The Effects of Changes in Mortality and Fertility on Age Composition," *The Milbank Memorial Fund Quarterly, 1956, 44.*

Jewett, S. P. "Longevity and the Longevity Syndrome," *The Gerontologist,* 1973, 13:1.

Kaplan, O., and R. Ontell. "Social Indicators and the Aging." In A. Schwartz and I. Mensh (eds.), *Professional Obligations and Approaches to the Aged.* Springfield, Ill.: Charles C Thomas, 1974.

Sachuk, N. N. "Population Longevity Study: Sources and Indices," *Journal of Gerontology,* 1970, 24.

Townsend, C. *Old Age, the Last Segregation.* New York: Bantam Books, 1971.

II | Social Institutions

CHAPTER 3

Social Processes and the Later Years

Do not go gentle into that good night,
Old age should burn and
  rave at close of day;
Rage, rage against the dying of the light.
And you, my father, there on that sad height

Curse, bless me now with your fierce tears, I pray
Do not go gentle into that good night.
Rage, rage against the dying of the light.

         DYLAN THOMAS

This chapter describes some of the more important social roles that operate over time and suggests the impact of changes in social roles upon older persons. In this context the student can begin to examine age norms and age grading and how these time-related social factors influence attitudes and behavior. One implication of the chapter is how, in our society, continuity and change constitute an application of the principle of complementarity with respect to the interaction of social norms and values in later life.

Differences in generational experiences must be taken into account when we assess the genesis and development of intergenerational bias and conflicts. Some of the more prevalent myths and stereotypes ascribed to aging persons are discussed in this chapter, thus providing an opportunity to explore the most basic and pernicious barriers to accurate evaluations of the real promise of later years, namely, the self-

fulfilling prophecies of many negative stereotypes about growing old that still persist. Because they are widely held by younger segments of society, these stereotypes become especially important inasmuch as many elderly, through social learning, accept them at face value and consequently lower their own expectations and goals.

The following case description describes a man here named James North. A good friend and intimate of the authors, he shared his life history with us. His story is a good introduction to an understanding of some of the social factors that are critical in social gerontology, although, because he is one individual, his case certainly does not exhaust the experiences of men in their later years.

James North is a sixty-eight-year-old Caucasian in his third year as a resident of a retirement home in Los Angeles. The authors were called in for consultation with the administrators of the retirement home because Mr. North was exhibiting such disturbing behavior as appearing at 4:00 A.M. by the bedside of other residents, introducing himself by strange names, refusing to eat for days at a time, and just sitting in a depressed stupor for extended periods of time. All of this was new and unusual behavior for Mr. North and the cause of grave concern within the facility.

In going over the problems presented by Mr. North, his physical condition was evaluated first. Nothing remarkable was in evidence; physiologically, all factors appeared to be within normal or acceptable limits. He had some trouble with glaucoma, but no direct physical basis for his change of behavior could be discovered from the records.

Assessment then focused on his psychological status. While he had been somewhat depressed in recent years, he had no history of bouts of extended depression. He had always been forgetful and sometimes distractable; yet, during two months of study he never missed an appointment. He did wander about at night but he only stood or sat by the bedside of fellow residents. There was very little from his prior psychological history and behavior to account for this new and deviant pattern of behavior.

Evaluation then focused on past and present social factors in his life. Not having located any specific physical or psychological antecedents for his change of behavior, the therapists now looked for an explanation in the ways he had previously and now related to other persons —a social explanation. Several elements in this man's social roles were uncovered which proved to be crucial ones. Mr. North had been a high school principal in the same community for forty years. This had involved three other roles he had pursued with vigor. He had been a far-sighted community leader, working with zest for his church, the Rotary Club's Eye Program, the Democratic Party, the sheriff's Boys'

Club, and other groups. He consistently took courses at a nearby university and after many years he had earned (with distinction) his Ph.D. His third role was that of husband and father.

All of these roles gave him a deep sense of personal value and satisfaction. But all of these roles were abruptly terminated when he retired and moved into the retirement community. The retirement community was located far from either a school or an adequate library. His poor eyesight made reading difficult. There were no classes at the retirement center that challenged him, nor were there individuals who might have become intellectual friends. He pinpointed his plight when he rather succinctly stated, ". . . there are no brains in this place."

The retirement community was run smoothly enough by an autocrat who said he loved "older folks." But he appeared to "love" them only when he could control and manipulate them. Consequently, there was no resident council, no resident committee—no way for Mr. North or anyone else to participate meaningfully in decisions regarding programs that would affect him. All of Mr. North's long training in community organization and volunteer activity was ignored. Finally, his wife had died six months after they had moved into the retirement facility and his children lived far away. So all of his forty-six years spent with family and with intimacy and warmth were also lost.

If Mr. North sat silently in the retirement residence by the bed of a female resident, it had much to do with the fact that he very much missed the long-accustomed warmth and comfort of sleeping beside his wife. In his depression and bewilderment he was reaching out. If he sat in a stupor and was depressed, it was because the past intellectual and social interactions were far more rewarding in recall than any attempt to participate in a currently sterile and unrewarding life routine devoid of intellectual stimulation. If he refused to eat, it was a mute protest against a life that had no further challenge as he saw it and for which he had little taste. All his major social roles which had given him his sense of identity and satisfaction were shrunken. Most of his usual sources of satisfaction were cut off. As these facts began to emerge, Mr. North's behavior became (for us) less "strange," "bizarre," or incongruous. We began to get a better grasp of what had happened to the social network, to his sources of past satisfaction, and what these events meant to him. A similar thwarting of interests and satisfactions happens to a great many older persons.

Changes in patterns of role enactment, in the amount and quality of social and intellectual stimuli, and in opportunities for meaningful work help to explain the life situation and the behavior of many older persons (Streib, 1971). These changes are related, of course, to demographic shifts, to age stratification, to intergenerational and facility contacts, and to friendship networks. These social factors certainly do not explain all of the variations between life-styles and satisfaction of older persons but they do explain many of them. The remainder of this chapter is organized to explore the salience of various social aspects of aging.

SOCIAL STRATIFICATION AND THE OLDER PERSON

In all discussions of demographic profiles, age is used as one of the most critical variables. Given the specific differences between those under fifteen, fifteen to sixty-four, and sixty-five and over, students of gerontology can focus on the similarities and differences of persons in different age categories, and determine how membership in the unique social structures associated with age groups influences attitudes and behavior.

Stratification is a complex topic. As the term is used in sociology it refers to a special category of belonging: to a limited group (or stratum) that determines to some extent one's values and attitudes. Obviously age itself puts constraints on individuals. The adolescent is all hormones and pimples; internal sexual promptings are novel and disturbing. Fifteen years later such feelings are accepted as normal. Fifty years later sexual drives may be more sporadic and sometimes surprising. A child of six may want to wield an ax like his father but he can't quite manage it. Perhaps his grandfather coming up the lane with his cane is feeling nostalgic for the days he swung that ax with vigor. Childbearing may be a joy or a burden, but, after fifty, it is no longer (for almost all women) either an expectation or a threat.

Physical changes and decrements are factors that set limits and can influence behavior. No one would suggest that changes in strength, glandular products, vital capacity, sexual drive, vision, hearing, and the like are not often critical contributors to changes appearing with age. But they do not necessarily form the major component in determining specific responses. In the case of James North, an analysis eliminated physical states as particularly significant in the assessment of his problems.

Position in the family often determines attitudes and values associated with behavior at given ages. In fact, the family is decisive in helping the growing generation adopt those values that are essential for smooth acceptance in their social class. Kohn (1969) explains the critical nature of the socialization process—how finely drawn are the influences of father and mother in this process and how the process is different for different social classes—concluding from his national study:

> In both the middle class and the working class, mothers have their husbands play a role that facilitates children's development of valued characteristics. To middle-class mothers, it is important that children be able to decide for themselves how to act and that they have the personal resources to act on these decisions. In this conception fathers' responsibility for imposing restraints is secondary to their responsibility of being supportive . . . .To working-class mothers, on the other hand, it is more important that children conform to externally imposed rules. In this conception, fathers' primary responsibility is to guide and direct the children.

We will test later the success of this socializing process in providing continuity of society's values and institutions as one tries to explain intergenerational relationships. But family structures and functions are also so definitive that age-graded norms and roles are assigned and regulated. The child and early adolescent are not expected to support themselves independently. They are dependents, but the young adult male, on pain of disapproval, has to support himself, his mate and, later, his children. As he ages in America, he must be industrious and frugal so that he can support himself when his work days are over. And work days must be over at a specified time so that his sons and grandsons have job opportunities. This rite of passage of mandated unemployment is known as mandatory retirement. Thus, every age has its defined objectives and social roles that determine the way to achieve, but the social environment in which these roles occur is changing and puts strain on the effort to achieve and be productive.

VARIATIONS IN LIFE EXPERIENCE

Those persons who are now fifty-five to seventy-five years of age were the cohort that experienced the Great Depression of the thirties, and their personal life-styles, economic attitudes, and political opinions were partially shaped by the deprivations and insecurities that attended the Depression. Subsequent cohorts lived through a period when jobs were abundant. They also lived through a period of rampant nationalism that accompanied World War II and the Korean War. Technology was changing too, so that each cohort was confronted by a different world. Their education was also different as the curriculum was adjusted to prepare the next generation for new jobs held in new circumstances. Young people carried special inhibitions, anxieties, and attitudes acquired during these periods of social turmoil into their middle and older years. Three-fourths of children now in training will enter into an array of widely different jobs that did not exist when they were born. This explains why it is sometimes difficult for parents to socialize their children either by encouragement or by constraint into a world substantially different from the one they knew in their own formative years. It may be even more difficult for aging grandparents to be current enough, in a world of such rapid economic and social change, to communicate easily with their grandchildren.

The problem of the impact of shifting cohort values is accentuated by what Bengtson calls the *generational stake* (Bengtson et al., 1976), the expectations that one generation has of another, expectations often in conflict. Thus parents expect their children to be similar in values and behavior to themselves—to carry on their traditions and thus give continuity to culture. But their children need to be independent, creative, and innovative—to adjust to their world as they perceive it. One of their developmental goals in late adolescence is to develop a sense of individual identity and personal competence, a need that may lead to their denying (at least in part) the validity of parental values and lifestyles that were formed in another era. Furthermore, in moving toward the achievement of independence young persons often substitute approval of their peers for parental approval. This solidifies cohort conformity but it jeopardizes intergenerational relationships and social continuity. On the other hand, if social, political, economic, and technological structures are changing, the revolt of youth may be an adaptive social mechanism.

What is the extent of continuity of values in our society with its rapid social change? The data in Figure 3–1 is instructive: Some 2,100 persons participated in the study and the report is based on data from 1,481 of the participants; 313 are members of the grandparent generation, 562 are from the parent generation, and 606 are young adults. Males and females are about equally divided. Bengtson's study shows that, regardless of environmental differences in the socialization process, there is continuity of social values. On the other hand, while the study shows continuity it does not account for differential attitudes and behavior. One study of the growth of sexual permissiveness bridges this gap (Reiss, 1971). Using a national sample to test his hypothesis, Reiss found that an adolescent's acceptance of a given level of sexual permissiveness is a product of influences that started out on a base line of the acceptance of parental attitudes, generally low on permissiveness and reinforced most powerfully by religious norms. Attitudes and pressures of the peer group tend to liberalize the level of permissiveness. The degree to which young persons can divorce themselves from guilt-inducing institutions and become involved as part of a more sexually permissive youth culture depends on their autonomy

Figure 3–1.   INTERGENERATIONAL VALUES

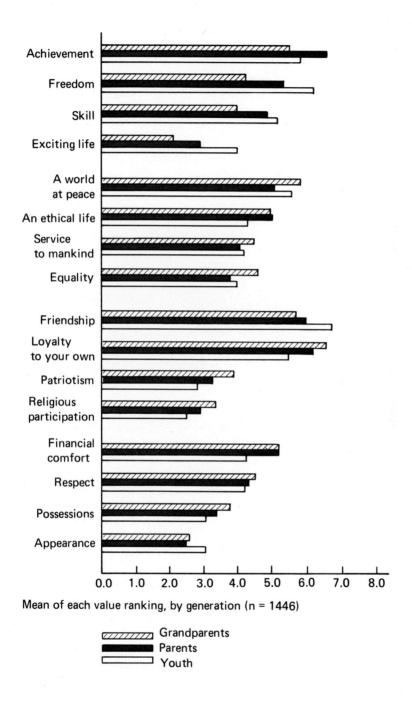

Mean of each value ranking, by generation (n = 1446)

SOURCE: Bengtson et al. (1976).

and degree of participation in the erotic behavior patterns of their youthful subcultures. Thus internal psychological pressures must be taken into account in determining causative factors with respect to intergenerational relations.

However, when the role position of young persons changes and they themselves become parents, now having to worry about pregnancy and venereal disease for their own children, their higher permissiveness level changes to a somewhat lower one. Still, the generational cohort to which one belongs in terms of placement of scales of cultural change and in terms of family position and responsibility are both critical in understanding social attitudes and intergenerational conflicts (Reiss, 1971).

How powerful are age norms in determining behavior? Obviously Reiss's study shows that they have a constraining influence but not rigid control. Other investigators think that most persons are aware of these age norms but regard them as guides society provides *for others.* Bengtson stresses the reasons why older persons find a greater stake in social norms than do the young: "... the old have a stake in continuing that which they found desirable or deemed appropriate" (Bengtson & Haber, 1975). He also believes that the sanctions society places on conformity to these norms is so great that if one is tardy in living up to life-cycle norms such as marrying late, one will hurry to have a first child:" ... to move toward the norm on the next event" (Bengtson & Haber, 1975).

What are the issues or questions inherent in the "generational stake" for different age strata? There is real potential for conflict both over national resources and between young and older workers.

When those over sixty-five made up but 3 percent of the population and were relatively well cared for by families that lived close by, there was little possibility of conflict, but now when we look forward to 12 percent of the population's being over sixty-five, and some 30 million persons all living a little longer, there is potential for bitter struggle. Maggie Kuhn's Gray Panthers, for instance, make it clear they will not settle for mediocre medical services or living conditions. Yet the tax on younger producers still in the stages of raising and educating their children may become so high that they will balk. Both employers and employees have already expressed great concern over the size of the proposed Social Security tax increase, which is necessary if that system is to be viable for the future. One of the reasons for the near-bankrupt status of the City of New York may well be the generous pension system it maintains for its large number of employees.

In the future the group from twenty-five to sixty must support for a much longer time both the young, who have an ever lengthening period of education, and the older persons, who are living longer. And

Older people find many ways to participate in the life of their communities.

through all this they, too, must remember that one day the system must support them!

There is much pressure from labor unions to force industry to provide liberal conditions for early retirement. Already 50 percent of industrial plants have such plans. Many universities with a high percentage of older, tenured professors are concerned about closing their doors to young, highly skilled, promising men and women. Two states, New York and California, have passed legislation to eliminate sixty-five as an arbitrary retirement date. More critical is the fact that when our current middle-aged group gets older they will be healthier and better educated. Continued education has enabled these persons to stay reasonably current in their skills and informational base. There is a growing discontent over an arbitrary retirement based on assumptions of inevitable decrements which have long ago proven to be mythological. We should analyze those myths.

MYTHS ABOUT OLDER PERSONS

The Social Myth

Social myths are defined sociologically as false social beliefs about social groups. Such myths not only predispose society to adopt negative attitudes toward older people, they also undermine the real potential of the elderly by lowering their own expectations. As we mentioned at the outset of this chapter, the basic problem of a social myth is its potential to make its victims act so that the myth becomes a self-fulfilling prophecy. Specifically, if older persons accept the common belief that they lose the capacity to function well, they themselves may come to believe what others think and say about them, and thus begin to function below their actual capacity. If an older person is told repeatedly that his or her sexual capacity is bankrupt when he or she reaches the sixties, that belief may make a male impotent or a woman frigid. At the very least it can cause elderly persons to avoid opportunities for sexual activities.

Thus, all the while attempts are made to lure older workers into earlier retirement, pressures continue to build on those with acceptable levels of health and skills to stay on the job and continue their careers. If society tells its oldest citizens that they have no further economic or political usefulness, they may withdraw from the economic or political scene. The same self-fulfilling process occurs when older individuals have occasions of forgetfulness (as we all do, regardless of age), but they are taught to regard this as a sign of senility, so that they retreat intellectually. It is worth discussing sexual, political, and intellectual myths in order to document the insidious and destructive nature of mythologies about aging. These topics are discussed in greater detail in other parts of this book. In this chapter we are interested in presenting ways in which the process of stereotyping the elderly is destructive.

The Economic Myth

It is widely believed that the majority of older persons are poor and economically dependent. "Not having enough money to live on" was judged a problem for older persons by 62 percent of the public, but only 15 percent of seniors thought it a problem (Harris, 1976). This myth has devastating consequences for any person approaching retirement and can produce dread on the part of their children. The myth results in a distorted picture of our older population, gives them a poor public image, and makes adaptation to aging difficult.

What are the facts? What is an adequate income? How many of our older persons live well? On the average, retired persons have an income in this and many foreign countries that is almost 50 percent of the income they had in the last years of their employment careers. However, inflation having been in double figures for the last few years, the value of the dollar total may be something less than 50 percent in purchasing power. Because one-half of all retirement income comes from programs such as Social Security or various other pension plans, the adequacy of those payments depends partially on payment levels and partially on the way in which those payments are adjusted to rising costs. Social Security payments are now geared to inflation—if living costs rise significantly, so do Social Security payments. This is not true of the majority of private pension plans.

The US Department of Labor has established levels of adequacy of income for both individuals and families. Those whose incomes are below those standards ($3,000 for couples) are described as living below the poverty level. Tables 3–1 and 3–2 give a graphic picture as of 1971 of the economic status of our older citizens.

TABLE 3–1. INCOME DISTRIBUTION OF 5 MILLION COUPLES WITH HEADS 65 AND OVER, 1971

Percentage of Couples	Income	Percent
83 under $10,000	$10,000 or more	17
50 under $4,999	$5,000 to $10,000	32
21 under $3,000	$3,000 to $5,000	30
1 under $1,000	$1,000 to $3,000	20
	Under $1,000	1

SOURCE: *New Facts about Older Americans* (June 1973).

TABLE 3–2. INCOME DISTRIBUTION OF 6.1 MILLION PERSONS AGED 65 AND OVER, LIVING ALONE OR WITH NONRELATIVES, 1971

Percentage of Couples	Income	Percent
87 under $5,000	$5,000 and more	13
69 under $3,000	$3,000 to $5,000	18
45 under $2,000	$2,000 to $3,000	24
26 under $1,500	$1,500 to $2,000	19
10 under $1,000	$1,000 to $1,500	16
	Under $1,000	10

SOURCE: *New Facts about Older Americans* (June 1973).

Tables 3–1 and 3–2 indicate that many older persons have incomes that allow tolerable standards of living. Seventy-nine percent of couples have incomes over $3,000 and almost 50 percent have incomes over $5,000. On the other hand, 21 percent of these couples are certainly living at what has been defined by the Labor Department as below the poverty level. The 6.1 million persons living alone or with nonrelatives are worse off. Forty-five percent have incomes below $2,000 and 26 percent below $1,500. It is difficult to imagine those 1,600,000 persons (the 26 percent) paying rent, buying adequate food, paying for adequate medical care, and maintaining a satisfactory lifestyle. But, overall, the majority of older persons seem to have adequate income.

The rules governing Social Security discourage older persons from working. For every two dollars they earn above $4,000 a year, one dollar is subtracted from their Social Security payment by the government. There is no earnings limit for retirees seventy-two and over.* In spite of all this, 15 percent of those over sixty-five (or 3.1 million) are in the labor force. This may encourage older persons to work, at least part time, providing something is done to counteract the very strong pressure in industry against the older worker. Those who work today after sixty-five represent one in four older persons, in contrast to the two of three older persons who were at work in 1900.

All persons engaged in the argument regarding the employment of older persons agree that many older persons need a better retirement income. Almost everyone who studies income and aging looks with chagrin at the high number of those living below the poverty level. Thus while it is inaccurate to say that all older persons are poor, nevertheless it is clear that more opportunities for work in the later years are needed.

A more subtle aspect of this myth is that older persons somehow are responsible for their own poverty. They should have saved more. They should have avoided frittering away their savings. Many younger and middle-aged persons feel that to raise Social Security payments or other pensions is an act of charity. These groups do not often stress the inadequacies of national planning or lack of national policies for our senior citizens. Yet those who are older built the nation. They availed themselves of whatever chance they had to save and to enroll in such programs as Social Security. They laid the foundations in industry and agriculture for the younger persons who may now elect to give them a much smaller share of current national income.

The myth that most older persons are unable to work because of

*Under newly passed legislation, the limit jumps to $4,500 in 1979, $5,000 in 1980, $5,500 in 1981, and $6,000 in 1982, after which the limit will be based on the rate of inflation. Starting in 1980, the earnings limit will no longer apply to persons age seventy and over.

weakness, physical problems, mental illness, senility, and so forth is often cited to justify mandatory retirement at sixty-five. The economic myth says not only that older persons are poor because they deserve to be poor but that they are inadequate employees. But the great majority of sixty-five-year-olds, male and female, are hearty and could contribute to the economic progress of the country. (See further discussion of this point in chapter 4.) There are pressing economic reasons for earlier and earlier retirement. There may be arguments cogent enough to raise the question as to the wisdom of mandatory retirement, but certainly such arguments ought not to be based on myth.

The Health Myth

The public image of older persons is well stated by Professor Edwin Markham describing in verse what he sees in Millet's painting *The Man with the Hoe:*

Bowed by the weight of centuries he leans
Upon his hoe and gazes on the ground,
The emptiness of ages in his face,
And on his back the burden of the world.
Who made him dead to rapture and despair,
A thing that grieves not and that never hopes,
Stolid and stunned, a brother to the ox?
Who loosened and let down this brutal jaw?
Whose was the hand that slanted back this brow?
Whose breath blew out the light within this brain?

Equally graphic is Shakespeare's summary of the last age of man: "Sans teeth, sans ears, sans voice, sans everything."

These portrayals of the "destroyed" older person are mythological today. It is true that there are about one million older persons in some 25,000 nursing homes, but this represents only about 4 percent of that population.

It is true that chronic conditions like arthritis, rheumatism, high blood pressure, and depression are more prevalent in the aging population than in younger cohorts, but it is also true that nine out of ten older persons are not homebound and live mobile lives of comparative independence. (See discussion in chapter 8.) It is also true that when reference is made to the greater incidence of impairment among those over seventy-five in contrast to the young, the reference is to the greater incidence of chronic ailments (Bengtson and Haber, 1975). While seven out of eight older persons have some chronic condition, this does not mean that they are incapable of employment, a rewarding sexual life, or independent living. Only 21 percent of the elderly say that health is one of their great problems. On the other hand, 50 percent of young people think that poor health is a very serious problem for those over sixty-five (Manion, 1972).

The myth about health adds anxiety to the way older persons view themselves and the years they have left. It distorts the debate about mandatory retirement and makes discussion of an adequate program of health maintenance difficult.

The Health Care Myth

A fourth kind of myth has to do with health care and health mainte-nance. It is widely assumed that, with the high financial investment the nation makes in Medicare and Medicaid, the health needs of the elderly have been adequately met. There is much impatience regarding the possibility of any national health insurance. We are not here pro-posing to give the arguments for or against such a plan; that discussion is properly reserved for a discussion of public policy. We are simply showing the basic difficulties of appropriate assessment of the needs of older people in the face of mythology. What are the facts? In 1973 the total annual health bill per aged person was $1,040. Medicare paid only 40.5 percent of this bill. Figure 3–2 illustrates the failure of our national health program to keep up at all with rising health costs of older persons. This means that because those living below the poverty line must spend such large proportions of their available income for such basics as housing, food, clothing, and medical care, nothing is left for leisure, education, travel, or anything else that might enhance life satisfaction.

Figure 3–2.   MEDICAL CARE PER AGED PERSON AND PROPORTION COVERED BY MEDICARE, 1966-1973

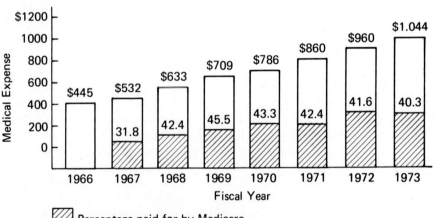

Percentage paid for by Medicare.

SOURCE: Social Security Administration.

The Sexual Myth

The sexual myth simply says that when men and women reach old age, the woman after menopause and the man after sixty, nature decrees that sexual drives and responsiveness are gone. What ought to be regarded as a perfectly normal episode of occasional impotence is interpreted by a man schooled in the myth as a true indication that his potency is permanently gone. Then his anxiety can lead to the self-fulfilling outcome of permanent impotence. Just so, the same kind of anxiety can make a female retreat from sex when the first signs of aging tissue cause some minor (treatable) distress. Of course, the fact is well established by Masters and Johnson that sexual joy can be part of almost every person's life until they die. But the deep-seated myth can destroy that potential and has done so, sad to say, for hundreds of thousands of aging persons (Gordon, 1976).

The Myth of the Aging Mind

One of the most devastating of all myths is the one that predicts that all older persons will gradually lose the acuity of their thought pro-

The need for and interest in closeness, affection, and intimacy can and usually do continue unabated throughout the life span.

cesses. This myth is particularly insidious because it forms the partial justification for mandatory retirement, for suspicion of the political and social behavior of older persons, and for relegating the "old ones" to insignificant life roles. It is generally believed that older persons think more slowly and more sloppily than do young persons. It is true that the intellectual *performance* of elderly persons becomes more deliberate, slows down. This has been demonstrated in many research studies. It is also true that the sensory deprivation many older persons experience significantly affects their cognitive and intellectual processes. But despite these and other more equivocal findings Schaie and others have concluded from extensive study that most of the so-called declines in intelligence are a myth (see chapter 9), that older persons can be as wise and insightful at eighty as they were at thirty and, perhaps, even wiser in making decisions. What is important to note here is the damage to self-esteem, social usefulness, and political involvement and the waste of basic contributions that attend these myths.

We have summarized a few of the social distortions and stereotypes about older persons from the point of view of the impact those myths make on life fulfillment of our senior citizens. It is apparent that gerontology has a major research and dissemination task in investigating such myths and providing the evidence that will enable older persons to take a more optimistic view of themselves and contribute more positively to their world.

THE LOSS OF SOCIAL ROLES

The social-role losses of older persons are numerous and cumulative. Women face early retirement when they reach the end of their child-raising careers. Not merely do their children leave home, but all the roles ancillary to motherhood—such as PTA member, Cub Scout board member, chauffeur to a dozen events, and so forth—go with them. The male who retires likewise gives up his daily associations and recreational linkages with his fellow workers, as well as his union or managerial association membership. He gives up a great many associated roles with the end of his work: the festive luncheon group role, the work-associated recreational role, such as member of the bowling team. And many times the end of his work career makes a serious impact on his friendship network, which previously was tied to his occupation.

As the couple ages, their friendship network is shriveled by the death and mobility of neighbors and friends. His co-workers are transferred. His pastor may leave. His doctor may retire. His siblings die.

All of the significant persons who were part of his life support system may go. Sometimes financial and health factors contribute to a narrowing of the circle of his friends and the range of his interests. One price we pay for extended survival is the disruption of the family and the friendship network.

It was because of their observations of such decrements in social life that Elaine Cumming and William Henry (1961) produced their much debated disengagement theory, which was discussed in chapter 1. Much of their data is relevant to our discussion of social factors; Table 3–3 illustrates the losses that occur.

TABLE 3–3.   ROLES OF INTERACTION BY AGE AND SEX

Sex and Age	Number Interviewed	Percent of Number Interviewed	
		Large Number of Roles	High Daily Interaction
Both sexes	211	41.7	47.9
50–54	36	61.1	72.2
55–59	34	61.8	58.8
60–64	34	58.8	58.8
65–69	31	38.7	45.2
70–74	50	22.0	34.0
75 and over	26	7.7	15.4
Males	107	42.0	46.7
50–54	19	68.4	78.9
55–59	18	61.1	50.0
60–64	19	47.4	52.6
65–69	12	50.0	50.0
70–75	25	20.0	32.0
75 and over	14	7.1	14.3
Females	104	41.3	49.0
50–54	17	52.9	64.7
55–59	16	62.5	68.8
60–64	15	73.3	66.7
65–69	19	31.6	42.1
70–74	25	24.0	36.0
75 and over	12	8.3	16.7

SOURCE: Cumming & Henry (1961).

It is obvious that as the number of roles diminish with age, high daily interaction goes down. This is social loss.

The loss of family roles and interactions is discussed in chapter 5. Although there is evidence of a new form of semiextended family, it is obvious that the high daily interaction rate goes down as the family disperses due to employment mobility, marriage of children and the new tasks of their newly formed families in raising their own children, and so forth. There are few family sociologists, regardless of their description of the contemporary family, who would not agree that older persons lose some family contacts and that often relationships with siblings and cousins are not as consistent or close as they once were.

What are the compensations for these social losses? Is it possible that older persons may find new interests and supports in association with other aged persons and thus build a meaningful reference group? To do so would be to develop an age consciousness so that the group would identify with each other and work both to increase sociability and to redress their problems. On the whole, older persons have not tended in the past to band together socially or politically. This is changing. One must not overlook the enormous success of the Gray Panther movement in assessing potentialities for the future of the aged. There are now in most major cities loosely organized groups of Panthers, their consciousness raised by young and old who are developing advocacy skills and new networks of influence. There are such groups as the American Association of Retired Persons; its local chapters become a coordinated social group working for mutual goals and serving each other through volunteer work. There are special religiously inspired groups, such as the Shepherd's Centers in Kansas City and Atlanta and HEAD groups in other eastern cities, which indeed seem to be significant alternatives to the social losses we have described. (These will be be more fully discussed in chapter 7.)

We are equally impressed with the possibility that congregate living supplies a new community. In a sense many of these give examples of retribalization where new friendships are formed, where volunteer effort builds a kind of quasi-family closeness. There widows find opportunity for heterosexual contact, businessmen can associate in a new form of social club that replicates their former service club experience. Such living arrangements do encourage change in the negative stereotypes of the aged. Careful research on patterns of neighboring among older persons shows both consistency and change in social relations (Rosow, 1974). New friendship networks create excitement and pleasure and at least some opportunities to use old skills in new ways.

Along with a loss of role there must also be a loss of status. Older people in America are not given the prestige or approval that came to them when they were middle-aged. If one asks them in a survey how old they are, a most characteristic response is that they are "middle-aged." Then if one asks how old their friends are, they say that they are all "old." It may well be that this way of responding reveals much about their sense of loss of position and status. But one cannot change the evaluation by society by claiming membership in another age group. The older individual loses his job, his position on the board of elders in the church, in his political organization, in the service groups in the community, even in some volunteer organizations. All of this tells him much about his lowered status and loss of power. Even if he is affluent he is likely to experience losses of role, position, and status. Indeed, some research indicates that the more affluent, influential older person is likely to encounter even greater difficulty than the average person in adapting to status change (Shire, 1972). It may well be that if other elderly begin to form a reference group for him in a senior citizen center, in a retirement community, in a Gray Panthers group, that he may find a new or renewed status which is meaningful among his peers.

SOCIAL INSTITUTIONS AND THE AGED

One of the classical sociological descriptions of an institution is that it is an idea and a structure. It is a structured and permanent way that society organizes to meet human needs. The institutions that seem to be a part of every primitive and advanced society are those of religion, education, economics, politics, and recreation. Because we treat the institutions of religion, politics, economics, and recreation in later chapters, our attention is focused here on the way the educational institutions meet the needs of the elderly.

There are four basic dimensions of social change that explain why it is imperative for society to turn rhetoric about lifelong education into specific action programs.

The first dimension has to do with demographic trends. We have already noted that in 1900 only 3 percent of our population was sixty-five or older. Families in 1900 rarely had both father and mother still living when the last child left home. Today, citizens who have already marked their sixty-fifth birthday comprise almost 11 percent of the population. They number 22 million persons. The achievement of zero population growth for the last years when projected thirty years from now gives us an estimate that well over half the population will then be over fifty years of age. If the task of education is broadly seen as that of creative adaptation, changing personal, social and cultural tasks, then the educational system has an obligation to refocus on the last half of life (Peterson, 1978).

The second dimension arises from an analysis of employment trends

Nutrition programs for the elderly provide good, hot meals—and more. They also provide opportunities for social exchange, which for most people is an important element in the enjoyment of food.

in our work world. Several years ago the Civil Service Commission established the period of life work as terminating at age fifty-five. The great debate in the Chrysler and mine workers negotiations over the past few years did not have so much to do with wages as with retirement. The negotiations were concluded when an agreement was reached that the worker who had been employed steadily for thirty years was entitled to a full pension at that time, whether the worker was fifty or fifty-five years of age. The steel industry has much the same rules. More than half the major industries in the United States now have provisions for early retirement. A comprehensive study of faculty retirement at the University of Southern California (Peterson, 1978) has shown that 35 percent of the current working faculty would prefer to retire early (see chapter 4). It might have been expected that cycles of depression and inflation would have stilled the voices of those wishing early retirement, but the best statistical evidence available is that there has been only a 14 percent drop in applications for early termination of work. Thirty-five percent of the faculty is a major proportion. The implications of these trends are that in twenty years, another 10 million persons "at leisure" may be added to the 25 to 30 million above sixty-five who will be retired at that time. Some of these individuals will wish second career training, but many of them will be an avid group seeking educational opportunities to give meaning to their lives (Hemistra, 1978).

The third dimension has to do with technological advances in research and development. Two years ago a student chose to replicate a dissertation done a quarter of a century before. When the original author wrote that dissertation, he hired three young men who were facile with slide rules and they worked for three months to put his statistics in order. After the young man who replicated the earlier research effort had his computer cards punched he spent exactly nine minutes feeding them into the computer. And he has much additional data to mine for years to come.

Even if a person elects to work after fifty, and is in a field where research is common, that person will have to spend much time in classes or the laboratory simply to keep up with younger colleagues. If one is beyond fifty years of age he may discover that unless he has studied strenuously to keep up his vocabulary, his information base, and his techniques, his value may be seen as more appropriate to yesteryear. Technological change makes it imperative that education focus on the constant upgrading of members of the work force so they do not become obsolescent. This will be true even when society changes the unrealistic rule of retirement at sixty-five.

The fourth dimension is the conclusion, drawn from psychosocial research, that age has nothing to do with intellectual acuity. Botwinik, Woodruff, Schaie, and Birren have all demonstrated that there is no significant intellectual loss simply because of age for most persons as they age. The store of information and vocabularies grows until one dies (see chapter 9).

Early retirement, the dislocations caused by technological unemployment, the need for the older persons who are employed to stay current, the growing demand for second career education, all make continued education for those past fifty imperative. The growing number of older persons who have time and energy to devote to social and political fields demands that they be educated so that their time and energy investments will be relevant.

Human beings can be vigorous all their years, and if they have lost that vigor, it can be regained (discussed further in chapter 8). DeVries (1975) has shown how only three hours of exercise a week can restore muscle, add significant strength to the heart, increase capacity to use oxygen, and in general help people to feel well and alert. Others have shown how important good diet is. But all such findings have to be disseminated in classes or groups before they become effective agents of change. It is rewarding for the scholar to know that the myths associated with aging are groundless, but it is more meaningful to work out ways by which education can serve to transform the health and outlook of millions of people.

Older persons want information on many subjects. They are terrorized by the growing violence in the nation. They are often prime targets for burglaries, con men, and grafters. Instruction in crime prevention can help them a great deal in terms of modifying their own behavior and thus finding peace of mind. Inflation robs retirees on fixed incomes of substantial proportions of the savings; many older persons can benefit from instruction in special techniques for coping with a shrinking income. Loneliness is a prime feature of aging. It is part of the etiology of depression. The excitement and adventure of learning go far to give some fellowship and relief from a sense of uselessness and thus from depression.

As a group, a larger proportion of older persons vote than do younger persons. They need updating on national and international issues. They would like to participate in life, but interest in music, painting, or other cultural pursuits requires cultivation. Left to themselves, many elderly feel aimless, frustrated, and out of the mainstream. In classes they have the help of experts, along with the stimulating support of others. Many of their needs are precisely those to which a relevant adult education program can speak. What is being done about it?

In California fifty-six community colleges have classes for the elderly, and fifty-two of these have gold card programs; thirty-six have advisory committees of older persons helping plan the locale of the programs. Many of these programs show innovative adaptations. San Jose has a nutrition program, Laney College has developed a Retired Senior Volunteer program, Cabrillo College has a stroke center, Porterville College has a mobile van for counseling, and Fullerton College has a Center for Creative Retirement. Similar educational programs are being developed across the nation.

It may be true that many older persons have not been socialized to the value of education. They grew up in a different time and yet they need the services and the inspiration of an educational program. This probably means that the educational system is faced with the task of aggressive recruiting. It is not enough to reach 30 percent. This recruiting will be partially achieved by new types of educational structures, locales, teaching, and evaluation methods.

Some of the implications for education are:

1. There is a potential student body of 22 million persons above sixty-five for adult education.

2. Older persons have the intellectual resources and motivation to remain contributing citizens.

3. Early retirement and displacement by technological development demand effort to help older individuals remain constructive, creative, and productive.

4. Science has provided us with useful information that can make the last half of life healthful and joyous, but older persons have had relatively little ready access to such information (Russel, 1978).

5. The growth of violence, criminal assault, graft; the ravages of inflation and loneliness invite the marshaling of resources through educational programs for those most hurt by these trends, the older persons.

6. Older persons have given enthusiastic response wherever informational programs have been instituted. There is a willing and motivated "student body" waiting for the response of gerontology and educators.

7. Academic programs of training as well as in-service training are critical to providing effective services to the older person.

8. Many programs are being developed by educational and community agencies that need to be upgraded and coordinated.

9. Most evidence shows that about 6 million of the older persons are self-motivated and will participate in any adequate service or educational program; the other 16 million must be cultivated and recruited.

10. In planning programs, in recruiting for the classroom or discussion, the inclusion of the older persons themselves as part of the planning process is essential.

11. As demographic trends show the diminution of the size of our infant and child population, the future of a well-financed and well-organized educational institution depends on our changing a youth-focused curriculum and structure to one that is responsive to the growing number of those in the last half of life.

SUMMARY

Beyond demography and social trends stands the bent figure of the man with the hoe. He is a caricature both in reality and in his potential.

The 22 million older persons and the 20 million more who will within three decades face crucial problems in midlife need not be bent and looking only at the ground. It is the challenge of gerontology to give an upward look and the light back to them. To do so involves institutional analysis and change: the challenging of current myths and changes of social policy.

There is, of course, some conflict over changing values from one generation to another, but the divergence of values is not as great as is believed. Greater conflict is seen in discussions about the use of national resources. Some of these conflicts can be reduced as social, economic, health, sexual social-role, and educational myths and stereotypes about older persons are dispelled.

REFERENCES

Bengtson, V., and D. A. Haber. "Sociological Approaches to Aging." In D. Woodruff and J. Birren (eds.), *Aging: Scientific Perspectives and Social Issues.* New York: D. Van Nostrand, 1975.

Bengtson, V. L., et al. *A Progress Report: USC Study of Generations.* Andrus Gerontology Center, University of Southern California, Los Angeles, 1976.

Cumming, E., and W. Henry. *Growing Old: The Process of Disengagement.* New York: Basic Books, 1961.

DeVries, H. "The Physiology of Exercise and Aging." In D. Woodruff and J. Birren (eds.), *Aging: Scientific Perspectives and Social Issues.* New York: D. Van Nostrand, 1975.

Gordon, C. *Human Sexuality: Contemporary Perspectives.* New York: Harper & Row, 1976.

Harris, Louis, and Associates, Inc. "The Myth and Reality of Aging in America." A survey for the National Council on the Aging, Washington, D.C., 1976.

Hemistra, R. "New Career Opportunities in Geronotology for the 1980's! A Crystal Ball." In M. Seltzer, H. Sterns, and T. Hickey (eds.), *Gerontology in Higher Education: Perspectives and Issues.* Belmont, Calif.: Wadsworth, 1978.

Kohn, M. L. *Class and Conformity: A Study in Values.* Homewood, Ill.: The Dorsey Press, 1969.

Manion, O. V. *Aging: Old Myths versus New Facts.* Eugene, Ore.: Retirement Services Incorporated, 1972.

New Facts about Older Americans. US Department of Health, Education, and Welfare, June 1973.

Peterson, D. "An Overview of Gerontology Education." In M. Seltzer, H. Sterns, and T. Hickey (eds.), *Gerontology in Higher Education: Perspectives and Issues.* Belmont, Calif.: Wadsworth, 1978.

Peterson, J. A. "Factors Involved in the Adjustment of Retired Faculty." Research monograph, Andrus Gerontology Center, University of Southern California, Los Angeles, 1976.

Reiss, I. *The Family System in America.* New York: Holt, Rinehart and Winston, 1971.

Rosow, I. *Socialization in Old Age.* Berkeley: University of California Press, 1974.

Russel, B. "Special Service Aspects of College and University Programs." In M. Seltzer, H. Sterns, and T. Hickey (eds.), *Gerontology in Higher Education: Perspectives and Issues.* Belmont, Calif.: Wadsworth, 1978.

Shire, H. "The Corporate Executive, Continuities, Education, and Schools of Business and Management" (unpublished master's thesis, Pepperdine University, Los Angeles, 1972).

Streib, G. F. "New Roles and Activities for Retirement." In G. L. Maddox (ed.), *The Future of Aging and the Aged.* Southern Newspaper Publishers Association Seminar Studies, 1971.

FOR FURTHER READING

Atchley, R. *The Social Forces in Later Life.* Belmont, Calif.: Wadworth, 1972.

Beauvoir, S. de. *The Coming of Age.* New York: Putnam, 1973.

Bengtson, V. *The Social Psychology of Aging.* New York: Bobbs-Merrill, 1973.

Binstock, R., and E. Shanas (eds.). *Handbook of Aging and the Social Sciences.* New York: Van Nostrand Reinhold, 1976.

Neugarten, B. (ed.). *Middle Age and Aging: A Reader in Social Psychology.* Chicago: The University of Chicago Press, 1968.

Riley, M. M., et al. *Aging and Society.* Vol. I. *An Inventory of Research Findings.* New York: Russell Sage Foundation, 1968.

Seltzer, M., H. Sterns, and T. Hickey, (eds.). *Gerontology in Higher Education: Perspectives and Issues.* Belmont, Calif.: Wadsworth, 1978.

CHAPTER 4

Economic and Vocational Factors in Aging

If you wanted to punish a man . . . so severely so that even the most hardened criminal would quail, all you have to do is to make his work meaningless.

FYODOR DOSTOYEVSKY

I t may be true that human beings do not live by bread alone. Equally true is the fact that they cannot live well without bread, without adequate shelter, and without recreation. Good nutrition, clothing, transportation, and adequate health care are also important factors contributing to life satisfaction in present-day society, and all of these cost money.

For this reason it is necessary that students of gerontology become familiar with the current economic circumstances of the elderly and those economic factors that affect them. Newcomers to gerontology can use this chapter to assess the adequacy of income of the elderly, examine sources of income, and evaluate the probabilities that the level of financial return for older persons will remain adequate. The student should also consider how certain public policies and social events (such as the rite of passage called retirement) affect the economic position of the aged in our society.

A basic question has to do with the willingness of other segments of the population to allocate funds to those who are no longer seen as "productive." We can categorize those segments of the population to whom money resources are allocated as the young who are being trained to take their place in the economy; those who are currently employed and producing goods or services; and those who are older, retired, and considered "nonproductive." Any society must divide up its monetary pie among these three sectors of the population. Throughout this chapter we will be analyzing the constraints and attitudes of these sectors and how they affect and are affected by such allocations. Some of the issues raised by this fundamental question are these:

1. What is the history of support for elderly persons in this country?

2. What provisions do the private and the public sectors make for retired persons?

3. How has inflation influenced those provisions?

4. What are the financial prospects for older persons today?

5. What do trends in employment, particularly trends toward early retirement, imply for the economy and what do they mean to the elderly?

6. Can the economy support on an adequate scale an increasing number of older persons who are unemployed?

7. Can the economy sustain the impact of Social Security, Medicare and Medicaid? Can it do so without reducing the high standard of living of the middle group, which underwrites both the young and the old?

How are some of the older persons in our country faring? Let us consider the case of Mrs. G.*

She was probably between sixty-nine and seventy-nine years old. She stood defiantly before my desk and challenged me.

"Don't give me that crap. You come with me to my apartment and *then* tell me how much the lot of the older person has improved. Are you timid? Why won't you come?"

I went. She lived in central Los Angeles, near McArthur Park. The Center had studied both the park and its relationship to nearby residents. I knew a little about her situation there, but really very little. So I went with her.

She went slowly because she did not walk well. Her left hip had been broken and never properly attended to. We came to her building and I let her lead the way, very slowly, up steps—six flights (the elevator was not working).

She had two rooms: small, untidy, cramped. The wallpaper hung

*Excerpts from a case report of a senior supervisor at Andrus Gerontology Center.

down in a fold where it had peeled off the wall. I wanted to tear it away
—I didn't (the landlord would have accused her of destruction). The
faucets didn't drip—they ran. I tried to tighten them (part of my education was two years as a plumber's helper), but in vain. The place was
dark. I offered to buy light bulbs and she laughed—evidently the wir-
ing was defective.

We talked about her social contacts. There were none except the
owner of a local store. If one day she didn't hobble down six flights he
would bring her a can of soup, bread, and milk. After rent and doctors'
bills were paid she didn't have any change left for streetcar fare to the
senior center or church.

In some desperation I told her I would take her to a social service
center. We would talk with a social worker. She laughed. She'd been
there. They would not listen. There were forms and more forms to fill
out, but she couldn't understand them and the workers were impatient.
She was hungry—and they seemed to be indifferent. So she left.

It's humiliating to admit failure, but I failed. Then I assigned a
bright, enthusiastic graduate student to Mrs. G. She failed, too. She
tried, but Mrs. G.'s suspiciousness and excessive demands and the
environmental and social barriers were too much. She failed—or we
failed—or all of us failed. I have no notion of what happened to Mrs.
G. Several months after this I returned, but Mrs. G. had disappeared.

Project FIND has uncovered thousands of cases like Mrs. G. These
are the forgotten isolates of our urban and suburban communities.
Nothing can obscure the fact that hundreds of thousands of our senior
citizens live in isolated, desolate rooms. They are the debris of an
industrial civilization, and such persons are the forgotten.

We cannot ignore the substantial number of aged living in poverty.
On the other hand, gerontologists are aware that in the last thirty years
basic economic trends show some improvement for older persons.
Fewer were below the low-income level in 1973 than in 1966. Table
4–1 shows the improvement.

While that figure may be encouraging in terms of a general trend, it
does not tell the story of the plight of special segments of the population. Older women, and especially black women, tend to be impover-
ished. Table 4–2 specifies the median income of these population
groups as of 1970. It is obvious that income at age sixty-five reflects the
lower base in preceding years.

Economic conditions for the older person are improving in this
country as a result of a number of factors. One contributor has been the
growth of private pension plans (Atchley, 1972). Until recently only a
relatively few persons benefited from such plans because they were
neither vested nor transferable. Recent legislation has improved the
financial return to the worker from private pensions. A second contrib-

TABLE 4–1.   PERSONS BELOW THE LOW–INCOME LEVEL BY AGE AND RACE FOR SELECTED YEARS, 1966–1973

Percent of Group below Low-Income Level	1973	1971	1969[a]	1966[b]
ALL PERSONS				
Total	11.1	12.5	12.2	14.7
65 Years and Over	16.3	21.6	25.3	28.5
Relative Concentration[c]	1.47	1.73	2.07	1.94
WHITE				
Total	8.4	9.9	9.5	11.3
65 Years and Over	14.4	10.9	23.3	26.4
Relative Concentration	1.71	1.73	2.45	2.34
OTHER RACES				
Total	29.6	30.9	31.1	39.8
65 Years and Over	35.5	38.4	48.1	53.4
Relative Concentration	1.20	1.24	1.55	1.34

[a]Data for 1973 and 1971 not directly comparable to data for 1969.
[b]Data for 1969 not directly comparable to data for 1966.
[c]Relative concentration is the ratio of percent of those 65 and over to percent of all persons in group.
SOURCE: US Bureau of the Census (July 1974).

utor is the new inclusion in Social Security of many self-employed groups, such as the farmer. A third contribution has come from recent legislation linking Social Security payments to the inflationary spiral so that real benefits are not lost because of rising prices. Basic to all of this has been the continued rise in the gross national product (GNP) of the country, coupled with the participation of the worker in shares of this expansion. Still another contribution has been the provision through Social Security of medical benefits through Medicare and Medicaid. More recently, the addition of a new program called Supplemental Security Income (SSI), which was instituted in January 1974 to augment the income of those below the poverty level, has helped improve to some extent the financial status of millions of elderly persons (see the later discussion in this chapter).

THE INCOME BASE IN EARLIER TIMES

But when we review the history of support for the older person in this country we find little that is really comparable to the present.

TABLE 4–2.   INCOME AND INCOME SOURCES OF BLACK, SPANISH, AND WHITE AGED IN THE UNITED STATES, AS OF 1970

	Black	Spanish	White
Median Individual Income			
Female: 65–69	$1,170	$1,270	$1,608
Female: 70–74	1,098	1,248	1,525
Female: 75+	974	1,189	1,362
Male: 65–69	1,956	2,659	3,817
Male: 70–74	1,711	2,101	2,892
Male: 75+	1,503	1,735	2,229
Percent Persons with Income under $2,000			
Female	83.4	77.3	67.5
Male	59.8	47.4	34.0
Percent Persons without Income			
Female	14.0	21.0	13.0
Male	5.9	5.8	2.9
Median Family Income by Family Type			
Husband (65+) Wife	$3,250	$4,373	$5,050
Female (65+) Head	$2,904	$3,897	$5,772
Percent of All Aged Families Living in Poverty	38.8	25.4	15.6
Percent of All Aged Unrelated Individuals in Poverty	71.7	58.1	48.8

SOURCE: US Bureau of the Census (1973).

Older persons had a different status and different roles at the turn of the century. In chapter 5 (on the family) we trace some of the changes moving the country from an extended to a semiextended or nuclear family structure. In the extended family, the father developed the farm or small business and production was controlled by him (Atchley, 1972). In his last years he reaped the rewards and benefits generated by his labors. It was his own farm or his own business until he died. He might bring his children into management but he made the major decisions. Thus, he did not depend on the largess of his children for support; they were dependent on him for their income. *That system is gone.*

The concept of family-centered production and distribution has for the most part disappeared. The children of today's oldster are much

Vocation helps us to define ourselves. Continuing in a work role is important to the aged in maintaining self-esteem.

less likely to work in the same occupation and more likely to live far away, so that his control is long since gone. Hill and Litwak and Sussman have made much of the contributions generations give to each other, and everyone is happy that these family connections exist to the extent they do. But the significant change has been in the nature of the socioeconomic structure of the community and nation (Hill, 1965).

It is primarily because of these changes that Social Security, Medicare, and SSI came into being. The transition from an agrarian to a highly industrialized economy has not been an easy one for older persons. During the period before 1900, most older persons who were alone and dependent were sent to county poor farms. In 1871 there were twenty-four county hospitals and almshouses in California alone, housing the poor aged, dependent children, and the feeble-minded and "insane." These institutions were often poorly ventilated, poorly maintained, and decrepit. Although they had to function in part as hospitals for the seriously ill, it was difficult to segregate the aged or children from the ill. After the turn of the century many counties developed county welfare boards, which made some attempts to improve care for the mentally ill, the physically ill, abandoned and retarded children, and aged persons. As the number of the aged began to increase from 3 percent in 1900 to 10 percent in 1970, and the social structure changed, special attention was focused on the elderly poor.

As early as 1915, states began to pass legislation enabling them to give Old Age Assistance. By 1929 there were some ten states and one territory, Alaska, that had enacted Old Age Assistance measures. They may have been called pensions in some states, but they were essentially welfare for the aged poor. By 1934 two territories and twenty-eight states had old age pension plans. The number of those covered grew from 70,000 in 1931 to 235,000 in December of 1934. However, in many states the right to establish pensions with state aid was optional for the counties of these states, and this did not work well. Only 28 percent of the population was covered in so-called optional states, as contrasted to 91 percent coverage in states where the law made it mandatory for counties to assume responsibility for old age pensions. In some states the state government contributed nothing, and counties found it difficult to assume the additional burden imposed by these pensions. When the Depression of the thirties came, resources of both states and counties were so low that they had difficulty meeting these additional costs. Another problem that led to inequity was the demand in many states that responsible relatives pay a share of the pension, depending on their own financial resources. Many children and relatives avoided any payment at all by loading their financial statements with exorbitant expenses.

The amount of money available to each person was very limited. In California it was regarded as extremely courageous when the legislature (in 1943) increased the monthly maximum payment from $40 to $50. This was the most generous allocation of any state in the nation. The federal government eventually increased its contribution so that the state could add $5 in 1946 and again could give another $5 raise in 1947, thus increasing the maximum to $60.

The period immediately after World War II (1945 through 1947) was a time of unrest and controversy over care of the aged. Social agitation increased across the country. A controversial figure was George McClain (the Great White Father to the elderly), who organized older persons in California and demanded $75 a month for the elderly and $85 for the blind. At the same time the Democratic Committee of Los

Angeles County asked for $80 per month and urged the elimination of the "relative responsibility" section. It is probably significant that George McClain's father had gone broke during the Depression and the senior McClain had had to apply for Old Age Assistance. He was granted a sum of $18 a month, but an inquisitive social worker soon discovered that McClain was a Christian Scientist and concluded that he had no need for medical expenses. Consequently his monthly stipend was cut to $15 per month.

McClain won an early election for the state senate the first time he ran but lost the subsequent one. Although he tried repeatedly after that, it was apparent he had lost his support. Nevertheless, the pattern has repeated itself in California, where older persons have for years been strong advocates of financial assistance to elderly citizens.

After Social Security was legislated in 1935, providing for a contributory scheme of pensions, it was widely predicted that more and more persons would be covered by that insurance and that fewer and fewer persons would need Old Age Assistance. This has proved to be true. As the Social Security Law was amended and more and more groups of people came under its umbrella of financial support, fewer and fewer persons needed Old Age Assistance. The SSI supplement to Social Security replaced Old Age Assistance, but in a more rational and comprehensive manner.

There is evidence, then, to support the conclusion that the past fifty years has seen increasing attention to financial support for the older persons in the United States.

RECENT INCOME AND THE WORK PICTURE

Older persons draw their sustenance from savings accumulated during their lifetime, from private pensions, from such public pensions as Social Security, Railroad Retirement or Veterans Retirement Pay, from SSI, as well as help from relatives and from work. We shall look at the income from work first.

When Social Security was inaugurated, the retirement age in the United States was arbitrarily set at sixty-five. In 1890 some 70 percent of sixty-five-year-olds were still working; in 1972 this had dropped to 21 percent. There were a great many factors involved in the change. First, the growth in productivity based on technological changes appeared to make it possible for the country to support those over sixty-five without their working. Second, that same technology reduced the number of jobs available in both factories and distribution processes so that the public concluded older persons had to become unemployed if there was to be a place for younger workers entering the work force.

Unions supported retirement because it enabled them to enlarge their membership by bringing young dues-paying workers into their ranks. Some workers, trained for jobs during an earlier period, found themselves obsolescent. The provision of Social Security made it possible for men and women who were in poor health to retire and relinquish the struggle of earning a living (Sheppard, 1976).

EARLY RETIREMENT

While sixty-five was arbitrarily set by the government and most industries as a mandatory retirement age, millions of persons used their savings or Social Security to retire earlier. There is a group of occupations in the United States where more than 90 percent of those aged fifty-eight to sixty-three are currently employed. Table 4–3 shows that the more highly skilled or trained stay on the job longer, while those less skilled or less well trained tend to leave their work earlier.

TABLE 4–3. 1969 LABOR PARTICIPATION OF MEN 58–63 BY OCCUPATION

Occupation	Percent in Labor Force
Professional	90
Farmer	88
Manager	87
Clerical	83
Sales	89
Craftsman	84
Operative	79
Service	79
Farm laborer	76
Nonfarm laborer	73

SOURCE: Schwab (August 1974).

Pollman (1971) studied 725 male workers from the automobile industry to discover why they retired early. Almost half of them cited their adequate retirement income as the reason for retiring. One-quarter ascribed their leaving work to health reasons. Twenty percent wanted more free time. Five percent were unhappy with their job, and another 3 percent were dissatisfied with their boss or did not like the people with whom they worked.

Professional persons also retire early. Studying retiring professors at the University of California, Patton (1976) found that during the last seven years some 43 percent of the faculty members retiring did so before the mandatory age of sixty-seven. Females retired at an average age of 64.0 and males at an average age of 65.6. Those with the rank of professor retired the latest, at 65.7, but associate professors did so at the average age of 63.2. Patton asked why faculty members retired early and received the following answers: (1) interests outside of the university; (2) a desire to change life-style; (3) poor health; and (4) pressures from administration or colleagues.

Peterson studied attitudes toward early retirement at the University of Southern California, surveying those currently between ages fifty-five and sixty-five. Some 36 percent wished to retire prior to sixty-five, the mandatory retirement age at USC.

Those who wished to retire at sixty-five or earlier wanted to leave the university because (1) they could pursue a different career; (2) they could pursue career-related activities; (3) they could pursue a special hobby; (4) they could pursue other leisure activity; (5) of health; (6) they were tired of teaching; or (7) they were tired of doing research (Peterson & Morey, 1976).

About the same percentage of professors (34 percent) wished to stay on at the university after sixty-five for a combination of the following reasons: (1) interest in their work (86 percent); (2) income (52 percent); (3) continued productivity (78 percent); and (4) "other" (7 percent). It is obvious from all three studies that the trend among professionals to leave employment before the mandatory retirement age is a significant one.

The great auto manufacturing and steel industries already have well-defined early retirement policies written into their contracts. In some cases workers can retire with full pension after thirty years of service. In others they may retire with a sizable but not maximum pension. This is true of civil service workers, who may now retire at fifty-five but not with the same pension they would receive at sixty-five. In a review of the negotiations between the 1.4 million United Steel Workers of America and the industry, *Time* (February 21, 1977) summarized the issues at stake:

When the bargaining begins this week for a new contract to take effect in August, the union is likely to call for a "lifetime security" program—some sort of guaranteed annual wage, a 32-hour week, earlier retirement, or a combination of all.

For that 25 percent of older persons who are still working, conditions become more difficult. If they become unemployed due to mandatory retirement, it takes much longer for them than for younger persons to find a new job, if they are successful in finding a job at all; only about 10 percent of older women are employed; more older persons work part-time. This is true even though studies show that older persons have the better attendance records, that they are not as transient as younger employees, that there is little difference in productivity when compared with younger workers. The bias against the older worker is not based on fact; it is a reflection of the major social myth that all older persons lose their skills, mental ability, flexibility, and dependability as they age.

These trends do not seem favorable for widespread full employment of retired people in their later years. Technology is concentrating jobs in fewer and fewer persons. Unions use their power to generate more and more instances of early retirement. We have yet to measure the effects of federal legislation (1978) in invalidating compulsory retirement. In fact, while estimates vary, most observers think that by 1985, the 21 percent of older persons fully employed today will further decrease. Unless present trends change, the obvious conclusion is that regular employment will become a much smaller item in income resources for the older person. This is to say nothing regarding the damage to the self-esteem of older workers which such trends represent.

SOCIAL SECURITY

Social Security, the national pension plan, is a program whereby both the employer and the employee contribute monthly to a reserve which will pay the retired person during his later years. The amount paid into government coffers to underwrite the program has so increased since its inception that those who have enrolled in the last five years pay far more than those who were originally covered. But they will also be paid much higher returns when they retire. Social Security has become the major source of income for most retired persons, and is now automatically adjusted to meet the problems of inflation. Each time living costs increase 5 percent, the amount given to pensioners increases a similar amount.

Nevertheless, the average individual payment through Social Security has not been high. In 1974 the average payment despite cost-of-living adjustments was $181 per month for the typical retired worker; $310 per month for the retired couple; and $177 per month for an aged widow.

Pensions for retired military personnel, firemen, policemen, and executives are far above these figures. There is a general inequity in the pension program in the United States. However, as the years pass and the amount levied on the employer and employee increases, the optimistic view is that benefits will also increase.

Social Security is the backbone of income for 50 percent of aged couples, and for two-thirds of nonmarried persons. One provision of this plan presents a special problem to older persons. Although they have paid their premiums during their working life and seem entitled to monthly payments, they are penalized by working for additional income. Older persons (up to seventy-two years of age) are allowed some $4,000 in earnings per year. Beyond that, for each two dollars earned, one dollar is deducted from their Social Security payment. The net effect is to penalize initiative and productivity in older persons.

SUPPLEMENTAL SECURITY INCOME (SSI)

A basic program of a federally administered program of Supplemental Security Income was enacted by Congress in October 1972. Its purpose was to bring assistance to the poor aged and to blind and disabled persons. Even before SSI went into effect, it was changed to define payment levels and to provide for state supplementation, Medicaid, and food stamps (US Department of Health, Education and Welfare, 1974). The law replaced grants to state-administered programs for Old Age Assistance (OAA), the blind (AD), and the totally disabled (APTO). SSI replaced these programs in order to establish a federal standard of income for all eligible aged, blind, and disabled in the nation (Schwab, 1974).

The payment schedule is quite specifically spelled out. If the recipient is single, his cash benefit is $140 per month if he has no other countable income. An eligible couple may receive as much as $210 per month. If an individual is supported in a hospital, nursing home, or extended care facility and these costs are covered by Medicaid, his SSI payment is limited to $25 per month. Couples will receive $50 per month in this case. Regular payments are reduced by one-third if the recipient is living in some other person's household and is receiving major maintenance from that person. If a person's monthly income is below $130 per month or a couple's monthly income is below $195, they may receive supplemental income. The total goal of a somewhat complicated accounting system is to guarantee a monthly income of $157.70 for single eligible individuals and $236.50 for eligible couples.

The estimates of the impact of this program vary. H.E.W. assumed that twice as many needy persons would receive benefits under the SSI program as under OAA—3.7 million in contrast to 1.8 million (H.E.W., p. 13). This would mean an increase from $10 to $60 per month for individuals and from $5 to $75 for couples. States that were paying less than the minimum SSI payments would be raised, but those paying more would continue to do so. But this largess is small compared to the increase in basic Social Security payments, which rose some 69 percent from 1969 through 1974. The federal guarantee under the program of SSI still remains substantially below the poverty line. This is partially because many states were already paying above the maximum SSI benefits and these remain stable.

Some of the goals and benefits of the SSI program are stated by the Select Committee on Aging of the House of Representatives as follows (US House of Representatives, 1976):

Replacement of the multiplicity of eligibility requirements of previous state/federal assistance programs with uniform national standards

More efficient and economic operation

Elimination of lien laws and relatives' responsibility

Higher monthly income for most aged, blind, and disabled.

A new term used in determining payment is "disregards." This means that a given level of income a person has will not reduce monthly payments. If a person earns income from work or business, the first $65, plus one-half of the rest, is not counted in determining the amount of the SSI payment. Some other "disregards" are occasional gifts, property tax refunds, and tuition. The limits on salable property held by a person are $1,500 for an individual and $2,250 for a couple. However, such properties as a house (used as a home), a reasonable amount of household goods, a car, and a life insurance policy with a cash value of less than $1,000 are not counted. If a person has excess resources he may sell those and become eligible. Food stamp eligibility for SSI recipients varies. Forty-five states automatically make SSI recipients eligible, but five states (California, Massachusetts, Nevada, New York, and Wisconsin) eliminate SSI recipients.

A major difference between Social Security and SSI lies in their sources of funding. Social Security payments come from contributions of employers, employees, and self-employed persons. SSI comes from the federal and state treasuries and is covered by taxes. Some individuals who receive Social Security payments are eligible for SSI payments, but as Social Security payments increase, SSI payments may decrease.

HEALTH COSTS

A major source of insecurity for the older person is concern over medical costs and medical crises. A long-term illness or a major operation becomes a financial catastrophe because it can wipe out a lifetime of savings. The federal government has tried to intervene to help allay the insecurity and the burden of medical costs through Medicare and Medicaid. These are medical insurance plans that require a monthly payment from the older person on the basis of which part of his expenses for medical care are paid.

Medicare has proven to be of great help but it leaves great gaps in alleviating the problems of health care for older persons. In fact, it covers less than half of total medical expenses. The Social Security Administration reports that in 1973 Medicare covered only 40.3 percent of the total health bill of $1,040 per aged person (see chapter 3). Critical needs that most older persons have are not covered, such as dental work, hearing aids, eyeglasses, and out-of-hospital care. Worse, it does not cover preventive medical care and some of the expenses involved in treating chronic conditions. This is critical because, given proper preventive care and reasonable medical attention and support systems, most of those sixty-five and over can avoid long hospitalizations or placement in nursing homes, which treat the aged as chronically ill. It is estimated that if such support systems were available it would be possible for 40 percent or more of the one million persons now in long-term-care facilities (nursing homes) to avoid institutionalization, at great savings to the government, to society, and to the individual.

ASSETS

The assets that older people have in the form of cash and equities in homes are very important hedges against the future. Yet in some ways they may be a liability. If a person has no regular income but has over $4,000 in cash, he is ineligible for SSI. Then the question arises for him whether he should give up that holding by spending it in order to qualify for a higher monthly income from SSI or keep it in case of catastrophic illness or other crisis. This might be a fortunate position to be in because most older persons do not have much; they possess a relatively insignificant amount of financial assets. Sixty-six percent of couples and 80 percent of unrelated older individuals had less than $5,000 in assets in 1967. But of this group, some 43 percent of the couples and 61 percent of individuals had less than $1,000. Of those who had less than $5,000, only 13 percent had an equity in a home, but

80 percent of those who had over $5,000 in equities had equity in a home (Schultz, 1976).

An equity in a home or some other financial asset may be a liability in terms of ultimate cost because high taxes turn out to be a great burden to an older person with a small cash flow. In 1970, the Bureau of the Census reported that older persons paid twice as much of their income (8 percent) for real estate taxes as did younger persons. This may be changing, and it is important to review what both the states and the federal government have done to minimize the burden of taxes for older persons.

Eighty percent of the states have given persons over sixty-five some property tax relief. Furthermore, one or more states give additional tax helps in the form of exemption of prescription drugs from sales tax and in such state income tax provisions as special allocation of income levels, higher personal exemptions, special individual deductions, special treatment of retirement income, and special tax credits (Schultz, 1976). The federal government has also made gestures toward relieving tax burdens on older persons by instituting a double personal exemption ($1,500 per individual or $3,000 for a couple); by levying no taxes on income received from Social Security; by giving retirement income credits if the individual is not covered by Social Security; and by forgoing capital gains entirely on home sales for $20,000 or less, and partially if the sale is for over $20,000.

PRIVATE PENSIONS

About 5 percent of total income of older persons in 1967 came from private pensions. Few older persons have benefited by their private pension programs: only 12 percent in 1967 were receiving funds from these sources. An example of what has happened to private pensions developed when the Studebaker Company went out of business. The company quit before the pension fund was adequately financed; consequently employees over sixty-five received a sum much reduced from what they had been promised and those below sixty-five simply lost their money. Most private pension plans have not been "portable" (transferable): If a worker changed jobs, and went to work for another company, he lost all of his pension credits. Schultz quotes one Labor Department official as telling the Senate Special Committee on Aging in 1970, with only a hint of irony:

If you remain in good health and stay with the same company until you are sixty-five years old, and if the company is still in business, and if your department has not been abolished, and if you haven't been laid off for too long a period, and if there is enough money in the fund, and if that money has been prudently invested, you will get a pension.

THE IMPACT OF INFLATION ON INCOME

Inflation robs older persons of their savings. Financial analyst Sylvia Porter observes that inflation hits older people more directly than any other age group because it erodes the value of a lifetime of savings and reduces the buying power of a fixed income from fixed pensions or other benefits—particularly in the case of such basic necessities as home maintenance, transportation, insurance, taxes, food, and medical care. The middle 1970s saw inflation at record levels, the highest in twenty-five years. In 1973, the rate was 8.8 percent and in 1974 it was 12.2 percent, so that in two years prices rose over 20 percent. At the end of 1974, one needed $155.40 to buy the same amount of goods it would have taken $100 to buy in 1967. Since then inflation has continued but at a lower rate. Nevertheless, there is a constant eroding of the value of dollars that have been saved for retirement.

What hedges do retired persons have to counter inflation? Of course, Social Security has been raised consistently to try to cope with this problem. But private pensions, savings and loan companies, and bank savings have no escalator clauses. This leaves the average older person squeezed between a fixed income and inflating costs. Middle-aged persons are able in some measure to escalate wages or profits to counter inflation, but the unemployed older person has few options for coping with this other than to deny himself necessities. This issue remains one of the most serious problems for retired people. Certainly every older person must find a trusted financial counselor to help him determine what steps are possible to safeguard his savings.

Since that report given to the Senate, a year was devoted by a Senate committee to special hearings on pensions, and the result was reevaluation of private pension schemes with new legislation aimed at correcting most of the previous pension problems. Consequently, a new report ten years from now might have a different tone than the one quoted from the Labor Department official.

INCOME FROM RELATIVES

There has been a much heralded emphasis among sociologists on the semiextended family. Students of family life are loathe to believe that America has lost its tradition of the larger intergenerational family and its support of family members. Litwak, Hill, Sussman, and many others have proclaimed in the most positive terms the flow of goods and services between family members. However, the facts are somewhat different, at least as far as income is concerned.

Only about 1 percent of aggregate income for older persons comes from sons, daughters, brothers, sisters, or any other relative. It appears that the older and middle-aged generation feel that the government has an obligation to support them rather than their depending upon each other.

THE OLDER PERSON AS A CONSUMER

The US Bureau of Labor Statistics provides a summary of the way older persons spend their money. They show these amounts for three levels of living: lower, intermediate, and higher. Table 4–4 indicates the limits of income for these three categories:

TABLE 4–4.   THREE LEVELS OF LIVING STANDARDS, 1973

	Annual Budget	Monthly Budget
Lower	$3,763	$314
Intermediate	5,414	451
Higher	8,043	670

SOURCE: US Department of Agriculture (1973).

The amounts in the table are then broken down into the sums spent on various items, as in Table 4–5.

It is obvious that about 80 percent (intermediate level) of the total available monthly allocation is spent on four items: food, housing, transportation, and medical care, leaving just 20 percent for all other concerns, such as clothing, personal care, gifts, and recreation. A further observation is that medical care takes an average of $38 for all three groups but this is 12 percent of the budget for those on the lower level and only 6 percent of the higher level budget.

By 1970 older persons were spending some $60 billion a year, or over 10 percent of the national total. As the proportion of older persons in the United States becomes larger and larger (and their income rises), it is quite possible, even likely, that they will become a more powerful and sought-after consumer group.

The elderly consumer on a fixed income is especially vulnerable to inflation. This is most keenly felt when marketing for food.

TABLE 4–5.   BUDGET FOR A RETIRED COUPLE—AUTUMN, 1973

	Lower	%	Intermediate	%	Higher	%
Food	$ 98	32	$133	29	$167	25
Housing	106	34	153	34	239	36
Transportation	20	6	39	9	70	10
Clothing	15	5	25	6	39	6
Personal care	9	3	13	3	19	3
Medical care	38	12	38	8	38	6
Other family consumption	14	4	23	5	46	7
Other items	14	4	27	6	52	7
TOTALS	$314	100	$451	100	$670	100

SOURCE: US Department of Agriculture (1973).

CONSUMERISM AND FRAUDS

Although advertisers may not pay much attention to the older person (Klippel & Sweeney, 1974), rip-off artists do. The US Postal Service has issued a series of warnings about schemes older persons should be aware of (Peterson & Payne, 1976):

1. Fraudulent solicitation of funds.

2. Work-at-home schemes involving an infinite variety of products and/or services to be manufactured, sold, or performed in the home.

3. Home improvement promotional campaigns, and the possibility "that an upsurge in the questionable sale of furnaces, insulation, etc., will be seen due to the present energy crisis."

4. Questionable business opportunities including distributorships, franchises, vending machines, and other lures to investors. The report adds, "Retired and disabled persons lead the list of individuals who are preyed upon each year to 'put their savings to work and supplement their incomes.'"

5. Land sale swindles, although "concerted attention" within recent years has reduced their numbers.

6. Matrimonial schemes directed at lonely people, including the elderly.

The swindles associated with the Maryland savings and loan scandals of 1961 were an example of fraud by mail. These state-chartered savings and loan associations in Maryland were not federally insured. They advertised a very high interest rate (twice the rate of more conservative groups). Thus they entrapped older clients all over the United States who subsequently lost their life's savings. Little comfort to them that officers of these corporate groups were tried for embezzlement and fraud. Along with this is the considerable concern about the high cost of dying as well as the medical care that precedes death. We will treat this aspect of the financial problems of older persons in a later chapter.

BASIC ISSUES INVOLVED IN THE ECONOMICS OF OLDER PERSONS

The allocation of funds for the older segment of our population involves two significant issues. The first—the allocation of funds for the livelihood and comfort of our retired people—has already been mentioned. As a matter of public policy, is it possible to lift the standard of living much higher than it is at present without penalizing the goals and satisfactions of both the younger and the middle-aged sectors of society? Already there are indications that, given the present base of income, Social Security will go bankrupt in a dozen years. One proposal is to augment Social Security funds by drawing on general tax income. The Senate passed a bill in February 1978 sharply increasing assessments on workers, but by March 1978 there was Senate committee discussion to modify those assessments by shifting some programs like Medicare to general tax support. But the federal budget already is and has been in deficit spending to an extent alarming to many. This means sharply increased taxes on those who are gainfully employed, which, in turn, may produce a somewhat lower standard of living. By the same token, the very same workers can look forward to being supported during the last fourth of their lives at a higher rate. The rates of withholding for Social Security would be effectively increased to make the system actuarily sound. In a sense, this is another and more direct way of dealing with the problem from the viewpoint of the worker. He would then not pay for his last years through higher taxes but through direct assessment. Social Security has become such a basic expectation of the American worker that there is little chance that it will ever be allowed to fail. But one way or another, it must be more adequately financed, either by taxes or by higher payments. The final decision about financing will have to be made sometime in the next decade.

The second issue has to do with equity in support for older persons —whether there should be equality in treatment through Social Security, SSI, and the like, for all older persons or whether some major differences in the circumstances and needs of individuals should be taken into account. In general, the income of a retired person averages about 50 percent of what it was when he was employed. But this is true whether retirement income is $200 or $10,000 for a couple. The interesting but difficult question here is whether individuals who have lived their lives in a lower income bracket require the same monetary support in order to achieve life satisfaction as those who had quadruple the income. Other questions having to do with home ownership, cash or other assets, earning capacity after employment complicate the issue. Does an individual who lives on a farm with the resources there of cow, garden, and crops require as much as the city-based person? Certainly our analysis has indicated that there is little equity when comparisons are made on a sexual basis, because the single woman is far worse off than the single man. And whites are far better off than all other ethnic groups. Regardless of the outcome of the analysis of this inequity, it seems obvious that even though there may be some justification for not granting total equality to all persons under all circumstances, much can yet be done to bring sex and race into a better position when determining the allocation of our resources.

SUMMARY

The economics of aging are complicated. When, following the Great Depression, the nation assumed the position that all persons were entitled to economic support, a new era in American life began. We have looked at the various sources of support for retired and aging persons. The general outlook is encouraging in that the number of individuals who exist below the poverty line has been lowered. A second encouraging factor is the change in public policy that now ties Social Security payments to costs, thus somewhat alleviating the erosion of income by inflation. Some of the major areas of rising costs, such as taxes and medical expenses, have been blunted in their impact by special consideration of the tax obligations of older persons and the institution of Medicare and Medicaid.

However, a look at all three levels of retirement income showed that support was marginal and certainly not productive of much security. Two basic issues for discussion and research have been raised: the first dealing with ways in which retirement income can be raised and who must pay the price, and second, as we look into the future, what final stance will be taken to assure some equity in the manner in which we provide for the elderly members of our society.

REFERENCES

Atchley, R. *The Social Forces in Later Life.* Belmont, Calif.: Wadsworth, 1972.

Hill, R. "Decision Making and the Family Life Cycle." In E. Shanas and G. Streib (eds.), *Social Structure and the Family.* Englewood Cliffs, N.J.: Prentice-Hall, 1965.

Klippel, R. E., and T. Sweeney. "The Use of Information Sources by the Aged Consumer." *The Gerontologist,* 1974, 14:2.

Patton, C. V. "The Latent Demand for Early Faculty Retirement" (paper presented at "Academic Planning for the Eighties and Nineties," University of Southern California, Los Angeles, January 22–23, 1976).

Peterson, J. A., and A. Morey. "Factors Related to Life Satisfaction of Retired Professors" (monograph, University of Southern California Libraries, Los Angeles, 1976).

Peterson, J. A., and B. Payne. *Love in the Later Years.* New York: Association Press, 1976.

Pollman, A. W. "Early Retirement: A Comparison of Poor Health and Other Retirement Factors." *Journal of Gerontology,* 1971, 26: 41–45.

Schultz, J. "Income Distribution and the Aging." In R. Binstock and E. Shanas (eds.), *Handbook of Aging and the Social Sciences.* New York: Van Nostrand Reinhold, 1976.

Schwab, K. *Social Security Bulletin,* August 1974.

Sheppard, H. L. "Work and Retirement." In R. Binstock and E. Shanas (eds.), *Handbook of Aging and the Social Sciences.* New York: Van Nostrand Reinhold, 1976.

US Bureau of the Census, *Census of Population, 1970: Detailed Characteristics.* Final Report PC (1)-DI, United States Summary. Washington, D.C.: Government Printing Office, 1973.

US Bureau of the Census. "Characteristics of the Low-Income Population: 1973." Current Population Reports, Series P-No. 94. Washington, D.C.: Government Printing Office, July 1974.

US Department of Agriculture. *A Guide to Budgeting for a Retired Couple.* Publication No. 194. Washington, D.C.: Government Printing Office, 1973.

US Department of Health, Education and Welfare. "Federalization of Old Age Assistance; Potential Impact on the Aged Poor." In *The Supplemental Security Income Program for the Aged, Blind and Disabled.* Social Security Administration, Office of Research and Statistics, Publication No. (SSA) 75-11851, Staff Paper NM. 17. Washington, D.C.: Government Printing Office, 1974.

US House of Representatives Select Committee on Aging. "SSI Questions and Answers." Committee Print. Washington, D.C., 1976.

FOR FURTHER READING

Bowen, W. G., and J. A. Finegan. *The Economics of Labor Force Participation.* N. J.: Princeton University Press, 1966.

Chen, Yung-Ping. "Economic Poverty: The Special Case of the Aged." *The Gerontologist,* 1966, 6:1.

Chen, Yung-Ping. "Retirement Income Adequacy." In A. Schwartz and I. Mensh (eds.), *Professional Obligations and Approaches to the Aged.* Springfield, Ill.: Charles C Thomas, 1974.

Heflin, T. L. "Social Security: Individual or Social Equity?" *The Gerontologist,* 1976, 16:5.

Kreps, J. *Employment, Income and Retirement Problems of the Aged.* Durham, N.C.: Duke University Press, 1965.

Kreps, J. *Lifetime Allocations of Work and Income.* Durham, N.C.: Duke University Press, 1971.

Schultz, J., et al. *Providing Adequate Retirement Income in the United States and Abroad.* Waltham, Mass.: Brandeis University Press, 1974.

Marriage, Family, and Community Relationships of Older Persons

If a man is moderate and contented
  then even age is no burden—
If he is not, then even youth is full of cares.

PLATO

Family, friendships, and community supports and assurance for the
elderly are of great interest and concern to gerontologists. This
chapter explores and discusses aspects of these relationships, so
critically important in the later years.

The student will note that the studies and statistics about marital
satisfactions in the later years are far from conclusive. This is true of
many other areas of concern in studies about aging, too. Expectations
about late-life marriage and remarriage are discussed in some detail.
This discussion also touches upon the common phenomenon of role-
reversal.

This chapter also directs attention to sexuality and sexual behavior
in the later years, a subject too long taboo and now widely discussed.
Attitudes of community, kin, and friends become enormously
influential in this regard.

Finally, this chapter is designed to help the student examine the role of ancillary community support and support systems directed toward the maintenance of competence in activities of daily living.

When I get older losing my hair,
Many years from now.
Will you still be sending me a Valentine,
Birthday greetings, bottle of wine.
If I'll be out till quarter to three
Would you lock the door.
Will you still need me, will you still feed me,
When I'm sixty-four.
You'll be older too,
And if you say the word,
I could stay with you.
I could be handy, mending a fuse
When your lights have gone.
You can knit a sweater by the fireside
Sunday mornings go for a ride,
Doing the garden, digging the weeds,
Who could ask for more.
Will you still need me, will you still feed me
When I'm sixty-four.*

The haunting verse of this popular song becomes all the more poignant when we ponder a case study like the following:

Don was referred for consultation because he had attempted to throw himself from a ten-story building. His story was simple. Two years earlier his wife had died. His two grown sons came for the funeral but stayed only three days when the demands of their work took them away again: one a thousand miles away, the other across the continent. Friends had hovered about for a week or so and then seemed to forget him. His sons called him by phone but had little to say to him. Most of his friends were couples, and he felt he didn't "fit into his social life" anymore. His apartment was pleasant enough, but he had little interaction with his neighbors, who were mostly younger than he was. Sometime earlier he had fractured his hip, so he found it difficult to get to his church. He called, but no one came to visit him. He found it difficult to get to the market regularly, his diet suffered, he got little exercise and no mental stimulation. After a time he became increasingly depressed, concluded there was "nothing left for him," and decided to "join his wife." Hence his attempt at suicide.

Cases like this, which with many variations in their details are repeated literally thousands of times, raise important questions for us

---

* From the Beatles' album *Sgt. Pepper's Lonely Hearts Club Band.* Song: "When I'm Sixty-Four." Capitol Records, Hollywood, Calif., 1967.

about the effectiveness of family and friendship support for a great many older persons, about family and community support and assurance for the isolated and the widowed. Before one can effectively help the "Dons" of our society, much needs to be known about his community, his friendship network, and his family.

THE FAMILY

There is some basic and reliable data regarding living arrangements of older persons. A final report on the 1970 census gives us this information.

TABLE 5–1.　LIVING ARRANGEMENTS OF THOSE SIXTY-FIVE AND OLDER BY RACE AND SEX: 1970

	MALE		FEMALE	
Living Arrangement	White	Black	White	Black
In families	79.1	69.6	58.2	62.2
Primary individual[a]	15.1	21.6	33.7	31.2
Other[b]	2.1	5.5	2.1	3.3
Institutionalized	3.8	3.2	5.9	3.2
Total[c]	100.0	100.0	100.0	100.0

[a] A household head living alone or with nonrelatives only.
[b] Includes lodgers, resident employees, and those living in group quarters such as covents or rooming houses.
[c] Totals do not add to 100 due to rounding error.
SOURCE: US Bureau of the Census, 1973b.

Almost 80 percent of the men and 60 percent of all persons older than sixty-five live in families, but these generally consist of husband and wife. Less than a quarter of these persons live with their children, and less than 3 percent are part of households comprised of parents, children, and grandchildren (US Bureau of the Census, 1973b).

In 1970 there were some 8,300,000 widows and some 1,700,000 widowers fifty-five years and older. In addition there were 500,000 divorced men and 1,000,000 divorced women who were still not remarried. While 22 million were married, a total of about 11.5 million were single and generally living alone or with nonrelatives (Peterson & Payne, 1975). Fewer than 5 percent of households include a parent or parent-in-law (US Bureau of the Census, 1973b).

These data suggest that the following issues are relevant for this particular analysis:

1. What is the degree of satisfaction or adjustment in those 22 million older persons who are married?

2. What is possibility of marriage for the 11.5 million persons who are single?

3. What is the degree of relationship between parents, children, and grandchildren when they do not live together?

4. What are the special problems of widows and widowers?

5. What other community support systems beyond the family are important?

MARITAL ADJUSTMENT IN THE LATER YEARS

It is difficult to determine in specific terms how older persons get along in marriage. There is much evidence that for many, marriage becomes staid and stodgy by the middle years and never recovers. There is other evidence that it recovers from middle-age "blahs" and is a good source of life satisfaction during the last years.

One longitudinal study relevant to this issue has been that of Burgess and Wallin, who interviewed a panel of one thousand couples when they were engaged, then three years later, and again after the couples had been married up to twenty years. Peter C. Pineo, who conducted the third phase of the study, chose the word "disen- /chantment" to summarize the adjustment of these couples in the later years of their marriage. He found losses on most of the indices that he used to measure interaction of the couples (Pineo, 1961). Blood and Wolfe's cross-sectional sample in their study of 556 couples was more representative of social class than the Burgess-Wallin middle-class respondents (Blood & Wolfe, 1960). (See Figure 5-1.)

A further study by Cuber and Haroff (1963) used a sample of very successful upper-middle-class Americans. They categorized their findings as falling into five classes of interaction patterns: conflict-habituated, passive-congenial, devitalized, vital, and total. Of all these types of interaction, only the vital has an aspect of "exciting sharing," and it is a small group. The largest group is that labeled devitalized. No final statistical findings are presented, but the strong inference is that most of the respondents fall in the first three conflict-ridden or devitalized categories.

Lowenthal's San Francisco study embraced a stratified-random sam-

Figure 5-1. WIFE'S SATISFACTION WITH LOVE AND COMPANION-
SHIP BY STAGE IN FAMILY LIFE CYCLE

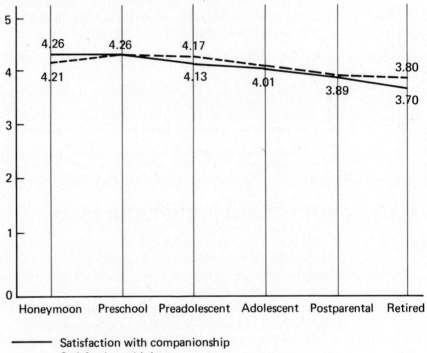

───── Satisfaction with companionship
── ── ── Satisfaction with love

SOURCE: Blood and Wolfe (1960).

ple of 280 respondents from eighteen census tracts. These respondents
were interviewed three times in order to locate etiological (causal)
factors in health or illness. She concluded that "an individual who has
been widowed within seven years, and who has a confidante, has even
higher morale than a person who remains married but lacks a confidante." The inference is clear that in old age a marital partner does not
necessarily offer profound emotional support to his or her mate. On the
other hand, marrieds have a higher satisfaction rating than widows
without a confidante. There must be some couples who continue to
function in vital ways with their partners. These studies indicate some
loss of communication and personal support in marriage through the
erosion of time (Lowenthal et al., 1967).

But not all studies show the same declining curve. Peterson's study
of middle- and upper-middle-class in-movers at Leisure World in Laguna Hills, California, reported a great deal of mutual decision making, mutual dependence, and stability in the 500 couples with an

average age of sixty-five whom he interviewed (Peterson et al., 1967). He suggests that the married couples were the happiest of any group in the community; and that they had achieved a method of problem solving satisfactory to both. His sample, however, is limited by its middle-class bias and by being self-selected as those who were moving into a retirement community.

A second (mostly positive) report is supplied by Feldman and Rollins, who studied 240 couples in various stages of the family life cycle. In contrast to Blood and Wolfe, they found that general marital satisfaction increases after middle age and continues high during the period of retirement. But they also report that "positive companionship experiences with their spouses at least once a day or more often" decrease to a low point during retirement. The life history events used to measure these companionship experiences are "laughing together, calm discussion with each other, having a stimulating exchange of ideas with each other, and working on a project" (Feldman & Rollins, 1970). Figure 5–2 from this study depicts such changes in companionship experiences. While it may be that enough other sharing modes account for general satisfaction, these marriages do seem dull without laughter, discussion, sharing, or working together.

Peterson's findings get some confirmation from Clark and Anderson, who stress the greater equality among happily married couples as con-

Figure 5-2. POSITIVE COMPANIONSHIP EXPERIENCES WITH THEIR SPOUSES

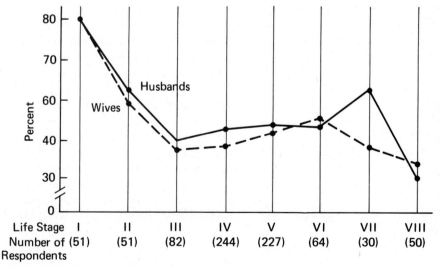

SOURCE: Feldman and Rollins (1970).

trasted to unhappy ones. These same happily married persons find marriage a source of comfort and joy when their children are all gone. They support each other in illness and loneliness. On the other hand, some long-married persons blame their mate for any troubles they may have and wish for termination of the marriage. Clark and Anderson found that unhappy couples cannot cope with illness. Lipman adds a further positive note in his study of the morale of couples in retirement. He feels that the retirement experience itself is instrumental in promoting the mutuality of sharing household tasks and the affective aspects of companionship, such as giving love, affection. He stresses that marriage in the later years moves away from dependence on such instrumental roles as striving for money and status, and moves toward new bonds based on mutuality of roles.

What we do make of these somewhat contradictory and incomplete studies? How can we answer our first question regarding the adequacy of the degree of satisfaction of marriage in the retirement years? The answer is that we cannot answer this question. All of these studies, while classic in the sociological literature, are limited by classbound and timebound samples. The samples are geographically limited, and the number of cases in each cell of the life cycle is very small, too small on which to generalize. The only safe conclusion is that we do not know much about marriage in the later years. We are reminded that Goode talked about remarriage after either divorce or widowhood as providing a better second than first marriage; one that was certainly "equal to good first marriages" (Goode, 1956). But the last careful 1974 census study of outcomes of second marriages indicates that some 50 percent of them will fail, and quite suddenly after remarriage . . . after an average marital interval of but three years. It may be that the 60 percent of first marriages and the 50 percent of current second marriages that persist may have a better quality than present older marriages because many poor ones will have dissolved. What we need are more comprehensive, more broadly based and longitudinal studies of marriage in the later years so that we might make more dependable inferences from their results. We must in the interim accept the notion that the conclusions of each of these studies are correct. Many older marriages will survive; some, as per Feldman and Rollins and Peterson, will be happy and offer good life supports and satisfactions. The sample is very small for those in the seventh stage (N=30) in contrast to other samples. Furthermore, there is a decisive contrast in judgment as to companionship—the *only* stage at which this occurs (Figure 5–2)! A great many will not be happy and, as Clark and Anderson (1967) suggest, will not be able to bring life supports or satisfaction to the mates in the marriage. It is probable, however, that many sour marriages will terminate because the social pressures against divorce are certainly lessened both in our laws and in the arena of public opinion.

RETIREMENT MARRIAGES

The second issue raised had to do with the possibilities of a rewarding marriage for the 11.5 million older single persons in our society. Remembering the hopelessly discrepant ratio between widows and widowers, it is not difficult to understand the fact that men are six times as prone to marry after age sixty-five as women. There simply are not enough men around for these women to marry. A great many older persons, of course, shun marriage. Lopata reports that even among her widows who reported happy past marriages, some 35 percent say they would not marry again (Lopata, 1973). Britton and Britton (1967) report that one third of a rural sample of sixty rejected the idea of remarriage for older persons.

Another impediment to remarriage in the later years is that Social Security penalizes many who have to give up part of their income in order to get a marriage license. So they often live together without license or, if you please, in "licentiousness." We shall analyze later in this chapter the roots of middle-aged children's opposition to their bereaved parent's marriage. This is another factor that may limit later-aged courtship. Also, loss of mobility, lessening of reserves of energy, and financial ease may inhibit some from exploring and cultivating a possible new relationship.

All of these reasons account for the fact that there were only sixty thousand marriages last year among older persons. Considering the vast army of single persons, this is minuscule. Retirement community promoters are frequently heard touting the marriages that have occurred in the past in their places of residence, but the aggregate is small.

If older men marry, whom do they marry? They continue the pattern initiated in their first and second marriages. They tend to marry younger persons. At least 20 percent of the grooms over sixty-five married brides under forty-five. Thus, as Sontag states, there is a double standard for love among older persons in that women are labeled as "old" at a much younger age than men (see further discussion of Sontag's argument in chapter 8).

And what happens to those who are either courageous or lucky enough to find a mate? How do these late marriages fare? McLain has provided us with a research study of one hundred couples where the bride was over sixty and the groom over sixty-five. While these couples were married in 1960, 1961 and 1962, they were not interviewed until 1966 so that the couples had had some time for adjustment and some perspective to their conclusions. McLain found six critical areas for late marriage adjustment: the authors have added two more (the last two are from their own counseling experience). McLain found a high degree of increased probability of success as he isolated certain factors that are troublesome and some that are helpful (McLain, 1969).

1. A retirement bride and groom must know each other well if their marriage is to succeed.

2. The marriage must be approved by children and friends to have a chance of success.

3. To be well adjusted in a retirement marriage, the couple must be well adjusted to retirement and other facets of aging.

4. Retirement is more successful if the couple does not try to live in a house in which one lived with another mate previously. There are "too many people" in such a house.

5. Sufficient income to underwrite the new marriage is a must.

6. Marital adjustment reflects the personal adjustment of both the new wife and husband. (Counselors would feel that this structure would apply to marriages of any age.)

7. Couples who expect their last years, spent together, to be happy must have a definite life plan for those years.

8. Every opportunity should be explored and utilized for premarital counseling, often involving families of the prospective bride and groom.

FAMILY RELATIONSHIPS AMONG THE ELDERLY

One of the major controversies in family sociology during the last fifteen years has been failure to agree on the basic structure of the contemporary family. This controversy has particular relevance to our topic because in one case the family is described as close and supportive, and in the other case, as somewhat farther removed and less supportive of the older person. Hill, Sussman, Litwak and others have pitted their research and theoretical formulations against the classic Parsonian formulation of the concept of the nuclear family. Basically they reject the notion of a small, nuclear family that is somewhat oblivious of the claims of extended members. On the other hand Parsons, Peterson, Townsend, and others have insisted that while there is a semiextended family, the relationships involved in such a family structure do not have the day-to-day or intimate meanings that are basic emotional supports for older persons. The number of actual contacts is dependent on the occupational mobility of the family, its social class location, and its emotional history. The critical question is posed in

Children need grandparents as much as grandparents need grandchildren, who discover their family "roots" in the reminiscing stories of their grandparents.

our series of issues when we ask: What is the quality of relationship between parents, children, and grandchildren when they do not live together? We shall try to answer this question in terms of financial contributions, helping behavior, and emotional support. The student should examine the sources of information critically because in this case *social desirability* factors predispose answers; much of the research is geographically (and hence, ethnically) biased, and distorted by social class limitations. Students will do well to measure carefully the adequacy of all such studies.

One study by Streib and Thompson done in 1965 using an eastern sample has been replicated by a California study utilizing the same scale (Streib & Thompson, 1965). It is unusual to find this kind of scientific replication using samples from two major areas of the country. The results of this scale, which tests attitudes of older members of the family toward their children, are reported in Table 5–2. These findings, on east and west coasts, illustrate the degree to which the "achievement motivation" has helped modify parental expectations of care from their children. It is also a measure of the degree of independence older persons are asserting. Only seventeen persons of more than four hundred elderly in the California sample reported ever having lived with their adult children, and fourteen of these went to great

TABLE 5-2. PARENTAL NORMS CONCERNING ACHIEVEMENT, CONTENT, AND LIVING ARRANGEMENTS OF CHILDREN

	AGREEMENT WITH STATEMENT	
Statement	Streib-Thompson %	Peterson, Larson and Hadwen %
Getting ahead in the world may be a bad thing if it keeps your family from being close.	49	67
When children are unmarried adults, it is nice to have them live at home with parents.	45	46
Children should not move away from their parents because of better financial opportunities elsewhere.	10	5
When parents get older and need help, they should be asked to move in with their married children.	8	14
Even when children are married, it is nice to have them living with parents.	5	2

SOURCE: Peterson et al. (1967).

pains to point out that this happened only because of a transitional period in the life of the parent and was regarded by all as temporary. When probe questions sought to discover under what circumstances any of the respondents would move in with their children, almost 100 percent said that under no circumstances would they ever consent to such a situation. These responses led the authors to generalize that for these two groups, the norms associated with the extended family are tenuous. Further analyses indicated that the persons in the California sample were not too enthusiastic about contacts with their grandchildren, preferring to see them only when they wished and for a limited time period. They seemed especially to resent being used as babysitters at the convenience of their own adult children.

In America, with its strong emphasis on privacy and independence, the relationship mode between kin known as "intimacy at a distance" may contribute most to good life adjustment of the elderly (Treas, 1975). When Murray (1973) studied 11,153 individuals fifty-five to sixty-three years of age, he found those living with relatives less happy. Kerchoff (1966) reports that retired married couples' morale was inversely related to the propinquity of their children. But there is communication; over 90 percent of the respondents over sixty-five had seen one of their children in the past month (Shanas, 1968). The majority of older persons live less than an hour's drive from some child (Sussman, 1976). The postal service, telephone, and airplane bring some sense of closeness or accessibility even in a mobile society.

A further analysis of the California sample indicated that there was no statistical association between familism and life satisfaction. Furthermore, about one-half of the children of the respondents in this sample lived far distant from them in California or in other states. The inferences of these data are supported by an investigation by Solomon of a lower-class group, which showed that most parents in this group take for granted separation and lack of intimate contact but rely on letter and telephone so that their children may be called upon in case of emergencies. The children do not play a daily or major part in their lives, but they are viewed as a kind of insurance against the exigencies of tomorrow. Undoubtedly Hill and Sussman and others are right to stress the value of the kind of relationship that is expressed by older persons in terms of gifts, baby-sitting (when possible), and communication; but this may be a negligible factor against loneliness.

Treas (1975) has summarized the controversy well and added some explanatory inferences which help to illuminate the issue:

> In reviewing all of the evidence on contemporary kin relationships, Peterson finds considerable support for the thesis that family "relations do not offer substantial intimacy or emotional support to aging persons." For many older people, contact with kin is too infrequent to provide companionship. Money and services may be exchanged with only minimal affect and interaction. While families may fall short of providing day-to-day social sustenance to the aged, youngerkind are sources of generative gratification and vicarious accomplishment. Parents view offspring as social heirs who extend their personal histories and validate their lives. Given this involvement, it is not surprising that older people feel their children should move away from them if better economic opportunities beckon (Peterson, 1970; Streib, 1958). This "developmental stake" in descendants encourages parents to minimize generational differences and to perceive greater closeness, understanding and communication between family members than do their young. Clearly, family satisfaction and solidarity survive even in a mobile and rapidly changing society such as ours.

There are special problems that characterize the relationship of older persons with their adult sons and daughters. One of these areas is called role inversion. If the sons or daughters come to feel that the parental figure is no longer competent, they may want to change their previously subservient role and become a parent of their parent. This reversal is often received with intense unhappiness by the older person, who may have no inclination to give up his or her independence, power, or authority. A case from another article by one of the authors illustrates this problem:

> John Broadus and his wife presented themselves to the therapist as prosperous, competent, and generous middle-aged persons. John went to great pains to explain that his eighty-year-old father and mother could no longer take care of themselves and he had gone to some trouble to discover a high quality medical facility for them. But, much to his chagrin, they would have nothing to do with such a move even though he described what happened indicated that he had a very great deal invested in this plan. In a sense, it developed, what he was doing now compensated for years in which he had spent little time with his parents. The vehemence of their rejection also reflected a bitterness born of neglect. John's wife took the side of the parents but revealed later that she resented the money John would spend on his parents. As it developed, the issue of the parents' giving up their home was only the arena in which were played out all of the resentments which had accumulated during the last twenty-five years, in which the parents felt neglected and scorned by John and his wife. Because dealing with a housing move was a superficial aspect of this case, it was handled as family therapy and all four persons were invited to work out a totally different way of dealing with each other.

In many cases the anxiety fostered by a younger person assuming the authority role becomes the focus of intervention. Such problems often underlie the complaints of a son or daughter of a parental resident in a nursing home. Children cannot deal open or directly with their feelings of guilt so they attack the nursing home because it is a handy and vulnerable target. Such behavior is often a displacement of a very personal sense of past failure or what is currently a poor relationship with that parent.

A second problem in the family has to do with opposition to the intended marriage of a widowed mother or father (McLain, 1969). The middle-aged child registers great indignation or consternation at the plan of his parent to remarry. A variety of psychological dynamics can be involved in such intrusions into parents' lives. One explanation focuses on a perceived threat to the possibility of an inheritance. The middle-aged offspring may be counting on receiving the bulk of the estate left by his father or mother but the new marriage is seen as threatening that expectation. In such cases the execution and revelation of a financial premarital agreement is often all it takes to eliminate the opposition. In such an agreement both the bride and groom specify

Middle-agers have become a "sandwich generation," needing to cope with the demands of their own children and those of aging parents.

how much of their resources will be committed to the marriage and how much must be reserved to give to the children as, perhaps, their departed mate would have wished.

In other cases, the anger or resistance toward the planned marriage of the elderly parent may stem not from monetary concerns but from complex emotional issues. It is not uncommon for some sons and daughters to believe that their surviving parent ought to dedicate the remainder of life to a ritual of single-minded devotion to the dead parent. Such stereotyped attitudes may stem from guilt associated with the child's own neglect and lack of demonstrated affection to the deceased parent. The child may now want the surviving parent to fulfill for him what he should have done a long time ago himself. More often than not, when a daughter or son says, "Oh, Mother, act your age; you are too old for that sort of thing," the response may simply be the reflection of stereotypic, mythological attitudes about appropriate sexual behavior in the later years of life. Yet such attitudes expressed to aging parents can be a source of embarrassment and chagrin, and produce further inhibitions on the behavior of the elderly parent.

Whatever the particulars may be of opposition to such free expression of the need for intimacy and sexuality on the part of a parent, the causes are often of such complex nature that only a sensitive and experienced therapist can deal with them in adequate fashion.

A third kind of role reversal has been suggested by Neugarten as characterizing relationship between the older husband and wife and complicating their relationship with their adult children (Neugarten, 1968). Neugarten gave a large sample in Kansas City some Thematic Apperception cards to try to tap the noncognitive patterns of older persons in terms of role perceptions. She found that many older women seem to have changed from expressive roles which have most to do with emotions to instrumental roles which have to do with jobs and decisions. Older men, on the other hand, often make the opposite kind of shift. Thus, as a husband and wife get older, they have to cope with a significant shift in roles. This can be most confusing to children who, by the time they have reached middle age, have learned to some extent to understand and cope with Father and Mother. Now they begin to discover that the familiar coping strategies do not seem to apply. They must learn to listen carefully and acquire new understandings of their parents. They may resent, for example, Mother's newfound independence as she begins to demand more voice in decisions, and loses some of the softness of her previous "mothering" role. As sociological studies established long ago, power in the family is associated with earning money, and when Father retires he loses a certain amount of status with his wife and the children, which loss may be reinforced by the kind of role reversal we are discussing.

THE WIDOWED AND SINGLE AND THEIR RELATIONSHIPS

No analysis of the older family would be complete if it neglected the problems of the more than 11 million single men and women in their later years. The gap in longevity between men and women is not being bridged yet by modern medicine so that as the older population increases in number the disproportion between the sexes also increases (Peterson & Briley, 1977). Furthermore, the salient circumstances of the high rise in divorce both for first and second marriages promises to make a new bulge in "singleness" statistics for older persons in the next twenty years. Any examination of relationship patterns, therefore, must take these trends into consideration, if the analysis is to be at all comprehensive and meaningful.

Unless there is a radical change in marriage customs which would permit some form of polygamy in which one man was related to more than one woman, there seems no alternative *in marriage* for the vast majority of single older women. What then are their prospects for some type of heterosexual life? There are some suggested remedies.

The proliferation of retirement communities may be one answer to the segregation of single older women. In these communities single women may find some wholesome associations with men (even though married) in educational classes, volunteer work, social activities, recreational activities, and neighboring. While an occasional swim or dance or card game with a married man is not the equivalent of living with him, nevertheless, this does provide contact and companionship. In many of these communities such men are perfectly willing to act as a kind of surrogate handyman and fix water sprinklers or the fence for their single female neighbors. This kind of friendship is not at all sexual but it does provide the basis for emotional support.

A second kind of relationship has developed between single men and single women which is sexual. Because the Social Security rules handicap older persons financially if they marry, many are simply having a long affair or even living together without the benefit of clergy. Certainly some of the 35 percent of widows who told Lopata that they so cherished their independence that they would never remarry are not going to give up completely their emotional closeness to either men or women (see report of interview in chapter 1). In other cases where a married couple has had a long and stormy relationship, the husband may find comfort in the arms of another woman. A few have tried communal living; some like it and some do not. Certainly there has been and will continue to be a large number of social experiments in which both older men and older women experiment with new forms of intimate association. We have heard more than one middle-aged child say to his older parent: "Well, you can have relationships but you certainly are no good at marriage. Don't try that again." It seems unrealistic to assume that new cohorts of older persons will be content to be completely celibate. What is the sexual potential of older persons?

THE SEXUAL PROMISE OF OLDER PERSONS

If the sexual fires of youth are completely banked and become only cold embers in old age we may be belaboring a lost cause. But this proves not to be the case. Since the early research of Kinsey et al., followed by the more precise findings of Masters and Johnson, and then elaborated by researchers at the Institute of Human Development at Duke University, University of Southern California, and others, it is now certain that older persons have much capacity to enjoy sex as long as they live (Masters & Johnson, 1966). It is true that the sexual impulse is not as dramatic in its demands as at eighteen years, but it is also true that sex for those in their senior years can be just as fulfilling as it was fifty years before—perhaps more so, because the imperative nature of the drive is generally modified so sex can be more psychologically and spiritually satisfying.

That older persons are capable of having normal and rewarding sexual experiences does not mean that there are no problems in the sexual sphere attendant to the later years. These are not generally serious but older persons need to know how to cope with them to increase their sexual fulfillment. An adequate analysis of the sexual promise and sexual changes associated with age is contained in the chapter entitled "Geriatric Sexual Response" in the book *Human Sexual Response* by Masters and Johnson (1966). Their findings will be summarized here. For females:

1. The vagina loses length, width, and vaginal-wall thickness and a "significant degree of involuntary ability to expand under sexual tension." But the loss is less for those females who have a consistent sexual relationship during middle and early later years.

2. Lubrication due to sexual stimulation is delayed in comparison to younger women, but for most women can be produced in one to three minutes.

3. Orgasms follow the general process as in the younger years, but their duration is shorter.

4. The intensity of reaction is diminished. But "the aging human female is fully capable of sexual performance at orgasmic response levels."

5. If there are conditions such as vaginal burning, pelvic distress, and painful uterine contractions associated with orgasms, these can be corrected by adequate endocrine replacements.

6. Women who have regular sexual expression once or twice a week maintain sexual capacity.

Findings for males:

1. The older the male, the more time it takes for full penile erection.

2. The erection may be maintained in older men "for extended periods of time."

3. Once an erection is lost in older men, it will not return as soon.

4. The number of expulsive contractions during orgasm are fewer for the older male.

5. In general the male loses, as does the female, some physiological efficiency as he ages.

6. The more consistent the male's sexual history during middle and early old age, the greater his chances for a healthy sexuality in his later years.

7. Most males over fifty who have a "secondarily acquired impotency" can be restored to potency. Impotency in the older male is accounted for by boredom with a dull and repetitious sexual regime; such great concentration on economic and occupational goals that no energy or time is left for sexual enjoyment; overindulgence in alcohol or food; physical or mental losses of either the actor or the partner; or fear of sexual failure.

Perhaps Masters and Johnson might have stressed the psychological aspects of sexual adjustment in the later years more adequately. Men and women are not simply tissue and hormones. They are individuals with long histories of interactions, of neglect or tenderness, so it may be difficult for them to anticipate or respond to love immediately. Some persons are injustice collectors, and they have their greatest glory in reciting the faults of others. Such conduct by older persons is not conducive to sexual responsiveness. Sometimes it takes intervention by a therapist to help older persons get over a traumatic past. But older persons need closeness, tenderness, touching so much that they sometimes make a good bargain to spend some time in therapy in order to achieve a good sexual relationship (see additional discussion in chapter 9).

PRIMARY RELATIONSHIP AND INSTITUTIONAL SUPPORTS IN THE COMMUNITY

In their study of the reasons that motivate persons to move into a retirement community, Peterson, Larson, and Hadwen (1967) were surprised to discover that one major reason for the move was the high ranking given the possibility of finding new friends. Friends and neighbors are primary relationships that supply many of the personal supports older persons need. Yet it is possible to remain in the same home for forty years and become entirely isolated. Family members, friends, and neighbors move and die, a beloved pastor is moved to another parish, a trusted doctor retires. Some loss of energy makes it difficult to take part in church or other voluntary activities that in previous years added excitement to life. So by virtue of continuity of housing and a discontinuity in both intimate relations and important activities, isolation occurs. Over 25 percent of the in-movers in this study put the possibility of new friendships as the most important reason for a move. A follow-up study of these same persons indicated that they were successful because the in-movers, on the average, doubled their friendship networks.

In summarizing favorable factors that lead to having many friends, Riley and Foner (1968) report that high socioeconomic status, good health, high density of older persons in the area, long-time neighborhood residence, and living in a small town rather than a large city are all practical factors.

Rosow (1967) has conducted a careful study of social integration of older persons. His study included twelve hundred people who lived in apartment buildings differentiated in terms of density, with some called normal where density of aged tenants was 1 to 15 percent, and dense where 50 percent or more tenants were aged. Age for women was sixty-two or older and men sixty-five or older. Three waves of interviews were conducted.

Rosow's basic hypothesis was that neighborhoods with a greater density of older persons would result in more friendships and that these friendships would come from their age peers and not from among young people. This finding explains much of the attraction and success of retirement communities in meeting needs for intimates.

One of Rosow's innovations was to categorize personality types and see what happened to them in these neighborhoods. The following table illustrates his method:

TABLE 5–3.   FUNCTIONS OF NEIGHBORING IN OLDER PEOPLE'S LIVES

Type	Contact with Neighbors	Desired Contacts with Neighbors
Cosmopolitan	low	none
Phlegmatic	low	none
Isolated	low	none
Sociable	high	no more
Insatiable	high	more

SOURCE: Rosow (1967).

Other significant findings by Rosow were that the isolated group might suffer morale loss if members of this group had opportunities for contact but could not make friends or neighbors. They needed help. If

New friends and activities help to counteract the loss of morale of many eld-erly people as their social roles decrease.

older persons lived with someone they rarely asked for help and had few relatives, then neighbors became their reference group and nursed them through both long and short illnesses. The critical nature of hav-ing intimates, friends, and neighbors is demonstrated by Lowenthal's work, which has been previously reviewed. Any retirement community or community with a high density of older persons has many advan-tages in overcoming loneliness and adding to the sense of well-being of its residents. The need to structure environments that can eliminate isolation and promote socialization is a high priority for older persons.

If we imagine the activities and contacts of any older person in terms of concentric circles, the core and predominant one has to be of spouse and family. The second consists of other primary individuals such as friends, neighbors, and significant others. There is a third circle that represents frequent and stimulating contacts in the community. This social arena presents such persons as the aged person's doctor, minis-ter, banker, investment counselor—individuals who have power and influence in the decisions older persons have to make. In this regard Newcomer's studies are useful in identifying community supports that need to be accessible in order for the aging person to be comfortable in his community (Newcomer, 1973).

TABLE 5–4.   SERVICE IMPORTANCE AND CRITICAL DISTANCE

Service	Importance	Critical Distance	Recommended Distance
Bus stop	1	1 block	Adjacent to site
Park/outdoor	2	1 block	Adjacent to site
Grocery store	3	1–3 blocks	1 block
Laundromat	4	On-site	1 block
Supermarket	5	4–10 blocks	3 blocks
Post office	6	4–10 blocks	3 blocks
Bank	7	1–3 blocks	3 blocks
Service center	8	1–3 blocks	On-site
Cleaner	9	4–10 blocks	3 blocks
Department store	10	4–10 blocks	3 blocks
Social center	11	4–10 blocks	3 blocks
Senior citizens' club	12	1–3 blocks	On-site
Bingo, cards	13	1–3 blocks	On-site
Arts, crafts, hobbies	14	1–3 blocks	On-site
Movies	15	Indeterminate	3 blocks
Parties, socials	16	1–3 blocks	On-site
Lectures, discussions	17	Indeterminate	On-site
Organized trips	18	Indeterminate	Indeterminate
Church	19	Indeterminate	Indeterminate
Physician	20	Indeterminate	Indeterminate
Public library	21	Indeterminate	Indeterminate
Dentist	22	Indeterminate	Indeterminate
Luncheonette, snacks	23	Indeterminate	Indeterminate
Bar	24	No importance	No importance

SOURCE: Newcomer (1973).

This judgment was made by six hundred housing tenants who were asked to judge the frequency of use by these twenty-four community services.

Regnier has added an important note to Newcomer's research findings. He suggests that there are a number of community characteristics that may modify critical distances to services because these factors may inhibit or motivate the older person in the use of the community supports. These Regnier (1975) lists as:

topography
street crime
land use
percentage of elderly
bus routes/public
    transportation

ethnic identification
traffic patterns
district designations
income/rent

Regnier suggests that in addition to identifying critical and important community services, positive environmental elements and accessible locations are important to assure full access to supports.

The institutions of the community are also basic. If there is an active RSVP program, older persons will be drawn into rewarding volunteer activity. If there is a stimulating series of activities at a local senior citizen center, the older person will have resources for keeping his hours busy and productive. If the local community college provides gold cards or special classes for the elderly, this is a resource to keep the mind from becoming atrophied. A great many communities are now interested in older persons and programs for them. In 1976 the Kiwanis Club made aging its national program priority. A great many federal agencies are concentrating on older persons (see chapter 6). The community has suddenly become aware of older persons. As most communities have a great many governmental and volunteer organizations that receive their mandates from state or federal authority, it is not surprising that many older persons are victims of competition for their participation. Warren (1972) has described the vertical and horizontal aspects of modern community organization. By vertical he means the way in which local organizations are tied to and directed by noncommunity authorities. By horizontal he means the way in which the organization cuts across the community in its membership. Because executives and paid staff of many local organizations gain status, promotion, and financial reward from state organizational leaders, they are competing with other organizations for the allegiance and support of local persons. In our analysis, one case is instructive:

> In a major southwestern city a local group was forming a voluntary association whose purpose it was to furnish such community and personal supports that the aged could remain in their homes and not enter institutions. Almost from the inception of their operation they ran into conflict with two other community groups; one was a national voluntary organization that thought that the new group would raid their membership, duplicate their services and undercut their efforts. The second was a governmental agency which was hard pressed to justify its existence. The leader of this group harshly condemned the new organization, saying that they were "cornering all the best leadership and loyalty of older persons in the community."

It has become apparent that there is need for some type of coordinating and pooling that might arbitrate and coordinate efforts for older citizens so that good efforts will not be duplicated and essential services overlooked.

Family, friends, neighbors, significant others, and community supports are important factors in serving older persons.* Much more research needs to be done on the effectiveness of community programs and on family responses to elderly members.

---

*Indeed, 75 to 80 percent of all social supports for the elderly in America come from family and friends. Professionals provide at most 15 percent and volunteers approximately 5 percent.

RECREATION AND LEISURETIME ACTIVITIES

There has been some very negative reaction to the emphasis on recreation for retired persons. Miller particularly has suggested that the involvement in the work ethic is so strong that any recreational effort after retirement will not make a significant alteration in role loss (Miller, 1965). He feels that leisure activities and roles cannot replace the work role to make retirement meaningful. It seems to us that a good many persons have made the leisure role a significant one even before retirement and that Miller overlooks this and also the fact that for at least some older persons recreation means a fulfillment of put-off dreams.

Several studies have analyzed what older persons do with their leisure time. The following table shows what five hundred middle-class Americans do with their retired hours. It is part of a study done by Peterson, Larson, and Hadwen of the motivations of persons who moved into a retirement community. The table indicates the importance of solitary and nonactive activities such as watching television, listening to radio, and reading. These are relatively passive uses of time.

But Table 5–5 indicates only what elderly people do now. It does not indicate what they would like to do. The same study asks what these persons would do if they had the opportunity for other types of activities. Table 5–6 shows other preferences.

A summary of the findings of the Peterson-Larson-Hadwen study shows that older persons wish to move beyond what they are doing, how they perceive themselves, and what potentials they have. These findings are:

1. The in-movers are aware of and vocal about significant losses in activity patterns.

2. The activities that involve mobility, energy, and physical effort are participated in fewer times by fewer numbers than those involving more passive, receptive attitudes.

3. There is a general dissatisfaction on the part of a large percentage of the in-movers with the activities now occupying their time. The group judges as most enjoyable precisely those activities that appear less frequently among the things they are doing. The passive leisure-time pursuits such as television watching and listening to radio are judged as very low on the list of most enjoyable activities yet they occupy more time than any other activity.

4. The reasons advanced for not enjoying desired activities include health, finances, and family change as important variables, but all of these are low in incidence compared to the large factor of "lack of opportunity." Three-fourths of the respondents were positive about

TABLE 5–5.   STATED PREFERENCE REGARDING MOST EN-
JOYABLE ACTIVITY

Activity	Number	Percent
Passive receptive	48	11.7
Watching TV	10	
Listening to radio	1	
Reading books	34	
Reading newspaper	1	
Writing letters	2	
Passive creative	110	26.8
Creative writing	8	
Stock market	1	
Do-it-yourself	16	
Sewing	26	
Gardening	13	
Hobbies	46	
Social participative	147	35.8
Playing cards	62	
Visiting, social	9	
Participative sports	71	
Dancing	5	
Social receptive	91	22.1
Movies	6	
Musicals, entertainment	20	
Spectator sports	15	
Cultural, museums	6	
Travel, tours	44	
No activity	3 3	.7
Volunteer work	5 5	1.2
Don't know	7 7	1.7
TOTAL	411 411	100.0

SOURCE: Peterson et al. (1967).

the importance of this factor in accounting for their feelings of
frustration.

5. A large number of those who wish new activities would like to
engage in what might be termed "educational ventures."

6. Health is a significant variable in accounting for the present situation. One hundred and thirty-six persons thought that health inhibited
their participation in desired leisuretime pursuits, particularly in physical activities and traveling. On the other hand, only seventy-six said
that their health problems were very serious.

TABLE 5–6.   STATED WISHES FOR NEW ACTIVITIES

Category	FIRST		SECOND		THIRD		TOTAL	
	N	%	N	%	N	%	N	%
Solitary	24	14.4	5	10.4	4	40.0	33	14.7
Educational	44	26.3	15	31.3	2	20.0	61	27.1
Social	26	15.6	13	27.1	3	30.0	42	18.7
Participative sports	42	25.1	6	12.5	0	—	48	21.3
Spectator sports	1	.6	0	—	0	—	1	.4
Travel	21	12.6	8	16.7	1	10.0	30	13.3
Volunteer	8	4.8	1	2.1	0	—	9	4.0
Political	1	.6	0	—	0	—	1	.4
TOTAL	167	100.0	48	100.1	10	100.0	225	99.9

SOURCE: Peterson et al. (1967).

7. Because of such factors as loneliness, health, and family problems, 266 persons felt depressed or blue at times, but 185 respondents said that this occurred quite frequently. One hundred and eight felt that they were more depressed now than at age forty-five, but eighty-eight persons felt they were less depressed.

8. This group perceived themselves to have been popular with their friends and co-workers, respected in their communities, and useful in their previous roles. They brought into retirement and to the retirement community a background of success and ego strength.

9. Those individuals who list more health problems and those who feel health restricts their activities have a significantly lower life satisfaction score than those with fewer problems or who feel they are not restricted.

10. Material analyzed from open-ended questions reinforces the conclusions of other sections of this report that marriage and the family are important variables in understanding life satisfaction of this group of respondents.

11. Almost 60 percent of the in-movers would like to engage in activities that involve being with other persons. Eleven percent prefer activities that are isolated and solitary, and another 25 percent prefer passive creative pursuits, which may or may not involve others.

One of the problems of leisure is that our Calvinistic society has so glorified achievement that to play and to enjoy it is to feel guilty. Havighurst feels that because the trend is toward investing less time and energy in work we may now speak about the ethics of leisure in that people will be partially judged "by their use of free time" (Havighurst, 1977).

Leisure patterns involve the following:

1. Challenging new experiences

2. Instrumental service

3. Expressive pleasure

4. Mildly active time filling

5. Ordinary routines expanded to fill the day or week

6. Apathetic

7. Literally has no free time (Havighurst, 1977)

As free time and wealth increase, it is probable that leisure will become a more significant part of life. If this is so, the next generation will have had far better socialization in the use of free time than the present generation of elders.

SUMMARY

This chapter began with the analysis of the case of an individual who was depressed and suicidal. When his case was analyzed, it was thought that most of his problems stemmed from social losses, from failure of society to provide alternative roles for those he had lost and other relationships that might replace the ones he had given up. This chapter has illustrated many of his problems and some possible solutions to those problems. The critical issue has to do with changes in social structure that might help such persons find new roles, new positions, new activities, and new interests to modify the losses of the past and to provide assurance for new roles.

REFERENCES

Blood, R. O., Jr., and D. W. Wolfe, *Husbands and Wives: The Dynamics of Married Living.* New York: Free Press of Glencoe, 1960.

Britton, J. H., and J. O. Britton. *The Middle Aged and Older Rural Person and His Family.* Lexington: University of Kentucky Press, 1967.

Clark, M., and B. G. Anderson. *Culture in Aging: An Anthropology of Older Americans.* Springfield, Ill.: Charles C Thomas, 1967.

Cuber, J., and P. Haroff. "The More Total View: Relationships among Men and Women of the Upper Middle Class." *Journal of Marriage and Family Living,* Vol. 25, May, 1963.

Feldman, R., and M. Rollins. "Marital Satisfaction over the Family Cycle." *Journal of Marriage and Family Living,* Vol. 32, No. 1, 1970.

Goode, W. J. *After Divorce.* Glencoe, Ill.: Free Press, 1956.

Havighurst, R. J. "Life Style and Leisure Patterns." In R. Kalish (ed.), *The Later Years: Social Applications of Gerontology.* Monterey, Calif.: Brooks/Cole, 1977.

Kerchoff, A. C. "Family Patterns and Morale in Retirement." In I. H. Simpson and J. C. McKinney (eds.), *Social Aspects of Aging.* Durham, N.C.: Duke University Press, 1966.

Lopata, H. Z. *Widowhood in an American City.* Cambridge, Mass.: Schenkman, 1973.

Lowenthal, M. et al., *Aging and Mental Disorder in San Francisco.* San Francisco: Jossey-Bass, 1967.

Masters, W. H., and V. E. Johnson. *Human Sexual Response.* Boston: Little, Brown, 1966.

McLain, W. *Retirement Marriages.* Monograph 3, Storrs Agricultural Experiment Station. Storrs, Conn., 1969.

Miller, S. J. "The Social Dilemma of the Aging Leisure Participant." In A. Rose and W. Peterson (eds.), *Older Persons and Their Social World.* Philadelphia: F. A. Davis, 1965.

Murray, J. "Family Structure in the Pre-Retirement Years." Retirement Study Report # 4. US Department of Health, Education and Welfare, 1973.

Neugarten, B. *Middle Age and Aging: A Reader in Social Psychology.* Chicago: The University of Chicago Press, 1968.

Newcomer, R. "Housing Services and Neighborhood Activities" (paper presented at the 26th Annual Meeting of the Gerontology Society, 1973).

Peterson, J. A., and M. Briley. *Widows and Widowhood.* New York: Association Press, 1977.

Peterson, J. A., A. E. Larson, and T. A. Hadwen. *A Time for Work, A Time for Leisure: A Study of In-Movers.* University of Southern California Libraries, Los Angeles, 1967.

Peterson, J. A., and B. Payne. *Love in the Later Years.* New York: Association Press, 1975.

Pineo, P. "Disenchantment in the Later Years of Marriage." *Marriage and Family Living,* Vol. 23, 1961.

Regnier, V. "Neighborhood Planning for the Urban Elderly." In D. Woodruff and J. Birren (eds.), *Aging: Scientific Perspectives and Social Issues.* New York: D. Van Nostrand, 1975.

Riley, M., and A. Foner. *Aging and Society. Vol. I: An Inventory of Research Findings.* New York: Russell Sage Foundation, 1968.

Rosow, I. *Social Integration of the Aged.* New York: Free Press, 1967.

Shanas, E. *Old People in Three Industrial Societies.* New York: Atherton Press, 1968.

Streib, G. F., and W. E. Thompson. "The Older Person in a Family Context."

In E. Shanas and G. Streib (eds.), *Social Structure and Family: Intergenerational Relations.* Englewood Cliffs, N.J.: Prentice-Hall, 1965.

Sussman, M. "The Family Life of Old People." In R. Binstock and E. Shanas (eds.), *Handbook of Aging and the Social Sciences.* New York: Van Nostrand Reinhold, 1976.

Treas, J. "Aging in the Family." In D. Woodruff and J. Birren (eds.), *Aging: Scientific Perspectives and Social Issues.* New York: D. Van Nostrand, 1975.

US Bureau of the Census. *Census of Population: 1973. Subject Reports.* Final Report PG(2). 4B. Persons by Family Characteristics.

Warren, R. *The Community in America.* Chicago: Rand McNally, 1972.

FOR FURTHER READING

Aldous, J., and R. Hill. "Social Cohesion, Lineage Type, and Intergenerational Transmission." *Social Forces,* 1965, 43.

Bengtson, V. L., and K. D. Black. "Intergenerational Relations and Continuities in Socialization." In P. Baltes and W. Schaie (eds.), *Personality and Socialization.* New York: Academic Press, 1973.

Black, K. D., and V. L. Bengtson. "Solidarity across Generations: Elderly Parents and Their Middle-Aged Children" (paper presented at annual meeting of the Gerontological Society, 1973).

Glick, P. "A Demographic Look at American Families." *Journal of Marriage and Family,* 1975, 38.

Hill, R., N. Foote, J. Aldous, R. Carlson, and R. MacDonald. *Family Development in Three Generations.* Cambridge, Mass.: Schenkman, 1970.

Kerckhoff, A. C. "Nuclear and Extended Family Relationships: Normative and Behavioral Analysis." In E. Shanas and G. Streib (eds.), *Social Structure and Family: Intergenerational Relations.* Englewood Cliffs, N. J.: Prentice-Hall, 1965.

Moriwaki, S. Y. "Self-disclosure, Significant Others and Psychological Well-being in Old Age." *Journal of Health and Social Behavior,* 1973, 14.

Schwartz, A. *Survival Handbook for Children of Aging Parents.* Chicago: Follett, 1977.

Shanas, E. "Family Help Patterns and Social Class in Three Countries." *Journal of Marriage and Family,* 1967, 29.

Sussman, M. B. "The Isolated Nuclear Family: Fact or Fiction?" *Social Problems,* 1959, 6.

CHAPTER 6

Social Policy: Its Political Implications for the Aged

> The dogmas of the quiet past are inadequate to the stormy present. The occasion is piled high with difficulty and we must rise to the occasion. As our case is new—so we must think anew and act anew.
>
> ABRAHAM LINCOLN

M any problems associated with the aging process have to do with individual biomedical changes, with family and friendship relations, and with individual psychological factors. All of these occur within a broad context of societal attitudes and concerns which are themselves factors influencing societal goals, programs, and priorities. Clearly, all these factors inevitably affect the lives of the elderly in many ways, from medical services to transportation.

Important issues discussed in other chapters are touched on in this chapter, too. Here they are discussed from the perspective of public policy and national and local governmental priority setting and decision making. The student will therefore consider such issues in the context of public policies that affect the aging, directly and indirectly, as woven into the fabric of the political process.

What is described in this chapter is the origin and development of *certain policies. What the student must explore and weigh are the advantages and disadvantages of such policies, how these need to be reversed or supplemented as the case may be, and how and by whom this can be done. The aged as a "special interest group," a "voting block," and as a political force must also be considered.*

On November 8, 1977, a seventy-three-year-old widow by the name of Isabella Cannon was elected mayor of Raleigh, North Carolina. This was her first political outing, as they say. The *New York Times* reported her victory the following day:

> Mrs. Cannon, a retired library administrator, defeated the incumbent mayor in a stunning upset vote. She said that she had no idea the campaign would be so strenuous, but that she had thrived on the very demanding schedule. Asked whether her age or sex had been any handicap with the voters, Mrs. Cannon said that she had rarely gotten a question related to her age or sex. She felt that was more a concern of the media than it had been for the average citizen.

Isabella Cannon is but one of many instances of older persons who are involving themselves in their later years in the arena of public policy and politics. The old age lobby has a loud voice in Washington and the state capitols, illustrating the growth of gray power as a political force in recent years. With respect to social policy, a number of terms are commonly used loosely and sometimes interchangeably. Social policy, public policy, and political policy are seemingly used by social scientists to refer generally to the same phenomenon. In this chapter, social policy refers to the general social attitudes of society as they influence legislation and public decisions. Social policy represents the general consensus regarding the major tasks that should be done for the elderly. Public policy is almost the same; it refers to the up-front aspects of social policy, the current statements of social policy as reflected in legislative bills and political pronouncements. Political policy is even narrower. It has as a point of reference only those matters regarding the aged that are the focus of political discussion and (in large measure) expediency. We shall use the term social policy to cover social and public policy and refer later and very specifically to political responses to social policy.

MODELS OF SOCIAL POLICY

Kerschner and Hirschfield (1975) have described several models that help to sort out the issues involved in social policy (which they label public policy).

These models can be stated in terms of the following issues:

1. Will the elderly be best served by a categorical approach (programs that are focused exclusively on the pressing and sometimes unique problems of the aged) or by a generic approach (where the aged are only one of many age groups affected by the legislation)? One example is mass transit. All age segments of the community use transportation, but the aging group may have special needs in terms of bus schedules, special equipment, and cost to the user. These writers argue that when Social Security, once limited to serving the aged, had to retool to serve the blind, the poor, the disabled, and dependents, the result was "greater inefficiency and inadequate service delivery to its recipients."

2. Will the elderly be best served by a holistic or a segmented approach? At present it is obvious that they are served in a highly segmented manner, with dozens of specialized agencies serving housing, health, income, or nutritional needs. The holistic approach would integrate all of these so that older persons would not have to patronize a large number of different agencies which generally are located in different geographical places. The same writers suggest that unfortunately we divide the aged person into segments much as a butcher does a side of beef.

3. Is the aged person well served by a social policy based on the immediate present and rarely on anticipated needs of tomorrow? Public policy seems often limited by legislative bargaining and sensing of what the constituency will buy at the moment rather than based on careful studies of long-term needs.

> The tragic elements of this approach, from a public policy perspective, are that most legislation in aging evolves not from a group of policy scientists drafting policies for the future, but rather from some pragmatic assumptions about what will be tolerated by the dominant forces in society (Kerschner & Hirschfield, 1975).

4. Are the aged in our society really well served by a social policy that is the patchwork product of reaction to crisis rather than the product of rational analysis? The Social Security Act, useful as it is, was a crisis product of the Depression which focused attention on older workers who had lost their jobs and incomes.

These writers attempt to assess the costs of our present "chaotic" policy building by an analysis of Medicare. They find that while it may have been politically expedient to create the program when it was passed, it was based on inadequate research, it overlooked the great need for preventive and home-based medical care, it resulted in higher costs and less care, and it did not succeed in bringing older persons comprehensive care at reasonable cost. Some untoward results were that at least 25 percent of the population in nursing homes ought not to be there and that less than 50 percent of the health costs of older persons are covered. Thus Medicare has turned out to be a very mixed blessing.

The writers summarize by saying:

> We are suggesting here that given the resultant stalemates of the dilemmas created by categorical versus generic approaches, holistic versus segmental programming, current political context versus future planning designs, and crisis versus rational planning, aging legislation has been caught in a morass of conflicting and competing interests and issues. The result of these fragmented approaches is that in most cases involving major aging legislation, policy makers have abdicated moral responsibility by passing laws based on flimsy and inaccurate data.

ADDITIONAL SOCIAL POLICY ISSUES

There are three other special policy issues fundamental to understanding policy decisions in the United States that were not stressed by Kerschner and Hirschfield.

1. Is it possible to define an acceptable proportion of the national budget to be devoted to older persons—in fact, to each of the major age groups in the country? Each age group in every country has its own special claims against whatever available resources exist. It is never possible to meet all of the needs or wishes of any age segment. Compromises are the basis for all allocations. In the United States to date, a minimum amount of the tax dollar flows directly to the elderly. The following chart (Figure 6–1) contrasts the percentage of the Gross National Product spent on social security in six different countries, including the United States. Social security in this chart refers to all services for the elderly, not to our particular financial system. The figure reveals that Israel and the United States allocate a much smaller proportion of their gross product to long-term care. In the case of Israel, very high defense costs squeeze out social programs, although there are many innovative programs for the elderly in that country. In the United States pressures for other needs and from other sectors of the public account for the disproportion.

2. Where should the financing and authority be vested in private industry or in the government? Robert and Rosalie Kane have just finished a study with the US Department of Health, Education and Welfare in which they have compared the long-term care in six countries to uncover implications for the United States (Kane & Kane, 1976). One of their conclusions is that there is little national control in

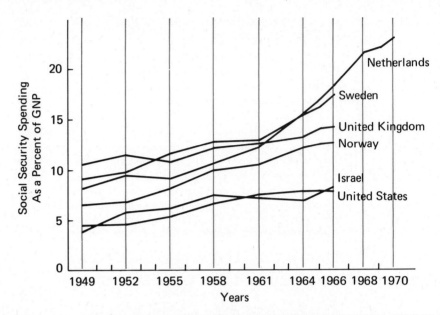

Figure 6-1. PROPORTION OF GROSS NATIONAL PRODUCT SPENT
ON SOCIAL SECURITY IN SIX COUNTRIES, 1949-70

this country in contrast to other countries and that private enterprise
motivated by the profit motive is basic to this country's system but not
in the other countries. They feel that any improvement in care must be
tied to the "entrepreneurial ethic" in this country. They also propose
some ideas about rewarding those homes that do best for their residents and penalizing those that do not give adequate care. They feel
that given the profit system, no other type of motivation or control will
work.

3. Is our society making adequate provisions for our ethnic aged?
Some poignant statistics indicate the problem. Because the average
black man's life expectancy in this country is sixty years, he is little
likely to collect one cent from all the contributions he makes to Social
Security. This issue is bound up with the reasons for the radical difference in death rates between white males living to age sixty-seven plus
and nonwhite males. Mexican-Americans often work as highly mobile
migrants and in occupations that do not have Social Security coverage.
Problems of language, social isolation, and cultural differences are
important ones for Orientals as they are forced into mandatory retirement. Benetiz (1973) summarizes some problems of the minority
elderly:

> For all the minority groups . . . there is little positive modeling of roles for
> the young with whom they come in contact. When there is a break in

intergenerational continuity it is hard, sometimes impossible, for the elderly to see what will transcend them. Many are left not with a sense of immortality through the existence of the next generation, but with a sense of loneliness and despair. . . . Benefits could be given earlier and other social policies could be devised to include alternatives particularly suited to the unique situations of minority elderly.

PROGRAMS THAT DOCUMENT SOCIAL POLICIES ISSUES

A brief history of national program efforts and legislation is instructive in understanding the basic nature of the issues that have been raised.

There have been three major national conferences designed to focus attention on and to define social policy about aging. The first was held in August of 1950 and was called together by the Federal Security Agency at the direction of President Harry Truman. Thurston Drake summarizes the objectives of this conference as:

1. To provide a forum for persons concerned with aging;

2. To reevalute the potentialities of older people;

3. To stimulate the exchange of ideas among interested people with a view to solving problems of aging;

4. To define the nature and extent of the problems;

5. To promote research in the various phases of aging; and

6. To transmit the findings to interested groups as guidelines for the development of policies with regard to older people.

Following the initial conference, the National Committee on Aging produced a report on the proceedings. These volumes were published by the Senate Labor Committee, and because of that effort a Special Staff on Aging was created in 1956. In that same year President Eisenhower established a special coordinating Federal Council on Aging, whose task was to make recommendations regarding the needs of older persons. All of these efforts produced a consensus that there was a need for a unified sense of direction and for more action in aging. This resulted in President Eisenhower's calling the second national conference in 1960, which was the first federally financed White House Conference on Aging. Preceding that conference, each state did a detailed analysis of the needs and circumstances of aged persons residing in that state. This careful preparation led to an acceleration of attention to state and local programs as well as a greater public focus on older people and their problems. The conference also recommended that a strong federal agency in aging be inaugurated and given the following directives:

1. A statutory basis and more independent leadership;

2. Adequate funds for coordination and other assigned functions through line item appropriation;

3. Responsibility for formulation of legislative proposals for submittal to Congress; and

4. Responsibility for periodic reviews and reports on the various federal programs, departments, and agencies working in behalf of older persons to achieve effective coordination and operation (Senate Special Committees on Aging, 1961).

As the result of this conference, Congressman John E. Fogarty introduced a bill in Congress that would create such an agency in the Department of Health, Education and Welfare. The agency was to help older persons through grants to states for community planning and training, projects, and training for research. While it was first proposed in 1963, it did not become law until 1965. It was called the Older American Act of 1965 and it established the Administration on Aging (AoA). It functioned as an independent agency until August 1967, when it was transferred to a new agency, the Social and Rehabilitation Service, which Kerschner and Hirschfield (1975) view as culminating in a loss of power for the AoA. They point out that:

A prime example of the destructive potential inherent in the reorganization effort is the experience of the ACTION agency. The decision in the spring of 1971 to transfer the Foster Grandparent program, the Peace Corps, VISTA, and the Retired Senior Volunteers Program to this new agency represents a loss of organizational identity and integrity. The rationale upon the part of the Administration was that such a restructuring would bring together, under one administrative "roof," agencies involved in essentially the same type of operation, e.g., volunteer efforts for special groups. What has occurred, in fact, is a gradual loss of morale, budgetary resources, and skilled and dedicated personnel.

Eventually a third national conference, the second White House Conference on Aging, was held in Washington in 1971. The need for the conference stemmed from the fact that despite great strides being taken in the sixties, "progress was at best sporadic and its momentum slowing. There was still no comprehensive set of national policies on which all levels and parts of government were working together to articulate" ("Toward a National Policy on Aging," 1971). The stated objectives for the 1971 conference were:

1. To initiate the development of specific, thoughtful guides and recommendations for policies and actions in aging at community, state, and national levels.

2. To draw these guides and recommendations from cross-sections of older people, providers of service, specialists on aging, key decision makers, and youth, in order that they may represent a broad and effective consensus.

3. To broaden the understanding, at community and state levels, of the needs of older people, and strengthen the willingness to act on the policy proposals that will emerge from the White House Conferences on Aging at all levels.

These objectives were to be approached through a three-year plan, with a follow-up after the conference. The first year, 1970, was called a Prologue year, in which older persons across the country would have an opportunity to present their needs through Older American Forums. The second year was called as the Year of Conferences (1971). Local and state conferences and national organizational task forces would gather to make policy recommendations that would be considered in November–December of the National Conference. The third year was regarded as the Year of Action (1972). The emphasis in 1972 was on the implementation of the recommendations of the White House Conference.

A great deal of planning and training went into each phase of this three-year program. The 1969 amendments to the Older American Act assigned to states responsibility for planning, coordination, and evaluation of various services and programs in those states. Each state was asked to make a "comprehensive study" of the income, health, housing, social, and other significant conditions of its older population. Many states were able to send these studies to Washington in time so that they became important research sources for the Conference. More than six thousand Older American White House Forums were held, with over 500,000 participants. Forum recorders noted major points of the discussions and voting on priorities of needs. These were all part of the section discussions of the Conference. The Conference affords us a valuable summary of social policy consensus as of that time. The recommendations of this Conference are as close to a clear statement of social and public policy as has yet been voiced in this country. As such, it is critically important to review those statements. We present them here in detail to highlight the basic policy issues and the intended national strategy in dealing with these issues.

Education

The Conference stressed the importance of existing educational opportunities and special educational programs' being opened to all older persons. Non-English-speaking aged and those from culturally different populations were also to be encouraged to participate in program planning. Moreover, such educational programs were to be designed to provide specific benefits to culturally different aged, as, for example, information about citizenship requirements, Social Security rules, and the like.

As a matter of policy, special effort was to be made to accommodate the elderly with low income and special health and disability problems. To this end particular consideration and maximum use could be made of subsistence allotment, free attendance at educational programs, special arrangements for transportation, noncredit courses, relaxed admission requirements, removal of any legal barriers, and not least, locations convenient and accessible to the elderly. Enhancing the utility and accessibility of public libraries as a primary community resource was stressed.

Increased opportunities for continued education require money and manpower and the Conference called for increased public expenditures in this regard. It called for a public policy that would funnel moneys into education for older persons, such education to include vocational and skills training, as well as training for more effective use of available services, cultural enrichment, and training aids in learning more successful ways of coping with problems and difficulties associated with aging.

It is also interesting to note that the 1971 Conference did not overlook the need for educational programs for the elderly to help them understand better the issues, procedures, and necessary required actions embedded in the political process. In other words, educational programs for the elderly should also help them learn how to effect political change.

As a matter of public policy, the Conference also declared for the preparation and presentation of appropriate materials and methods to inform and raise public awareness of aging issues. The mass communications media as well as the classroom, the Conference declared, should be the means by which a better understanding of the aging process and the resources of older persons could be achieved by society at large.

Statements about education specifically referred to the need for what was called preretirement education and to the need for special education and training for professionals who work with elderly persons.

Employment and Retirement

A large number of recommendations for policy regarding work and retirement roles and activities were formulated. Although these represent an optional state of affairs for the older persons, the continued gap between preferred policy and practice remains all too evident.

Calling for a more equitable distribution of services to all age groups, the Conference recommended that federal, state, and local employment programs expand their services to provide more job recruitment, job counseling, and placement services to older persons. Hiring or employment discrimination on account of age was firmly rejected, a notion that finally came to legislative fruition some seven years later with the passage of the law moving mandatory retirement to age seventy and eliminating it altogether for government workers (see chapter 4). The policy aim of the Conference was to remove chronological age as the sole criterion for retirement and to allow for a flexible program of retirement earlier for those who so desire.

Associated recommendations called for programs that would guarantee a retirement income adequate for maintaining a decent standard of living and/or some training required for reemployment. A transferable ("portable") pension was an important element of these policy recommendations. Another was the recommendation for modifying the rules so that Social Security beneficiaries are not unduly or unfairly penalized because of additional income earned.

Among the new federal agencies recommended by the Conference to help the elderly cope with financial problems were:

1. An Office of Aging in the executive branch of government

2. A national pension commission

3. A national job bank for retirees

4. Local centers to bring together older persons and potential or prospective employers

5. A new portable pension plan to be administered through Social Security

6. Retirement counseling programs to supplement pension programs.

Specific federal legislation called for by the Conference included laws to exempt older persons from federal taxes, and incentives to employers to establish and maintain adequate retirement plans.

The Conference issued a general policy statement that relates to this issue as a preamble to its section on income:

There is no substitute for income if people are to be free to exercise choices in their style of life. The income of elderly people in the past left the greater number of them with insufficient means for decent, dignified living. . . . The economic situation of the elderly, if past experience is repeated, will improve more slowly than that of younger groups even with an upturn in the national economy. Immediate action to increase the income of the elderly is urgent and imperative.

Public policy, according to the 1971 Conference, should work for a cash income in accordance with the "American standard of living . . . using the intermediate budget for an elderly couple prepared by the Bureau of Labor Statistics for all elderly." Obviously the phrase "American standard of living" is too vague and ambiguous to serve as a useful standard or criterion. The Conference was able to be more specific by recommending that a basic "floor" of income for older people be provided by Social Security and payments from general tax revenues, and that this floor be not less than $3,000 a year (that was in 1971 dollars); that widows' benefits under Social Security start at age fifty; that adjustments in Social Security payments be made with respect to the differences in longevity for various ethnic groups; that various improvements in private pension plans be made; that remission of property taxes for poor elderly be made; that benefits of Medicare-Medicaid programs be increased; and that a national health security program be established.

As discussions of income in other chapters point out, although the financial well-being of the elderly in America overall has improved to some degree, the well-intentioned policy statements of the 1971 Conference remain a tantalizing and unrealized prospect for too many elderly Americans caught between fixed incomes and financially crippling rates of inflation in the cost of living.

Physical and Mental Health

The policy statements in this area of concern of the Conference touched the conventional bases in its general statements. For instance, the Conference called for adequate health assessment of elderly persons, educational programs to preserve and maintain health, appropriate preventive, outreach, and supportive services necessary to maintain or restore physical and mental health, adequate rehabilitative services, and long-term care when disability occurs. Specifically, the Conference recommendations included:

1. A coordinated health system for the entire population, with special consideration given to the aged

2. A comprehensive national health plan

3. Health education for all ages

Many elderly women who are excellent cooks welcome the opportunity of having someone other than themselves to cook for.

4. Programs of training in aging at all levels of education for health professionals and specialists

5. Adequate funds to be divided between research, service, and education

6. A Center for Aging to be established in the National Institutes of Mental Health

7. An interdisciplinary committee on the protection of individual rights.

To date, only item 6 has been effected in the form of the National Institute on Aging (NIA). Public action continues to lag far behind these formulations of public policy, insofar as they indeed do represent public policy. Especially is this true in the area of mental health of the aged, as the discussions in chapters 9 and 12 indicate. The issue of how to define or even characterize health needs of the elderly, especially the institutionalized aged, is a subject of considerable debate and controversy today.

Nutrition

Although closely tied to the general subject of health, nutrition and the elderly proved to be a topic about which the Conference was able to generate policy statements that, in turn, have produced very specific action, especially at the federal level. The general policy statement in the preamble to the report said in part:

> Adequate nutrition is necessary to insure older Americans the right to enjoy life, liberty, and the pursuit of happiness. . . . Provision should be made to meet the social as well as nutritional needs of older persons. . . . Assistance should be provided to make possible the preparation of meals for themselves and others. Community meals, however, should be an alternative. . . . All nutrition programs should be supplemented by adequate educational measures. . . . The search for more efficient and better means of providing for the good nutrition, health, and happiness of older persons should be a continuous process (including research, evaluation, and communication). Recommendations clearly include elderly in small towns, rural and isolated areas and elderly in minority groups, older Indians, and other non-English speaking groups.

Among the specific recommendations for policy and action, the Conference stated that funds should be furnished for rehabilitation of the malnourished aged, to prevent malnutrition among those approaching old age, and for a major effort in research on the effects of nutrition on aging and disease in old age. Another element in nutritional policy for the aged is the establishment of standards for food and nutrition services with respect to the quality, nutritive value, and methods of preparing and serving foods. A portion of resources should be allocated for nutrition education and counseling.

Of major significance are the recommended policy that nutrition programs should stress the psychological benefits of group eating and the policy that would require federally financed housing to provide nutritionally sound eating programs. The Conference also called for new standards for food wholesomeness and safety to be established by federal and state government agencies.

Housing

The Conference's policy statement on housing for the elderly is straightforward and comprehensive.

> A national policy on housing for the elderly worthy of this nation must embrace not only shelter, but needed services of quality that extend the span of independent living in comfort and dignity, in and outside of institutions, as a right wherever the elderly live or choose to live.

The specific recommendations under this general statement of policy attempted to get at the housing problems that existed then and which exist currently.

The Conference proposed that a fixed proportion of all government

funds should be earmarked specifically for the elderly, with a minimum production of 120,000 units per year. Eligibility for housing was
to be based on economic, social, and health needs, while housing production was to be based on documented need.

A range of varied living arrangements was to be developed, recognizing the variety of preferences, needs, life-styles, and circumstances
among the elderly population. The range should include long-term-
care facilities for sick elderly and those for disabled, facilities with
more limited medical, food, and homemaker services, congregate housing with accompanying dining and personal services, and housing for
independent (self-maintenance) living.

The Conference proposed that housing programs should include
supportive services for residents as well as elderly living in adjacent
areas. Mechanism for local property tax relief should also be provided.
Procedural delays in producing housing for the elderly should be eliminated and minority and hard-core-poor elderly should have high
priority. Multidisciplinary teams should be formed to establish guidelines for all federal agencies involved in housing programs for the
elderly.

Minority nonprofit groups should be encouraged to provide housing.
Housing taken away from the elderly should be replaced. Neighborhoods should be preserved through rehabilitating procedures. Special
housing programs with special funds should be provided for the
unique needs of rural aged and native Americans.

Loans should be made available to the elderly to help those who
wish to stay in their own homes. Families should be encouraged by
financial incentives to provide for elderly in their homes. Rent supplements should be increased and their scope broadened. A direct loan
housing program should be funded and implemented.

And finally, the Conference recommended that standards for physical and environmental security be developed. Along with this went the
recommendation that research regarding the health, physical, psychological, and social aspects of the environment should be conducted
and the results widely disseminated.

Spiritual Well-Being

The emphasis the Conference placed upon policy statements relating to spiritual well-being indicates the role religion occupies in America and in the lives of elderly persons (see chapter 7). The policy
statement produced by the 1971 Conference is as follows:

As delegates to the White House Conference on Aging in the section concerned with spiritual well-being, we call attention to this fact of life: to

ignore, or to attempt to separate the need to fulfill the spiritual well-being of man from attempts to satisfy his physical, material, and social needs is to fail to understand the meaning of God and the meaning of man. Whether it be the concerns for education, employment, health, housing, income, nutrition, retirement-roles, or transportation, a proper solution involves personal identification, and human dignity. These come fully only when man has wholesome relationships with both fellow man and God. . . . Therefore, the White House Conference states that all policies, programs, and activities recommended in a national policy of aging should be so developed that the spiritual well-being of all citizens be fulfilled.

As a matter of public policy, the Conference stated, government should cooperate with others to help meet spiritual needs but with due concern for the separation of church and state. Part of that cooperative effort would be to provide research and professional training in the area of spiritual well-being to those who would provide services to the elderly. The Conference also declared that government should provide financial resources for the training of clergy, professional, and other workers to develop competence in satisfying the spiritual needs of the aged.

The Conference insisted that it be public policy that institutions licensed to care for the aged have a chaplaincy service and that spiritual consultation in private homes be made available to older persons who wish it; that interfaith programs should be planned for the entire aged population through multipurpose community centers; and that religious organizations should serve as referral agencies, as advocates for the elderly affirming the rights of the aged, including the right of all aged to die with dignity.

The National Interfaith Council on Aging, coordinating the work of religious groups covering a hundred million members, resulted from these recommendations (see chapter 7).

Transportation

The following excerpt from the preamble may be taken as a statement of public policy with respect to transportation:

The elderly, like everyone else in society, must depend upon the ability to travel for acquiring the basic necessities of food, clothing, and shelter as well as employment and medical care. The ability to travel is also necessary for their participation in spiritual, cultural, recreational, and other social activities. To the extent the aged are denied transportation services they are denied full participation in meaningful community life.

The availability and accessibility of convenient and cheap transportation is a major problem for many older people. Although they are apprehensive about using public transportation, it is generally their only means of shopping and reaching activities and friends.

Recommendations for policy specified that the federal government adopt a policy of increasing transportation services particularly for rural, handicapped, and poor elderly. A parallel policy should provide that when programs are planned for the elderly, transportation services be an integral part of such programs.

Further recommendations were that standards be set for design of transport vehicles for use by the aged and that crosswalks, shelters, traffic control, and so on, be designed with the aged in mind. Other recommendations proposed government underwriting of transportation services so that the elderly as well as the handicapped be permitted to travel at half fare. This recommendation suggested that the Highway Trust Fund be converted into a General Transportation

Fund. It was also recommended that nationwide driver's test standards be prohibited from discriminating on account of age, that a national policy for guaranteed liability insurance to cover volunteer drivers be set, and that insurance companies be prohibited from increasing auto insurance rates or canceling insurance solely on the basis of age. Subsidies for volunteer drivers of elderly persons were also recommended, as was no-fault insurance.

Some progress along these lines can be acknowledged by the fact that bus and other transportation services in a growing number of cities as well as some airlines now offer discounted fares to older persons. No-fault insurance has begun to be considered, even hotly debated, and while national standards for the design of transport vehicles have not been adopted, some bus companies have come to recognize the need for vehicular design that does not penalize handicapped or elderly persons.

The Conference's concern for public policy that addresses itself to protecting the individual rights of older persons and keeps open the widest possible range of options is indicated by the following statement of social policy endorsed by the Conference:

> National policy should guarantee to all older persons real choices as to how they spend their later years . . . to maintain their independence and their usefulness. . . . Attention must be given now to identify and provide those services which make it possible for older persons to remain in, or return to, their own homes or other places of residence. Whatever the type of resource required to assist them in maintaining the living arrangements of their choice, whether institutional or community based, appropriate standards for those resources must be established and strictly enforced.
>
> Action is needed in forging a national social policy on protection of the older person's rights and choices that will be reflected in provision of a wide range of facilities, programs, and services, whether preventive, rehabilitative, supportive, or developmental in their focus. To this end, there must be strategies for achieving action now, including federal fiscal support, to implement the policies which follow.

The specific recommendations under this general policy statement called for protective services, consumer protection, federal funding for a guaranteed full range of legal services, new methods of police protection for the elderly, and governmental coordination of services and standard setting for all delivery of services.

Planning

An important and unique section of the White House Conference was devoting to planning. The statement of policy formulated by the

Conference is interesting and important and is worth the student's attention.

Planning, which aims at the long-range needs of the elderly and attempts to look into the future to anticipate needs which may arise in years to come, is needed. Many of the needs of our present older citizens will be the same as those of Americans who are now you. When they are older, some needs may be different. Great social changes, which may take years to accomplish, may be needed. Inflation, overcrowding, population growth, environmental concerns, mobility and growth of government, and the lessened ability of an individual citizen to plan for the future make planning needed for today, tomorrow and for years to come. . . .

The following policy proposals represent the feelings and attitudes of Delegates representing all sections of America. Elderly Americans, planners, citizens involved in both the planning and delivery of services to the elderly were represented in each Section of the Conference. Planning to identify and state the needs of the elderly, planning to develop methods of meeting those needs, planning to find the means to generate support and galvanize the nation to action—each step of the way needs clear guidelines. The policy proposals herein may assist in finding our way.

Specific proposals asked for are:

1. Significant involvement of nongovernmental sectors and consumers in the decision-making process in planning, which is comprehensive and coordinated

2. A separate entity within the executive branch (Office of the President) to facilitate planning and advocacy in aging

3. State governments to provide comprehensive planning in aging in each state

4. Planning that makes service programs more responsive to the needs of elderly

5. Planning for aging that gives priority to minority groups who suffer most because of past discriminatory practices

6. Planning to insure responsibility, accountability, and responsiveness

7. Planning linked to budgeting so that executive public officials with responsibility for aging programs participate in the budgetary process

8. Reordering of national priorities so that the aged receive a fair share of national wealth.

One important outcome of these policy recommendations was the development of the Area Agencies on Aging (the so-called triple-A's). Their initial mandated task was that of coordinating existing services to the elderly. Subsequently the AAAs have become involved in providing services to their communities' aged.

Conclusion

What do we make of these very basic public policy statements? In the first place, there are a number of common themes that appear again and again in these reports. Let us see if we can identify some of them as more general statements of public policy:

1. National priorities must be reordered. If the American public in its general policy orientation is still a youth-centered nation, then it will not be likely to give to older persons a just share of the national wealth or attention when major decisions are made.

2. In reordering national priorities, attention is called again and again to the poverty of a great many older persons and the need to use some method of giving adequate financial support to older persons if they are to make any choices about their life-styles or to find adequate supports.

3. Income may be a great problem, but most of the reports had direct emphasis or codicils on the need to protect the independence of older persons. No matter how many recommendations were made to intervene in behalf of the health, housing, mental health, nutritional aspects of older persons' lives, such interventions must not be made at the cost of neglecting the dignity and self-determination of our aged population.

4. Most of the reports, whatever their point of reference, ask that the government structure be reordered so that the aged be given a position of strength and visibility in the federal government.

5. The principle of self-determination is everywhere evident. All reports suggested that future social policy be evolved only when the aged of all sectors are involved in decision making and planning.

6. There is a common theme that is expressed over and over, sometimes almost with despair. Society is now so complex that no "person or single agency" can ever operate effectively alone. Consequently the need for horizontal and vertical coordination and mutual planning.

These inferences from the total report indicate that social policy is in the process of change, that great basic new directions are needed if the growing population of aged is to have consideration in the future. What has happened to policy since the White House Conference? Two observations can be made. One deals with the effectiveness of such national advocacy as the White House Conference represented and a second deals with current salient public issues of policy. No one can deny that the White House Conference coalesced many efforts at improving the conditions of the aged, gave solid guidelines for governmental action, and resulted in positive programs. Let us review a few of these:

1.   There is now a national nutrition program with programs that pay attention to the need for the social values of eating together in thousands of nutrition centers across the country, and the Meals-on-Wheels program that enables thousands of persons to stay in their homes and apartments.

2.   The focus on transportation resulted in federal funding of programs to insure mobility of older persons who otherwise would not have access to medical, shopping, hospital, recreational, or cultural facilities. It resulted, furthermore, in many volunteer activities that go far to meet the needs of isolated urban and rural persons. Furthermore, laws now passed make the facilities of transportation and the facilities that serve the aged more felicitous to their moving about with comfort.

3.   The emphasis on spiritual well-being resulted in the Interfaith Coalition, a group of churches and synagogues representing more than 100 million members that are now mobilized to stir their organizations into a service mode for the aged.

4.   There is now established an Executive Office of Aging, manned by a distinguished gerontologist, Dr. Robert Butler, with direct access to the executive branch of the government. There is a new agency called the AAA, whose purpose is to facilitate the coordination of local, state, and federal programs as well as to monitor them.

5.   While fifteen years ago one might have identified a dozen universities or colleges that had courses in their curriculum to deal directly in educating the aged or in training people to work with the aged, there are now over one thousand institutions paying some attention to the aged (see discussion in chapter 11). Of course, many factors were involved in this change, but federal subsidies and grant programs have provided incentives.

As far as we know, no one has yet made a comprehensive analysis of the degree to which the policies enunciated at the 1971 White House Conference are now a recognized part of our public stance and are already illustrated in direct action programs. Students seeking a valuable research program could do no better than to take one of the sections and make a sober study of the degree to which those social policy statements have in fact become national policy, as evidenced in legislation and augmentation in both private and public sectors.

The second observation has to do with what has happened to some of the issues that caused most or little debate at the 1971 White House Conference. Many salient issues that confront the American people, that exercise the writers of editorials, and that demand a restatement of public policy, were only mentioned in 1971 but they did not demand the attention they do now. Most of these are emergent issues and consequently demand new social policy decisions.

As of the beginning of 1978 they are:

1. *The ways we deal with death.* This was not a paramount issue in 1971. It was mentioned and there were courses given in dying and death. Now courses are given everywhere, and the great issues are the high cost of funerals, euthanasia, the right to die, the living will, the applicability of the hospice concept to America, the meaning of death itself from a psychological and medical point of view.

2. *The age of retirement.* New York City, Seattle, Los Angeles, the State of California have all passed bills denying the right of the city or state to fire an employee because of age. A bill before the House in Washington has now passed and been signed by the president. Major newspapers are debating the issue on their editorial pages. Since the thirties, social and public policy decreed that it was right for a person to retire at sixty-five. This is now being challenged, and steps are being taken to change that policy.

3. The social policy recommendations we have read make various suggestions regarding amendments to *Social Security.* Many of those recommendations were accepted and the amount that a retired person may earn now without penalty, $4,000, is to be raised to $4,500 and then to $5,000. But a far more serious matter has entered the political arena. Social Security may not be fiscally sound. It may require subsidization from the general tax revenue unless rates are changed. This dilemma is clearly related to the age of retirement, because if any substantial number of workers were to stay regularly employed and defer collecting Social Security, such a change would contribute to its fiscal soundness. On the other hand, half of our industries now have early retirement provisions for their workers, which would reduce moneys paid into Social Security. It is a complex and difficult problem but there is no question that a basically new social policy must be enunciated with respect to Social Security to make it sound for the future.

4. *A national health insurance plan.* The idea of such a plan was on a low burner at the White House Conference. It was suggested and recommended, but it did not occupy a position of primary consideration on the part of most delegates. Today the enormous costs of medical and hospital care are such a burden that there are at least three major proposals for such a plan, differing in orientation and degree of involvement on the part of the government. Nevertheless, such proposals attest to the possibility of a major change in social policy in terms of national planning to meet the health needs of our people. As of now

that decision must be debated, a consensus found and then implemented. The soaring costs of medical care clearly make the issue a very important one now, especially for elderly Americans.

5. *Inflation.* Inflation continues to hold center stage for young and old alike. It was a prime source of reference in 1971, although there were few attempts to diagnose anything but its critical impact on aging persons. Today the national debate has to do with whether to try to hold down inflation or employment, or whether there is another alternative. The brave words said about both unemployment and the evils of inflation do not cure the problem, and older persons are losing their savings with every percent the inflationary rate rises. There is still no well-defined national policy articulated by the Carter Administration, by the Republicans, or by any other responsible group as to how to cope with these twin problems. But there is wide discussion and perhaps a policy will emerge. In the meantime some small stopgap attempts to protect the elderly against inflation have been made. Some states are deferring taxes on houses of those above sixty-five years and the state takes a lien on such homes. But few persons feel confident today about their private pension plans, their savings, their future Social Security payments when inflation booms and booms.

THE POLITICAL RESPONSE OF OLDER PERSONS

If we are to look at the total picture of the formation of social policy as it affects the aged it is important to assess the degree to which older persons have power and to analyze the ways they use that power.

The political orientation of older persons is generally more conservative than that of younger cohorts (Hudson & Binstock, 1976). This is illustrated by closer ties to the Republican Party, although this relationship is complicated by the variable of social class. One important explanatory concept comes from an analysis of the stability of political orientation, which shows that "older persons tend to retain political orientations they have developed earlier in life" (Hudson & Binstock, 1976).

Older persons take more interest in national affairs and in national political figures than younger persons when education is held a constant. Voting participation increases with age, reaches a high point around sixty, and then declines slightly—that is, it does not decline to the point where it began to increase in the thirties (Hudson & Binstock, 1976). Leadership positions in government are generally held by older persons (Hudson & Binstock, 1976). All of these patterns may make the political impact of older persons somewhat conservative—but that conservatism may be abandoned when specific issues regarding the

The elderly are more conscientious about voting than are the younger generations. They have also discovered how to make use of their political "clout."

welfare of older persons are being considered. Much of the political
impact of older persons is exercised through need-based organizations
such as the National Council of Senior Citizens, the National Retired
Teachers Association, the American Association of Retired Persons,
and the National Association of Retired Federal Employees. Probably
over half of all persons in the United States belong to one of these
groups. NRTA-AARP itself reported over 11 million members in 1972.
These groups have powerful and sophisticated political lobbies and
advocacy groups. They have ready access to Congress and the White
House. NRTA-AARP also has legislative councils in every state watching age-related legislation, lobbying, and educating the organization's
state members. Yet Pratt and Binstock both suggest that these organizations will not "engender a marked reordering of public processes or
public priorities" (Hudson & Binstock, 1976).

How much does the term "senior power" mean? When the number
of persons over sixty doubles in the next four decades, will this aug-
mented group have greater political control? The answer from political
scientists like Cutler, Pratt, and Binstock is, probably not. Binstock
argues convincingly that senior power will be limited because the

aging do not vote cohesively as a block (Binstock, 1974). No one can "deliver" the elderly vote.

SUMMARY

In America social policy has to be flexible and mobile because in a rapidly changing economy and society problems change in intensity and sometimes in applicability. Training for leadership in the field of aging certainly demands a new dimension as far as adjustment to social trends is concerned. If one is to have an effective voice as an advocate he must remember that the unexpected is today commonplace and a static law of yesterday may be simply irrelevant today. He must regard the innovative as the normal. This makes it difficult to change social policy to adapt because of the complexity of our bureaucratic way of life, our slowness to change law, even if we can influence social policy.

Older persons are interested in national, state, and local affairs and demonstrate that interest in their voting behavior. But because they do not vote cohesively, the power inherent in their numbers is diluted and they are not thought to represent potentials for major social changes.

REFERENCES

Benetiz, R. "Ethnicity, Social Policy, and Aging." In R. Davis and M. Nieswander (eds.), *Aging: Prospects and Issues.* Andrus Gerontology Center, University of Southern California, Los Angeles, 1973.

Binstock, R. "Aging and the Future of American Politics." *Annals of the American Academy of Political and Social Science,* 1974, 415.

Hudson, R., and R. Binstock. "Political Systems and Aging." In R. Binstock and E. Shanas (eds.), *Handbook of Aging and the Social Sciences.* New York: Van Nostrand Reinhold, 1976.

Kane, R., and R. Kane. *Long-term Care in Six Countries: Implications for the United States.* Department of Health, Education and Welfare (NIH) publication no. 76–1207. Washington, D.C.: Government Printing Office, 1976.

Kerschner, P., and I. Hirschfield. "Public Policy and Aging: Analytic Approaches." In D. Woodruff and J. Birren (eds.), *Aging: Scientific Perspectives and Social Issues.* New York: D. Van Nostrand, 1975.

FOR FURTHER READING

Cohen, N. "Aging, Disengagement, and Opinionation." *Public Opinion Quarterly,* 1969, 33.

Cottrell, F. "Aging and the Political System." In J. C. McKinney and F. de Vyver (eds.), *Aging and Social Policy.* New York: Appleton-Century-Crofts, 1966.

Kent, D. P. "Government and the Aging." *Journal of Social Issues,* 1965, 21.

National Council of Senior Citizens. *Legislative Approaches to the Problems of the Aged: A Handbook of Model State Statutes.* Washington, D.C.: National Council of Senior Citizens, 1971.

Schmidhauser, J. "The Political Influence of the Aged." *The Gerontologist,* 1968, 8:2.

CHAPTER 7 | Religion and Aging

> If life is a matter of getting older then it is bound to be a
> sad and mournful business, because you are leaving in the
> dust behind you life's glories dead. On the other hand, if
> life is a matter of growing older, deepening your affection,
> extending your field of knowledge, heightening your sense
> of beauty, expanding your areas of service, bearing your
> suffering more nobly, sensitizing your awareness of God's
> presence, then it is a joyful, and not a mournful, business.
>
> DR. MELVIN SHEATLEY, JR.
> in the *Los Angeles Times*, August 6, 1967

*Understanding the aging process requires some familiarity with all
significant aspects of life. The degree to which religion is an
influence upon individuals in later life is an important variable which
the student of gerontology must consider.*

*We acknowledge that relatively little empirical research has been
done on religious beliefs and practice of the aged. This chapter helps
the student develop some systematic way of considering the role or
status of religion on the aging person's life. The chapter directs the
student to an examination of religious behavior, beliefs, and practices
(rituals) and in which ways these have bearing upon life satisfaction in
the later years. Discussion is also focused upon activities of religious
organizations that are directed toward the elderly in terms of programs
and direct services to the aged.*

*One consequence of such study, the authors believe, may be to
stimulate the serious student of gerontology to test further some*

assumptions about the role of religion, formal and otherwise, in the
complex interplay of factors involved in successful aging.

One of the authors had a singular experience a dozen years ago. He
had arranged to spend an entire day in Chartres Cathedral watching
the colors reflected by those jeweled windows change with each position of the sun. During the afternoon vespers were held and some fifty
people, mostly old, attended. At the close of the service one older
woman got down on her knees and crawled to the statue of the Virgin
Mary, put her arms around the statue's feet and wept. After some time
she got up, her face radiant, and marched out of the cathedral. It was
almost identically the scene that Henry Adams had created in his book
describing the sixteenth century, *Mont Saint Michel and Chartres.* For
that woman, life must have been hard indeed. She looked like a woman
who experienced the hard life of a peasant, but there was comfort and
meaning in that place for her, as Adams said there had been three
hundred years before.

Some time after that incident the same author went into St. Patrick's
at noon time, during a mass, and watched hundreds of New Yorkers
use the corridor of the church as a warm and handy way to cross the
street. Most of them did not pause, did not cross themselves, did not
kneel. But some did and some seemed to walk away with a new serenity. Has the meaning of religion changed for human beings? Is it still a
refuge from the storms of life and an affirmation of the profound meaning of life for our older people?

Alfred North Whitehead spoke about the importance of science and
religion in his book *Science and the Modern World* (1942):

> When we consider what religion is for mankind and what science is, it is no
> exaggeration to say that the future course of history depends upon the deci-
> sion of this generation as to the relations between them. We have here the
> two strongest forces which influence men, and they seem to be set one
> against the other.

This chapter affords us a look, as objectively as we can, at the relationship between religiosity and aging. We say as objectively as possible
because of all historical institutions religion has received less attention
by competent scientists in the field of aging (if not in all fields) than
has any other major institutional aspect of life. An excellent text, for
example, *Aging: Scientific Perspectives and Social Issues* (Woodruff &
Birren, 1975), devoted a mere five lines to religion and aging, and those
comments have more to do with attitudes toward death than any review of investigations about how religion influences aging. The more
recent *Aging in Mass Society* (Hendricks & Hendricks, 1977) goes a bit

Religion continues to be a major source of satisfaction and comfort to many of the elderly.

further. It includes about two and a half pages of a general discussion of religion and aging. One wonders at this lack of attention. Perhaps it is because the editors looked at the studies in the field and found them so lacking in meaningfulness or utility that they decided to omit the subject entirely.

Why this neglect by the psychological and sociological researchers? It may be partially explained by the difficulty involved in establishing operational definitions of religion or religious experience. Or it may be that young social scientists, many without experiential background in religion, often choose to ignore the subject because of its complexities. Or others, with a bias against the different definitions of truth and truth seeking they encounter in dealing with religion, may think the whole subject peripheral and unworthy of serious scientific study. Still others, seeing what they interpreted in the last quarter of a century as the increase of secularization, may have decided not to spend time or energy in analyzing an area of life that may become less and less important. A further point of explanation may rest in some reluctance on the part of foundations or government agencies to fund this type of investigation. It ought to be of some interest to the student to try to discover why one of the oldest and most basic institutions in all cultures is so neglected by our best scientists.

A brief look at some demographic data indicates how salient is the religious thrust in lives of Americans. The Census Bureau in an analysis of 35,000 households—surely a significant sample—discovered that fewer than 3 percent reported no religious connection or interest. About 50 percent attend some kind of religious meeting regularly. Those facts alone make the matter one deserving attention on the part of the inquisitive student of gerontology.

It is necessary to break down the general question of the relationship of religion and aging into much more definitive and specific questions if we are to throw some light on this field of inquiry. Some of the questions are:

1. What, if any, are the characteristic patterns of religious participation over the life cycle?

2. Is religious behavior or are religious beliefs more important in assessing a relationship between religion and aging?

3. Does religious behavior or belief make a difference in measures of life satisfaction?

4. In what specific ways do practices or beliefs contribute to the happiness, serenity, or adjustment of the older persons during his last years?

5. Does religion as such enable older persons to face their dying days and their death with greater ease or comfort than those who do not believe?

6. Is it possible to differentiate the benefits that come to participants—to distinguish the social aspect of religion from aspects of religious experience that are sacred?

LIFE CYCLE RELIGIOUS PARTICIPATION

We are asking whether there are any characteristic patterns of religious participation that follow men and women through the life cycle. Do they attend church more during one period of life than another? Bahr (1970) has carefully tried to do this by charting religious attendance by age group. He identifies several models. The one we shall refer to here is the "traditional" model. Thus, formal practice of religion is presumed to decline between ages ten and thirty, reaches its lowest point from thirty to thirty-five, and then shows a steady rise until old age. It falls off during the last years when mobility is lost. This pattern gets some support from Fichter, Mauss, and Glock (Fichter, 1954). A recent Gallup poll gives some support as it shows that 42 percent of

In general, people do not become religious just because they get old. The continued practice or neglect of religion appears to be more related to early training and characteristic life style.

adults of all faiths attended church in what is described as a typical week but adults fifty and over had a slightly higher attendance—45 percent. There is contrary evidence from Orback's (1961).

There are problems with this research because it is cross-sectional in nature. To compare religious practices of present thirty-year-olds with present sixty-five-year-olds is an essential failure in scientific logic. These are two different cohorts (see discussion in chapter 1). They grew up in somewhat different cultures with different family and community influences. The degree of secularization may have been different for them. What this really tells us is not at all that older persons get more religious or are more religious than younger ones. It tells us only that there is some difference in religious participation between generations. We do not know from this research how those sixty-five and older participated when they were thirty, and we cannot tell from these studies how the thirty-year-olds will behave during their later years.

Furthermore, from these studies which correlate age and religious participation we know little about what religion means to each individual. Quite possibly it may mean to a thirty-year-old, newly moved to Los Angeles, that he needs social roots and he may find some social opportunities in his church participation. Or he may be a rising young manager wanting to achieve an executive position in his work, and his church and other community activities are part of his scheme to become a vice-president of his company.

A friend of one of the authors came from a family that had been part of the Congregational tradition for six generations, but when he aspired to become a bank president it appeared to him to be a wise strategy to join the Episcopal church. In other words, a simple correlation between attendance and age may mean little if we do not investigate the motivations, attitudes, and beliefs associated with the behavior. This has rarely been done in this type of study. We need to know what antecedent variables (what other social facts that influence) explain the behavior. We have learned a little from these studies, but they raise many more intriguing possibilities for study in depth and mandate more attention to explanatory factors.

BELIEFS AND PRAYER

It may be, as Whitehead suggested, that participation in religious rituals is not a measure of religiosity; rather, religion is what we do in our solitariness, when we are alone. Barron (1958) did a survey of the urban aged in which he interviewed some 1,206 older persons. He found that Bible reading played a relatively minor part in their lives. Only some 17 percent said they read the Bible either regularly or occasionally. In another study which followed this one only 20 percent of the 495 persons who had faced crisis had prayed to God for assistance, and almost no one had talked deep problems over with a minister. When Barron broke down this sample into age cohorts, he found that the cohort between thirty and thirty-five either prayed or talked with their minister as often as did the sixty- to sixty-five-year-olds. Barron got his sample from what he called thirty-five representative cities, but he does not report in his article whether he took a representative sample in these cities. The cross-sectional sample is legitimate, but we wish we knew more about whether it was also representative of the varied social classes, ethnic backgrounds, and so on.

FACING DYING AND DEATH

Our question here was whether or not religious practices or beliefs help older persons face the inevitability of aging and death. Mathieu (1970) analyzed data from a rural, northwestern state, from a middle-sized western city, and from a retirement community to find some answers to this question. About one-third of his sample said that they received help from their religious group or their beliefs. Barron asked about the degree of faith in the concept of immortality in his group. He found that such a belief remained about the same through ages thirty to fifty-five and then declined for the group from sixty to sixty-five. In an earlier study by Havighurst and Albrecht (1953) of Prairie City, some 90 percent of the respondents said they believed in an afterlife. All of this evidence suggests the influence of urbanization. At least one hypothesis is that when the secularization that goes with urbanization increases religiosity wanes and thus, in a rural city like Prairie City, faith is still triumphant. It would have been valuable if Mathieu, Barron, and Havighurst had included scales on urbanization and secularization so that hypotheses could have been tested. As it is, we do not know whether these results show biased sampling, differential definitions in questions asked, or secularization. By way of generalizing from these studies all we can say is that for some individuals from some population strata religion gives some comfort in the belief of immortality and in the practice of prayer and Bible reading.

RELIGIOSITY AND LIFE ADJUSTMENT

There have been some early attempts to relate religiosity and life satisfaction. These studies seek to know if the more committed or more religious folk evidence better adjustment in their later years than those who do not attend. Havighurst and Albrecht concluded from their contacts with their respondents that those who attend church are better adjusted and have better health. One may facetiously account for this as the result of better nutrition obtained at church dinners. More scientifically, we may turn the equation about and wonder if healthier persons are more mobile and therefore can attend more religious affairs. Or are they already better socially adjusted and, thus, attend social functions? Until we have systematic study of these questions and can put all the factors into our explanation, we can only speculate about the answers.

Barron asked an "adjustment" question, too. He wanted to know the things in life that gave older persons most satisfaction and comfort. Some 39 percent (close to Mathieu's statistic) stated that religion and their church did so. But family and friends were cited more often in this study than any other factor.

There is a more recent study by Palmore and Blazer (1976) that is more methodologically elegant because it is a longitudinal research effort. This study concluded that religious activity decreased over time, but that religious attitudes remained stable; that there is no relationship between religiosity and longevity, but that there is a positive relationship between religious participation and personal adjustment, and that "religion plays a significant and increasingly important role in the personal adjustment of many older persons."

This conclusion was tested by a study in San Francisco by Clark and Anderson (1967). They defined their interest as follows:

> [Religion is] a sphere of human activity where wisdom remains an asset for those in positions of responsibility and leadership. . . . We foresaw that older persons would express a greater need for spiritual comfort and the assurance of immortality.

They matched thirty-nine community respondents with forty hospital respondents; all were randomly selected. Their findings were that:

1. Hospital subjects cherished the functional support they received and community respondents stressed the social values of participation in the church.

2. Both groups agreed as to the existence of God.

3. Community respondents stressed the creative, benevolent nature of God, but the hospital respondents emphasized the judgmental and punitive aspects of God.

4. Healthy community respondents were less certain about immortality than the hospital group.

5. There was no evidence that religiosity increased with age.

The largest recent study of aging was a national survey by the National Council on Aging (1975), who retained Louis Harris and Associates, Inc., to conduct a wide-ranging study for them. The survey included questions regarding religious activities. One general conclusion was that attendance at church and synagogues is slightly higher among those over than among those under sixty-five. A second finding was that the importance people ascribe to religion increases with age. Seventy-one percent of the public sixty-five and over feels that religion is very important in their lives, compared with only 49 percent of those under sixty-five. However, this study recognized that two different cohorts were being compared. The Harris survey, therefore, does not suggest that religion has been or will be important to all those who in the future live beyond sixty-five; it simply states that religion is important for this particular group. These conclusions come from the data set forth in tables 7–1 and 7–2.

TABLE 7–1.   THE IMPORTANCE OF RELIGION IN YOUR LIFE

	18–64	65 +	18–24	25–39	40–54	55–64	65–69	70–79	80+
Very important	49	71	34	45	58	65	69	71	73
Somewhat important	33	21	40	35	29	25	22	21	19
Hardly important at all	17	7	25	20	12	10	8	8	6
Not sure	1	1	1	°	1	°	1	°	2

°Less than 0.5 percent.
SOURCE: Louis Harris and Associates (1975).

TABLE 7–2.   ATTENDANCE AT A CHURCH OR SYNAGOGUE IN LAST YEAR OR SO

Total Public	Percent Attended Last Year	Percent within a Week or So	A Month Ago	2–3 Months Ago	More Than 3 Months Ago	Not Sure
18–64	75	71	13	7	9	°
65+	77	79	9	5	7	°
18–24	67	60	18	8	14	°
25–39	73	72	11	7	10	°
40–54	78	70	15	8	7	—
55–64	81	79	11	4	6	—
65–69	80	79	9	5	6	1
70–79	78	79	10	4	7	°
80+	68	76	10	6	8	°

°Less than 0.5 percent.
SOURCE: Louis Harris and Associates (1975).

One of the classic studies in the field of religion is that of sociologist Gerhard Lenski (1961). Lenski used a Detroit area sample in order to determine the effect of religious commitment on the life of individuals. That sample is one of the best in terms of the comprehensive way it includes all elements of the population. Lenski's study showed the importance of the impact of religion on most persons' lives. To do this study he found it necessary to distinguish two categories of inquiry. The first had to do with the involvement of persons in a socioreligious group (or the corporate type of religious activity). The second stressed the individual actions of persons in such private and solitary religious activity as meditation, Bible reading, prayer, or "daily devotions." He measured the influence of both types of religious behavior on behavior. While he was not stressing any age group, he did discover that in the later years religious participation in organized groups declines but the influence of religious belief does not (Lenski, 1961).

Charles Y. Glock (1962) has devoted considerable time to analyzing all of the dimensions of religiosity. He feels that any analysis that does not do this may miss much of the significance of religion in the lives of persons. Thus his study endeavors to cope with the complexity of the phenomenon of human individuals in their relationship to the religious enterprise. Glock's typology is even more detailed than that of Lenski. He defines five ways in which an individual can be religious (and thus influenced in his life-style by religious activity or belief):

1. *Religious belief:* what persons believe; the doctrines, creeds, basic thoughts

2. *Religious practice:* participation in rituals such as church worship and the variations of such rituals

3. *Religious feeling:* the experiential, the assurance factor in facing life

4. *Religious knowledge:* the intellectual aspects of awareness of the history and beliefs of a particular religious tradition

5. *Religious effects:* the rewards and responsibilities that are attendant on religious commitment.

Payne-Pittard (1966) had the advantage of both the Gerhard and Glock studies as she began her effort to measure the impact of religiosity on life patterns and satisfaction. She also had the advantage of a thorough orientation to sociological theory. We shall, therefore, describe in some detail her study of religious commitment because it represents, to date, the most thorough effort to relate religiosity and life satisfaction. It might serve, therefore, as a methodological model for further study of this important area.

Payne-Pittard stressed the importance of socialization of a new member of a social system learning skills and role orientations "appropriate for participants in an organization" (Havighurst & Albrecht, 1953). Adequate socialization provides the motivation for such role performances as will make the system function. Merton's typology of the adaptation of any person or group to culture goals shows what variation there is in achieving those goals (Clark & Anderson, 1967). Every system, be it religious or secular, is concerned with such appropriate socialization that participants will have a high degree of commitment to the "tasks, goals, values and beliefs of the system" (Lenski, 1961). But commitment is composed of a "cluster of categories—cognitive, moral, motivational, actional, cultural" (Lenski, 1961). Payne-Pittard's study focuses on measuring "the effect of the socialization process as it is evident in the degree of commitment" (see Table 7–3).

Payne-Pittard next constructed a "Commitment Scale" to measure the individual, collective, and actional aspects involved in a religious institution. Eight categories of commitment measure these three aspects. They are:

1. *The cognitive category:* the way an individual responds to the beliefs expressed in creeds and doctrines

2. *The emotional category:* the way the participant expresses his feelings of love and loyalty for the church

3. *The moral category:* the way in which a participant's choices are affected by the "official morality" of his church

4. *The motivational category:* the degree to which the participant's responses indicate responsibility for the work and achievement of the goals of his organization

5. *The actional category:* the way in which the participant is involved in the activities of his organization (church)

6. *The group identification category:* the way the participant views his relationship to members and groups in his church

7. *The hierarchical category:* the way the participant views and participates in the decision-making processes of the church

8. *The reference group category:* how a participant's commitment to the church influences his interactions with other special groups.

When Payne-Pittard had developed a comprehensive conceptualization of the various components of the relationship of a person to the religious institution, she developed items to which participants could respond in order to measure those categories. One scale used was Dwight Dean's "Alienation Scale" and another was Russel Dynes "Church-Sect" scale. Seven of Dean's items were adapted for her study. Other items were adapted or constructed from her theoretical material. Then a panel of ten judges was selected to judge whether these items could, in fact, discriminate between high and low commitment. The choice of an item was determined by three criteria: the percentage of agreement (by the judges); the frequency distribution of disagreement; and the distribution of the items among the categories. Three tests composed the pretest instrument: the commitment test, a religious knowledge test, and the social characteristics of the respondents.

A pretest of some fifty respondents resulted in choosing forty items for the scale to be used in the study.

The final test was administered to a sample of attenders above age fifteen in church schools in four rural churches and one large urban church. The rural sample produced 123 complete (usable) forms, which was 93 percent of the church-school attenders on a "specified Sunday," and 282—79 percent—from urban church-school attenders. The results are shown in Table 7–3.

TABLE 7–3. COMPARISON OF SCORES ON THE COMMITMENT TEST AND THE AGE OF RESPONDENTS

Commitment Score		Total	AGE OF RESPONDENTS				
			15–19	20–24	25–44	45–64	65 and over
Low	N	107	33	10	29	21	14
	%		(24.9)	(9.0)	(29.6)	(34.1)	(9.2)
Middle	N	180	46	14	45	61	14
	%		(41.8)	(15.1)	(49.9)	(57.5)	(15.6)
High	N	117	15	10	38	47	7
	%		(27.2)	(9.8)	(32.4)	(37.3)	(10.1)
Total	N	404	94	34	112	129	35

Chi square is 212.8547 d.f. 8, P less than .01, V is .43.
SOURCE: Payne-Pittard (1966).

This summary shows a positive association for youth, a negative one for young adults, a positive one in middle age, and a negative association in the older adult group. The scale has again been revised, the categories clarified, and the instrument is now being used in national studies. Research is a slow, difficult process. The refinement of instruments is only one major task. Since this 1966 study, Payne-Pittard has used the revised scale with a national sample of 1,000 persons in 1968. The results paralleled the findings reported in Table 7–3 for her earlier samples.

THE RESPONSE FROM THE INSTITUTION OF THE CHURCH

The material presented in this chapter so far has detailed an analysis of what individuals have received from the institutions of religion. Let us now reverse our perspective and ask how institutional religion has responded to the needs of older persons, how alert it has been to demographic changes in which older persons have become a major part of the population, and to a society that has relegated older persons to a depressingly low status. As demographic analysis indicates, we are a graying population. It is obvious that any institution that hopes to serve the population will have to pay attention to older persons. This is as true of the church as it is of our educational institutions. How has the church been meeting the challenge of this population?

We shall use as our basic information a study done by the National Interfaith Coalition on Aging on seminary training of clergymen. The Interfaith Coalition on Aging was a direct by-product of the 1971 White House Conference on Aging. That conference stressed the need for all religious groups in this country to study and implement ways those institutions could serve the aged. The Coalition is a nonprofit corporation formed in 1972 by Roman Catholic, Protestant, Jewish,

Clergy are a good source of individual and family counseling of elderly persons.

and other faiths. From 1973 to 1978 the Interfaith Coalition was involved in a research and demonstration project called a Survey of Programs for Aging under Religious Auspices, funded in part by HEW. Part of its mission has been to study education for aging in the seminaries.

The seminary represents the only major socializing and educational effort on the part of the churches or synagogues to prepare its young leadership for professional service. It is obvious, then, that the curricula of seminaries may be examined to discover those areas of life that are regarded as critical by the church. In making its survey, the Interfaith Coalition intended to have some impact on the way the church perceived its responsibility to older persons. It was also trying to measure the degree of commitment churches had to their older members.

The sample of seminaries consisted of 135 schools (National Interfaith Coalition on Aging, 1976). A total of 37 seminaries of the 135 said they had at least one course in aging and nine had two or more courses. Some 285 courses were mentioned, but in most of them aging was only a part of a larger emphasis where gerontology was not the main focus. Seventy-five institutions said that at least one course in gerontology was available at another institution and fifty-four indicated that over half of their students enroll in at least one course having some substantive content related to aging. But, again, how much focus there is on gerontology was not ascertained. Not a single seminary student was competing an internship in a placement setting related to aging. The summary of the study is worth noting:

> In view of the fact that the respondent schools collectively place about 10,000 graduates every year in positions of influence and responsibility among more than 100,000,000 people, it is important that every effort be made to infuse the learning experience of future clergy with the realistic needs and characteristics of older persons in their constituency.

The church is obviously suffering from cultural lag. This term is used by sociologists to account for institutions that base their response to society on past needs. The church has great programs for children and youth but it has neglected older persons. Yet the evidence is that older persons continue to turn to the church for social and spiritual support.

If churches in general have not trained their leaders nationally to meet the needs of older persons, some individual churches and groups have pioneered in doing so. One of the most obvious ways in which the churches have tried to be helpful is to provide special housing for the elderly. A great many of 1,200 retirement communities and high rises have been sponsored by churches—Methodist, Presbyterian, Jewish, Congregational, Lutheran, Baptist, and Episcopal religious groups have been engaged for decades in underwriting pleasant retirement housing for the older person. The church has endeavored to find leadership for these institutions that would be responsive to the needs of older persons. Some of the housing is focused on lower-class persons but the majority seek to serve the middle class or the class from which their members come.

A few churches have been engaged in supplying services that permit older persons to remain in their communities and to avoid inappropriate institutionalization. One example is the Shepherd's Center in Kansas City, Missouri.* The Center is the product of the charismatic leadership of Dr. Elbert Cole, a Methodist minister, who rallied the cooperation of some twenty-four churches and synagogues in a geographically limited area of Kansas City to develop a center. From the beginning, the Shepherd's Center was dependent on the leadership and participation of older persons themselves. The number of services and their administration are designed by a board of older persons who themselves operate the Center.

The services of the Center are designed to keep older persons in their homes or apartments as long as they wish to stay there. Some of the services are:

1. *Meals on Wheels:* If an older person is ill and cannot get to the store or prepare meals, a group of forty men are on call to deliver one hot meal a day. Men were selected for delivery service partly because almost all of the recipients are women and these deliveries by men offer at least some heterosexual contact.

2. *Education:* Dozens of classes are offered at the Center. Individuals can learn to play bridge, study French or the Bible, participate in group therapy, or enjoy a travelogue. On Fridays some specialist in aging or government speaks to from five hundred to a thousand of those gathered to take these classes.

3. *Preretirement education:* Once a year the Center puts on a program designed to help those ending their work careers to understand the new roles essential for adjustment during retirement.

4. *Transportation:* A group of volunteers are steadily available to help older persons get to their doctors, banks, or churches.

5. *Handyman service:* A large group of retired painters, carpenters, plumbers, handymen are available at a very low cost to do minor repairs for older persons in the community.

*Material for this section comes from one of the authors, who participated in a study analyzing older volunteers and who conducted interviews at the Shepherd's Center with both leaders and volunteers.

6. *Telephone service:* One of the clergymen in the community is always by his phone to answer any calls at any time of night. Thus, an older person does not need to fear isolation in case of a heart attack or severe pain.

7. *Friendly visitors:* The Center is aware of shut-ins and tries to maintain contact by having persons regularly visit those who otherwise would be lonely.

8. *Protective service:* The Center holds seminars on special problems of older persons. The one on protective services helps older persons become aware of how they can protect themselves from burglaries, attacks, and fraud.

9. *Health fare:* At least once a year the Center rallies about health services, doctors, and nurses to help its community focus on health maintenance.

There are other services but these give some indication of how the older persons have themselves focused on the problems of aging and what programs they have initiated to help themselves and their friends and neighbors find a fulfilled life and remain in the community. Since the original Shepherd's Center in Kansas City, two others, modeled after this program, have sprung up in Atlanta and New York. The Catholic program for aging, HEAD, is in many ways a replication of these kinds of services. Many Catholic and Protestant groups in the East have been stimulated by HEAD to much more comprehensive programs for older persons.

Most religious groups are now beginning to pay particular attention to the needs of the elderly in their neighborhoods and in their temples and congregations. Special note, for example, should be taken of the Councils on Aging of the Jewish Federations in Los Angeles, Baltimore, New York, Chicago, and other places.

The Point Loma Presbyterian Church in San Diego has a comprehensive program for the elderly in its parish. Out of that program has come a most intelligent and effective mouse, Samantha (a puppet), which is doing much nationally to educate churches in their responsibility for older persons.

Another source of help and inspiration is the gerontology centers located in different parts of the country. They are mounting continuing education courses and institutes for the clergy and others in such courses as death and dying, thus giving effective training to some clergy in an important aspect of their relationship with older persons. Some have held general institutes on gerontology nationwide. As the result of the Interfaith Coalition, many churches are organized in major metropolitan communities in interfaith committees to alert the churches to the opportunities they offer.

Most of the programs we have discussed have a sense of advocacy regarding the economic, social, and health plight of many older persons. They are mobilizing the older persons to become active in both community and national political action. Maggie Kuhn's Gray Panthers is a group of militant individuals who have responded to her demands that older persons organize to help themselves.

THE NEW RELIGIONS

One of the novel aspects of religion in our time is the rise of nonassociational forms of religious participation. These new forms have emerged with some power in the last twenty years. They are cultlike and "ecstatic-experience" based. Three groups can be identified: Christian-related groups, mysticism, and the occult. Some of these groups are "The Jesus Movement" (six hundred establishments with thirty thousand members); Protestant and Catholic Charismatic (neo-Pentecostal) groups; some one thousand groups reported by the Notre Dame Charismatic Communication Center. The second group turns to mysticism, groups led by Hindu gurus, swamis, and Buddhists. Best known are the Krishna Consciousness Society, Mehr Ba Ba, and Nichiren Sosho. No membership figures are available for any of these. The occult may be represented here by astrology and witchcraft-satanism. It is thought that some ten thousand astrologers serve 40 million persons. There are probably fewer than three thousand witchcraft-satanism members in the United States.

All of these movements indicate a powerful religious movement outside the traditional modes of established churches. With a few exceptions, the aged are not part of the new religions. This is important because these radical departures from traditional religion might be viewed as giving impetus to some degree of intergenerational rifts and tensions, new misunderstandings.

SUMMARY

Religious beliefs and practices are an important part of the life of older persons. In a housing study, Hamovitch, Peterson, and Larson (1975) asked how important it was to elderly persons that their housing be located close to services and facilities. Choices varied: some chose first to be close to shopping areas, others to transportation. For life-time-care facilities, it was proximity to churches. Respondents were also asked what types of professional services they wished to be close to. For the entire sample, medical facilities were first in importance and religious facilities second. Thus judgment by almost two thousand interviewees indicates what importance they put on religion.

Except for a few studies, most of the research about religion and aging has been so oversimplified as to lose significance. Some new studies are more elegant in terms of theoretical sampling and analytical methodology. But given the importance of religion to many older persons, this is clearly an area of critical importance. The church has been tardy in responding to the problem, but new thrusts are coming from the Interfaith Coalition, from such novel alternatives to institutionalization as Shepherd's Center and HEAD, and from individuals such as Maggie Kuhn. The seminaries have lagged in providing either a theological background or practical programs and internships in aging, but the work of the Interfaith Coalition and new demoninational programs may rectify this.

REFERENCES

Bahr, M. H. "Aging and Religious Disaffiliation." *Social Forces*, 1970, vol. 49, no. 1.

Barron, M. L. "The Role of Religion and Religious Beliefs in Creating the Milieu of Older Persons." In D. Scudder (ed.), *Organized Religion and the Older Person*. Gainsville: University of Florida Press, 1958.

Clark, M., and B. G. Anderson. *Culture in Aging: An Anthropology of Older Americans*. Springfield, Ill.: Charles C Thomas, 1967.

Fichter, J. *Social Religion in the Urban Parish*. Chicago: The University of Chicago Press, 1954.

Glock, C. Y. "On the Study of Religious Commitment." *Religious Education, Research Supplement*, 1962, LVII.

Hamovitch, M. B., J. A. Peterson, and A. E. Larson. *Housing Needs and Satisfactions of the Elderly*. Los Angeles: Andrus Gerontology Center, University of Southern California, 1975.

Louis Harris Associates. *Myths and Realities of Aging in America*. New York: National Council on Aging, 1975.

Havighurst, R., and R. Albrecht. *Older People*. New York: Longmans and Green, 1953.

Hendricks, J., and C. D. Hendricks. *Aging in Mass Society*. Cambridge, Mass.: Winthrop, 1977.

Lenski, G. *The Religious Factor*. New York: Doubleday, 1961

Mathieu, J. "Religious Aspects of Death and Dying" (doctoral dissertation, University of Southern California Libraries, Los Angeles, 1970.

National Interfaith Coalition on Aging. "The Religious Sector Explores Its Mission in Aging." Athens, Georgia, 1976.

Orback, H. "Aging and Religion." *Geriatrics,* October, 1961.

Palmore, E., and D. B. Blazer. "Religion in a Longitudinal Panel." *The Gerontologist,* 1976, vol. XVI, pt. 1.

Payne-Pittard, B. "The Meaning and Measurement of Commitment to the Church." Research paper No. 13, Georgia State College, Atlanta, 1966.

Whitehead, A. N. *Science and the Modern World.* New York: Macmillan (Mentor Books), 1942.

Woodruff, D., and J. Birren (eds.). *Aging: Scientific Perspectives and Social Issues.* New York: D. Van Nostrand, 1975.

FOR FURTHER READING

Brewer, E. D. C. "Church and Sect in Methodism." *Social Forces,* 1952, 30.

Cox, H. *The Secular City.* New York: Macmillan, 1965.

Fichter, J. H. *The Catholic Cult of the Paraclete.* New York: Sheed and Ward, 1975.

Glock, C. Y. "The Role of Deprivation in the Origin and Evolution of Religious Groups." In R. Lee and M. E. Marty (eds.), *Religion and Social Conflict.* New York: Oxford University Press, 1964.

Mindel, C. H., and C. E. Vaughan. "A Multidimensional Approach to Religiosity and Disengagement." *Journal of Gerontology,* 1978, 33:1.

Payne, B. P. "Voluntary Associations of the Elderly" (paper presented to the Society for Scientific Study of Religion, New York, 1973).

Stark, R., and C. Y. Glock. *Religious Commitment.* Berkeley: University of California Press, 1968.

Yinger, J. M. *The Scientific Study of Religion.* London: Macmillan, 1970.

III | Physiology and Psychology

CHAPTER 8

Physical and Health Factors in Aging

When I was forty, my doctor advised me that a man in his
forties shouldn't play tennis. I heeded this advice carefully
and could hardly wait until I reached fifty to start again.

JUSTICE HUGO BLACK

*This chapter is intended to review the major changes in physical and
health factors relevant to the process of aging.*

*While many of these changes are reflected in terms of group-derived
statistics, individual variations must be kept in mind. A casual reading
may give the erroneous impression of inevitable and regular decline in
all aspects of physical functioning. But the student should recognize
the fact that great variability is observed within individuals and from
one older individual to another.*

*Changes and losses do occur, but ordinarily these changes are very
gradual, sometimes imperceptible. Yet their effects tend to be
cumulative because they are interacting.*

*Given these cautions, the student can examine changes observed in
the various sense modalities as well as the general process of physical
adaptation in later maturity. The student must also consider some
basic prevention strategies so that the theme of physical "loss" is not
presumed to be necessarily a prelude to irrevocable and irreversible
loss of functional capability.*

177

The following description has been taken from a detailed case study done by a senior counselor in gerontology. Names, dates, and places have been changed, but the essential facts and circumstances are true.

Mr. M.L.Z. is an eighty-nine-year-old white male of eastern European origin. He lives in a mid-sized nursing home in the Middle West. Much of his daily activities revolve around his circulating among the facility's residents, chatting, playing cards, reading to them, and "fetching things." Most important of all, Mr. Z. carries his old battered violin about with him and at the drop of a hat will play a tune or break into song in a surprisingly strong, clear, melodic tone. He claims to be able to sing songs in any one of seven languages and with the least encouragement will try out several for anyone who will listen.

Although Mr. Z. is a small (5'3"), frail-looking, completely bald gentleman with facial scars and wearing extremely thick-lensed glasses, he seems to be known and well-liked by practically all residents and staff of the facility where he resides, and by many visitors as well.

He recalls a colorful history. Born in eastern Europe, he "escaped" at the tender age of fifteen and a half to avoid compulsory military service, fled to Russia where he was inducted into the army and sent to duty in Siberia, where he lived for about six years. After subsequent duty in a border patrol, he deserted, made his way across Europe, and eventually to the United States. Here he took odd jobs, educated himself, and in time "got into show business": he became a vaudeville prompter. His contacts in entertainment took him in due course of time around the world. Yet time took its toll.

He tells of marrying a woman with whom he lived for "almost forty years." They had no children and she died some fifteen years ago. Following her death, he began to experience a series of physical difficulties. An operation for cataracts left him with the need to wear very thick glasses. At one time he had a toupee made, which he has not worn for some time. One leg was amputated because of a diabetic condition and he now wears a prosthetic leg. In addition, he wears a hearing aid, false teeth, and, for the past year, a heart pacer. Several years ago he experienced what he calls a "small stroke," which left him "mixed up" for a few days. But he "worked this out," he reports, by "walking a lot," of which he does much.

Yet for all of this, Mr. Z. maintains what is apparently a cheerful, optimistic view of life and circumstances, while he pursues his "hobby" of energetically helping his fellow residents keep their spirits up and their interests high.

Mr. Z. says he has never smoked and drinks only on "occasions" or holidays, and then only in limited fashion. He scorns food fads, eats "mostly" fresh fruits and "lots of vegetables"; he loves fish and drinks a lot of tea. Through it all, Mr. Z. clearly is very highly regarded and seen as filling a very important role in that facility as a storyteller and entertainer.

What is it that gerontologists would say about Mr. Z., or what do they ask about older persons like him?

1. Are such aged to be characterized as chronically ill, or are they persons with disabilities (chronic ailments)?

2. What do physical changes mean to the older person?

3. How do physiological changes affect behavior?

4. From a physical point of view, is Mr. Z. typical of the old in our society?

5. What are the physical changes experienced typically by the aged?

6. Is decline in physical health an inevitable accompaniment of old age?

CHANGE AND LOSS

The most obvious fact about aging with which all gerontologists can agree is the element of change. Many, if not most, changes associated with aging may be placed in the matrix of loss. Indeed, the characteristic most commonly used to describe aging is multiple loss. At the same time, gerontologists emphasize that loss itself is neither a function of nor intrinsic to the aging process but rather is *associated with* the aging process.

Physical and health factors represent a major category of change and loss variables. These factors influence the course of aging itself in individual cases and also exert substantial impact upon how senescence is personally experienced. There is good reason, then, why health factors have captured much of the attention of gerontological researchers. Outcomes from such research provide much raw material for those who develop public policy and those who initiate programmatic planning and provide direct services to the elderly.

AGE-ASSOCIATED ACUTE AND CHRONIC DISEASE

Surveys repeatedly show a higher incidence of disease and disease-related incapacities associated with advanced age. Much of this is accounted for by chronic conditions, in contrast to acute episodes: collagen (connective) tissue changes, diminution of cardiovascular and pulmonary competence, decline in the acuity of the various senses, chronic arthritis, loss of teeth, and the like.

TABLE 8–1. NUMBER OF ACUTE CONDITIONS* PER 100 PERSONS
PER YEAR, BY AGE, SEX, AND CONDITION: JULY 1969–JUNE 1970

Sex and Condition Group	All Ages	Under 6 Years	6–16 Years	17–44 Years	45 Years & Over
MALE					
All acute conditions	196.9	352.1	261.6	176.0	106.4
Infective and parasitic diseases	24.6	53.5	40.3	17.0	9.1
Respiratory conditions	107.1	205.7	134.6	97.3	56.7
Upper respiratory conditions	61.4	140.7	79.5	48.5	30.2
Influenza	39.1	44.3	48.0	44.4	23.2
Other respiratory conditions	6.7	20.7	7.2	4.4	3.3
Digestive system conditions	10.2	10.9	15.2	9.9	6.3
Injuries	33.5	35.7	45.7	35.0	20.7
All other acute conditions	21.5	46.3	25.8	16.9	13.6
FEMALE					
All acute conditions	212.2	340.8	264.5	208.6	138.0
Infective and parasitic diseases	24.3	57.5	34.8	22.0	9.0
Respiratory conditions	118.5	193.3	155.2	111.9	76.3
Upper respiratory conditions	69.9	135.5	105.2	57.6	38.5
Influenza	43.0	43.3	45.1	49.5	33.8
Other respiratory conditions	5.5	14.5	4.9	4.8	3.9
Digestive system conditions	11.8	14.9	16.0	11.9	7.7
Injuries	22.3	21.4	25.6	22.5	20.0
All other acute conditions	35.3	53.8	32.8	40.4	25.0

*Excluded from these statistics are those conditions that do not involve restricted activity or medical attention.
SOURCE: National Center for Health Statistics (1972).

Table 8.1 shows the incidence of acute diseases from childhood for males and females. These data show that acute episodes of illness are more likely to occur in younger rather than in older populations. The corollary to this is that certain chronic conditions are more frequently associated with late life, as shown in the table. Clearly from this we see that acute episodes tend to diminish and chronic conditions increase along the time dimension.

High blood pressure, heart ailments, rheumatism, and arthritis show up as the most prevalent chronic disabilities affecting individuals from mid-life and beyond. Although they can also contribute to some limitation on activities, such disabilities as asthma, hayfever, and diabetes are less prevalent chronic conditions in later life.

Figure 8-1.   PERCENTAGE OF ADULTS WITH VARIOUS DEGREES OF LIMITED ACTIVITY, 1970

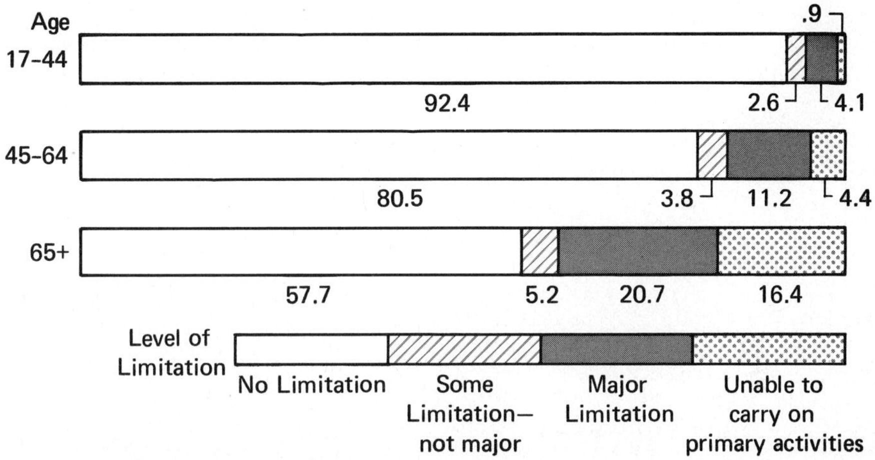

Age

.9 ⌐

17-44

92.4   2.6 ⌐ └ 4.1

45-64

80.5   3.8 ⌐   11.2   └ 4.4

65+

57.7   5.2   20.7   16.4

Level of
Limitation

No Limitation   Some   Major   Unable to
                     Limitation—   Limitation   carry on
                     not major   primary activities

SOURCE: *Limitation of Activity Due to Chronic Conditions, United States, 1970,* Vital and Health, Statistics, series 10, No. 80 (Washington, D.C.: Government Printing Office, April 1973), Table p. 5.

ILLNESS AND FUNCTIONAL CAPABILITY

A general perspective on such findings supports the view that older persons are more likely to exhibit chronic ailments and thus show a higher incidence of various kinds of "permanent" disabilities. Nevertheless, in spite of pervasive attitudes that still equate old age with sickness/incapacity, gerontologists recognize that by far the largest proportion of the elderly retain at least adequate levels of health and, from a physical point of view, remain remarkably functional. According to a US Vital and Health Statistics Survey (Figure 8–1), although some 37 percent of persons sixty-five and older experience some kind of limiting chronic disability, more than 62 percent of all older people are able to carry on most kinds of activities of daily living. Only 16.4 percent, according to the same survey, are judged unable to carry on primary activities of daily living. Obviously this is in sharp contrast to the popular view of old people as generally "sick and disabled."

Differentiating the fine line between being a person with a disability and being a disabled person becomes particularly important for planners and rehabilitation specialists. It will also make a great difference in general expectations of later life and perceptions of the capabilities and potentials of the aged. The fundamental issue has to do with how we choose to define "sickness," "ill health," and being "chronically ill."

The World Health Organization (WHO) and other organizations like the American Medical Association (AMA) correctly insist that health is more than simply the absence of disease. Yet most definitions of health, including those of WHO and the AMA, are deficient on at least two counts (Carlson, 1975). First, health is too often measured against some objective and extrinsic standard (e.g., "absence" of pathology, freedom from overt disability). Second, health is erroneously conceived of as a static state of an organism, rather than as a dynamic conflux of conditions.

Health is *not* merely the absence of disease; in fact, it often cohabits with disease (Carlson, 1975). A person with chronic diabetes or arthritis or a heart murmur or defective vision may be said to be, therefore, not sick, but merely a different person, that is, a person with certain constraints on activities. Within those limitations such a person can be as healthy as anyone else. This is precisely the point made by Beatrice Wright (1958) two decades ago: Being a person with a disability is not the same as being disabled. Ray Charles, the blind musician, is a person with a disability. He is hardly a disabled person. Apropos of this, studies indicate (Maddox, 1964) that older persons tend to assess their personal state of health more on subjective, functional grounds (e.g., ability to "get around") than on the basis of more objective criteria (e.g., physician's diagnostic evaluation).

Following Carlson's formulations, then, any redefinition of health must include at least four major elements. The first is an environment which is supportive and harmonious. The rationale for this has been detailed elsewhere (Schwartz, 1974). The second element is readily obtained resources to assist the individual in becoming or staying healthy. This simply recognizes the fact that some contingencies lie beyond the individual's immediate control. The third element is self-esteem, which includes the need of someone to care. The fourth element is the individual's own participation in and responsibility for health. That is, health is likely to elude those who maintain a strictly passive, uninterested role with respect to health.

It is precisely these issues and these values that have raised serious questions about care taking of institutionalized elderly and the criteria established to monitor and evaluate nursing homes. At issue is the appropriateness of care-taking patterns and enormous sums of money being spent inappropriately in Medicare and Medicaid programs (Tiberi et al., 1977).

Although the vast majority of institutionalized aged are usually labeled "chronically ill," repeated surveys indicate that most conditions identified are chronic conditions of one kind or another. Few of these

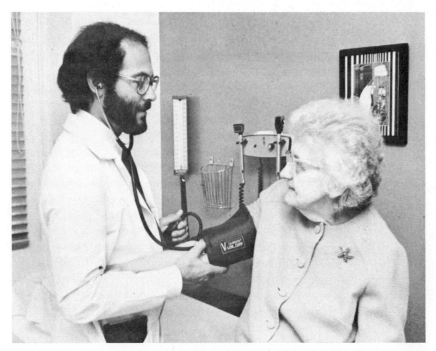

Health is a major concern but not necessarily the highest priority of elderly people. Unfortunately, traditional medical training is not calculated to make many physicians comfortable in dealing with the old. This Los Angeles geriatrician is an exception to the rule.

conditions (such as chronic diabetes, chronic arthritis, poor vision, poor hearing, and the like) can be treated and cured by medicine. These chronic conditions are limiting factors. What is called for are interventions and compensations that will enable the institutionalized aged to function reasonably well and with satisfaction within those constraints. In other words, the great need of such aged is for the psychosocial components that make living worthwhile, not merely possible (Cosin, 1975; Schwartz, 1977).

Public funding for the most part pays for *physical* treatment and care, and administrators of skilled nursing facilities do for the most part what they are reimbursed for (namely, providing physical care). Since state licensing and inspections of skilled nursing facilities have become a nationwide feature (within the past decade), the criteria for monitoring and inspecting long-term care of the aged has developed along the lines of the acute hospital or medical model. Increasingly this is seen to be inconsistent with and even antithetical to the primary needs of institutionalized aged.

It is worthwhile for students of gerontology to examine and appraise physical and health factors in aging within this context. This will provide a useful perspective on the nature of the impact of physical and health factors upon the aging individual.

OBSERVABLE INDICATIONS OF AGE

Usually the most obvious indicators of aging are changes in physical appearance. Hair tends to thin out and to gray or whiten. The skin begins to wrinkle. With age the ears become longer, the earlobes thicken, and the nose becomes somewhat broader. Skin discolorations (liver spots) appear, most frequently on the back of the hands. Imbalance in the hormone chain tends to produce a "neutering" effect; that is, a slight increase in body and facial hair growth in women, with a concomitant slight decrease of the same in men. Pitch and tone of voice are usually less stable. There is a tendency toward loss in muscle size and tone; thus the muscles begin their characteristic sag. The skull also appears slightly larger in size.

These are unmistakable, observable signs that such individuals have left their youth well behind them. Unfortunately, in our society, these very signs generate negative attitudes and produce some less than desirable effects. In nonindustrial societies, most people are not sure exactly how old they are. When the span of human lives is divided into long periods of stable responsibilities and clearly marked social and vocational roles, the exact number of years one has lived seems to be a rather trivial matter. In more highly industrialized, complex technological societies, where, by contrast, roles are less stable and less clearly marked and fixed, people seem haunted by the numbers game of chronological age. When keeping the scorecard of birthdays, for most purposes anything above a low total is considered bad news. Youth becomes the metaphor for vitality, vigorousness, productivity, assertiveness. Old age becomes the metaphor for depletion, illness, incompetence, and passivity (Sontag, 1972). And now especially when more people are living longer, what amounts to the latter half (or more) of everyone's life is shadowed by the poignant apprehension of irretrievable loss, decay, and devaluation as a worthwhile human being.

This can most easily be seen in much of the humor about the elderly. Examine a sample of birthday cards addressed to middle-aged celebrants and you discover the snide, pejorative references to aging. Many of the roles assigned to TV actors portraying the old depict them in unreal ways: either as benignly witless or as doddering, mean, forgetful incompetents. Cases in point are the cruel caricatures that have been presented with some frequency on the Johnny Carson and Carol Burnett shows, both of which have been severely criticized by aging advocates for this very reason.

The prestige of youthfulness afflicts almost everyone in our society. Men are just as prone as women to periodic bouts of the "blues" about growing old. Susan Sontag has made an insightful case for what she calls "the double standard of aging" (1972). Her thesis is based upon these observable "cosmetic" signs of age. Society is much more permissive about aging in men, she argues. That is, men are "allowed" to age without penalty in several ways women are not.

> This society offers even fewer rewards for aging to women than it does to men. Being physically attractive counts much more in a woman's life than in a man's, but beauty, identified as it is for women with youthfulness, does not stand up well to age.

Perhaps this accounts for a society that "combats" age and its appearance with creams, dyes, lotions, face lifts, and the denial of age through euphemisms of language and pejorative humor about aging.

HEIGHT AND WEIGHT CHANGES

Human anatomical changes with age have produced considerable data which must be accepted only with considerable reservation because of the preponderance of cross-sectional analyses. The comparative aspects of decreased height over time among different groups show rather small increases from age twenty to forty but a decline in stature generally about the fortieth year which tends to be progressive in succeeding decades. Lifetime loss in height will be approximately 4.9 cm in females, 2.9 cm in males (Rossman, 1977).

Studies of weight related to age in industrialized societies also support the well-known notion of increase of weight in the middle years with a decrease in old age. The incidence of obesity is more prevalent in higher- than lower-income groups.

In the 1965 US Health Examination Survey (cited by Rossman, 1977), males achieved maximum average weight between thirty-four and fifty-four years, with subsequent decline in average weight through seventy-nine years of age. Weight changes for women were different. For women, weight levels continued to climb for two decades longer than in men and the decline into old age was proportionately less.

SENSORY MODE CHANGES

The Visual Sense

Gerontological researchers in this area refer to two dimensions of vision: visual perception and visual communication. Visual perception refers to those processes within the individual that are necessary to sense, interpret, and respond to visual information. Visual communication refers to those physical and psychosocial processes involved in transferring visual information between individuals, and within groups (Fozard et al., 1977).

As age increases, the likelihood of visual impairment increases. The visual capability of three out of five persons over seventy-five is likely to be affected to some degree, and more often in females than in males. The National Center of Health Statistics reports that by age sixty-five about half the population have 20/70 visual acuity or less. This is about five times the number of those with 20/70 vision at age forty-five.

A study by the National Society for the Prevention of Blindness (1966) revealed that the incidence of legal blindness (defined as an acuity of 20/200 or worse) increases from about 250 to 500 to 1,450 per 100,000 persons respectively in age groups forty to sixty-four, sixty-five to sixty-nine, and sixty-nine years and over.

Such surveys highlight the visual problems of aging but do not tell much about the causes or the practical significance of such problems. They also demonstrate that losses of visual acuity and blindness are by no means universal phenomena of aging. The same holds for other sense modality changes in aging.

Many of the practical problems of vision encountered by the elderly are related to glare and poor visibility. Such circumstances can only exaggerate any visual losses that come from structural changes in the seeing apparatus.

The lens increases to the point that by age eighty the lens is 50 percent larger than it was at age twenty. At the same time the size of the pupil decreases, therefore reducing the amount of light reaching the retina. This, along with the diminished ability of the eye to adjust to changing amounts of light, can seriously interfere with visual perception. Cataracts (clouding of the lens) and glaucoma (excessively high intraocular pressure), too, can increase the hazards to vision in older persons (Fozard et al., 1977).

Another observable effect associated with aging is the restriction in the use of one's eyes—for example, restriction on the range of upward gaze in older individuals (Snyder et al., 1976). There are no limitations in the lower range of gaze but studies do show a rising incidence in

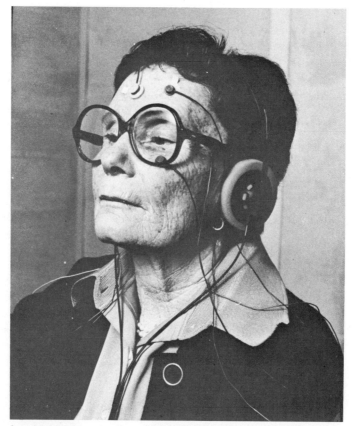

Psychophysiological testing has enabled researchers to uncover many important clues as to the nature of physical and health factors in later life.

constriction in upward gaze for monocular vision in ages five to ninety-four years. The practical significance of this for an older individual's perception of signs, landmarks, storage space, safety hazards, and the like, which are placed high in the angle of vision, is quite obvious.

The Auditory Sense

Hearing loss can usually begin in the early twenties and increases, especially in the upper tonal registers, as age increases. As is the case with vision, hearing deficits are not a universal age-related phenomenon (Corso, 1977). Yet unilateral and bilateral hearing impairments and deafness do occur with some frequency. Approximately 13 percent of those sixty-five and older show advanced signs of presbycousis, and approximately 30 percent of the older population show some signs of hearing loss.

The auditory system consists of the ear and its associated neural pathways which are organized into subsystems running parallel to each other. With advanced age, deterioration may occur in the neural structures at any level as well as in the peripheral components directly involved in sound transmission. Presbycousis represents neural loss, whereas otosclerosis adds a component of conductive hearing loss. Surgery for the latter condition may be quite beneficial but will not completely restore hearing in most cases.

Because hearing plays a major role in communicating and interpersonal relations, any impairment frequently produces negative consequences for both the psychological and social adjustment of elderly persons (Corso, 1977). Commonly the number and intensity of social contacts become the earliest casualties. Unlike the commonly recognized visible "signals" of blindness (dark glasses, white canes, seeing-eye dogs), a mild to moderate hearing impairment is not readily apparent to others. No response at all or an inappropriate response because of missing a few words here and there in a conversation can easily be misconstrued by others as "confusion," "senility," or even as antisocial behavior, rather than simply as a hearing deficit. The self-consciousness and embarrassment of those experiencing such impairment often induces them to avoid social situations and contacts, which in turn leads to greater social isolation.

Not least among the difficulties and obstacles that hard-of-hearing or deaf elderly face are household and safety hazards. Appliances that utilize auditory signals (bell timers, buzzers, telephones) obviously are inappropriate and usually useless. For the hearing person, water basins, toilets, garbage disposals, motorized heating units, and the like are ordinarily judged to be functioning adequately from the *sound* of their operation. These common auditory cues are missed by those with severe hearing loss. A warning of threats to safety which is inherent in traffic sounds, auto horns, and smoke-sensor units is missed and thereby creates special penalties and hazards for the hard-of-hearing elderly. Obviously, these are important factors that service providers must sensitively attend to and take into account.

A related form of such loss is aphasia. When external auditory signals fail to reach the brain centers because of neural or conductance loss, the resulting state is called a "receptive" aphasia. Auditory stimuli that are processed properly but that are not effectively translated by the individual into appropriate responses are referred to as an "expressive" aphasia.

Although this kind of event is associated with brain damage, experience has shown that a knowledgeable therapist/helper can successfully, with persistence and skill, retrain the sufferer of such damage in such a way as to regain much, and in many instances all, of his previous ability to perform.

The Olfactory and Gustatory Senses

The modalities of taste and smell are closely linked in their dependence upon each other and will therefore be treated together in the following discussion.

It has been conventional to measure these sense modalities in much the same manner vision and hearing are measured: namely, via psychophysical increased (or decreased) units of differences in acuity. The appropriateness of such methodology has been questioned. Taste and smell appear to be poorest in discriminating differences of concentrations of a single substance and best in discriminating distinctions between qualitatively different substances (Engen, 1977).

When an aged resident in a nursing home complains that the food doesn't taste good, or when an elderly mother is very reluctant to bake her "famous" cookies because she says "they don't taste good anymore," these persons may be speaking the literal truth of the matter. The number of taste buds may decrease as much as 75 to 80 percent by the time we reach eighty-five, but data on this is inconclusive. Consistent evidence also indicates a diminishing ability with advanced age to discriminate sweet, bitter, sour, and salty tastes, although there is less reduction in sensitivity to sour. The sex of the individual and state of health appear to be important factors in determining differential taste sensitivity in the later years. When taste preference is measured (sweet seems almost universally liked and bitter disliked, for example), individual differences along the line of long-standing habit and specific need of the moment also play an important part.

Findings on the sense of smell suggest that odor preference may be largely a result of cultural influences. There is some lessening of smell sensitivity with age but the evidence is not conclusive—that is, the sense of smell does appear to remain stable in older persons.

In spite of the difficulties in measuring these sense modalities and the lack of conclusive findings as to cause for change, gerontologists recognize that many older persons do not taste food exactly as they did formerly. Many older persons, too, may not as quickly recognize and respond to noxious odors that can warn of potential hazards to safety and well-being (e.g., toxic fumes and poisonous substances). In practical terms, an older person with a failing appetite may not necessarily be merely "cranky" but may be reporting literal fact that food doesn't taste the same. What food providers need to consider, therefore, is not more bland food but rather the need for tastier, spicier food, depending, of course, upon individual life-style and preference.

In a clinical context, evaluation of taste and smell responses must take into account a number of possible contributing elements, including (but not limited to) individual preference, familiarity with the substance, state of health, emotional stress or dysfunction (such as grief or depression), and the possibility that expressed distaste or loss of appetite may be symbolic or symptomatic of other life dissatisfactions. Lack of or ill-fitting dentures (which make it painful to bite down), a decline in ability to salivate, and shrinking gums can also contribute to eating problems and diminished satisfaction.

The Tactile, Temperature, and Kinesthetic Senses

Changes along these dimensions should not be thought of as a function of aging per se. These changes can be understood and accounted for within the context of the whole anatomical and physiological picture. Further, it is a mistake to anticipate that such deficiencies are going to occur universally in the aged.

Sensitivity to all stimuli applied to the feet starts to decrease at an earlier age than that applied to the forearm. In 5 to 10 percent of elderly tested there is some decline in sensitivity to vibration, temperature, pain, and light touch in the upper extremities; this occurs in more than 40 percent of individuals when sensitivity in their lower extremities is tested. Loss of sensitivity to light touch occurs in only 25 percent of elderly persons. Nor is it unusual to find some loss of sensitivity in one mode (such as kinesthesia) but little or no loss in the other modes (Kenshalo, 1977).

The criteria for thermal comfort does not appear to change with advancing years. But the capability of the body's temperature-regulating system to cope with temperature changes does seem to diminish. Thus an elderly woman who complains of a chilly room and insists on a shawl when younger people in the room are quite comfortable may not necessarily be acting in querulous fashion. By the same token, an elderly man awakening in the middle of the night may be responding to too many blankets or an overheated room. A rise in body temperature of as little as one degree can be enough to waken a light sleeper.

Convincing evidence of change in cutaneous pain sensitivity with advanced age is still lacking; the findings on this issue are mixed. What complicates such research is the well-accepted fact that pain is more than a sensory phenomenon. Clinicians especially are familiar with the cognitive (intellectual/symbolic) and affective (emotional) aspects of personality that exert significant influence upon how each individual responds to various kinds and intensities of pain stimuli.

Such factors, if they are to be correctly assessed, must be teased out and identified in the clinical setting, whether it be a medical or psychosocial one. Studies have shown for example (Kenshalo, 1977) that highly anxious patients report pain at lower stimulus intensities than do nonanxious patients. Also, particular instructions to experimental subjects can make both age and sex differences disappear and reappear. Subjects not informed that an experiment involves the experience of pain report higher pain thresholds than those so informed.

With respect to the sense modalities in general, then, deficiencies and impairments can and do occur with increasing age. But these are not universal phenomena nor do they occur regularly in a given individual. They represent a relatively modest proportion of the elderly and they reflect marked individual differences between elderly persons as well as differential sense thresholds within individuals.

AGING AND PHYSIOLOGICAL ADAPTATION

A major hypothesis regarding physical and health factors in aging questions the effectiveness (or failure) of a variety of control mechanisms that are known to regulate the interaction of different organ systems and tissues with advanced age (Birren & Renner, 1977). Primary control mechanisms operate either via the endocrine system or the nervous system in conjunction with the vascular system.

The corticosteroids, for instance, can have numerous and various physiological effects. They influence electrolyte and water balance, moderate metabolism and the functional capacities of the cardiovascular system, kidneys, skeletal muscles, and the central nervous system. They also influence the capacity of the body to cope with change and stress. As a contrasting comparison, one might examine the breakdown of causes of death in the United States. Table 8–2 very clearly shows how diseases of the heart and circulatory system have become in a disproportionate way by far the major cause of death from middle through old age in our country. No doubt that is why such diseases, associated with the circulatory system and exacerbated by stress factors, have given rise to the label "diseases of the industrialized west."

This phenomenon should also strongly suggest to the student of gerontology the major influence of psychosocial factors and their central role in the total picture of physical well-being of the population from the middle through the later years of life. Thinking of the older person as a social being, then, let us look now at some subsystems from the physiological point of view and quite literally try to imagine how the physical and psychosocial dimensions interrelate, especially in old age.

Physiologically, the human body is an intricate mechanochemical system which controls a constant flow of energy in the form of incom-

TABLE 8–2.   DEATH RATES PER 100,000 POPULATION IN THE UNITED STATES DURING 1973

Cause of Death	1–14	15–24	25–34	35–44	45–54	55–64	65–74	75–84	85 and Over
						AGE			
Major cardiovascular diseases	1.6	4.0	14.3	73.3	268.1	762.6	1,914.5	5,229.4	12,914.7
Malignant neoplasms, including neoplasms of lymphatic and hematopoietic tissues	5.6	7.2	15.4	54.9	181.4	428.6	778.2	1,208.1	1,457.7
Influenza and pneumonia	2.2	2.0	3.7	7.6	14.6	31.0	79.9	228.3	875.5
Diabetes mellitus	0.1	0.4	1.7	4.4	11.4	33.1	82.0	171.1	227.0
Bronchitis, emphysema, and asthma	0.1	0.2	0.5	1.9	8.3	32.2	79.8	134.2	123.9
Accidents	24.1	71.0	51.6	45.3	49.2	52.2	75.2	157.0	404.9

SOURCE: US Public Health Service (1974).

ing nutrients, water, and gases and outgoing waste products, water, heat, and gases. Such a paradigm, suggested by Abbey (1975), provides a useful framework for the study of physical factors in aging.

Consider, for example, the shape of a fairly typical elderly person. Arms and legs are relatively thin while the trunk, particularly around the abdomen, is fat. In the context of heat control or conservation, the spindly arms and legs with marked decrease in blood circulation act to prevent heat loss, while the fatty tissue around the belly tends to conserve heat in the area of the major organs where it is most needed.

The body gets rid of excess heat arising from cellular activity by sweating, and by vasodilation of the periphery. The elderly person with a compromised heart and vasculature (circulatory system), therefore, does not tolerate well extremes of heat and cold. An elevated temperature is ordinarily more serious in an elderly person because in addition to reduced energy reserves, vascular adaptation is much more limited. If the arteries are atherosclerotic, the capillary beds of the lungs are decreased and thickened alveoli all work to limit gaseous exchange (the normal process of breathing). The overall cardiopulmonary system can be said to be less resilient, and possibly because of less sensitivity to adaptation "signals," cannot adjust properly to the increased demands in rate and volume.

The heart becomes the central actor in this physical health drama. With advancing years the heart muscle typically shows a decrease in size and strength. It does not fill as well nor squeeze as tightly, factors probably related to the body's decreased ability to convert nutrients to mechanical energy as efficiently as it did when it was young. By age sixty-five cardiac output decreases approximately 30 to 40 percent. Cardiac rate remains stable, but under conditions of exertion the heart rate takes longer to increase and the rate is not as fast as it formerly was.

Prolongation of the period of contraction occurs and aortic elasticity diminishes considerably in the later years. With exercise, an increase in cardiac output can result in a rise in arterial blood pressure. This makes the blood-pumping mechanism less efficient and less able to adapt to stressful, demanding situations.

The circulatory problems of aging are well known. Perhaps less well known (and associated with the familiar "midnight jitters") is that insomnia is often related to diminished cerebral blood flow accompanying lessened mental or emotional stimulation. In such instances a sedative can actually be dangerous. Much better would be something warm and sweet to drink (like hot chocolate) and someone to talk to for a while. In such instances a gentle backrub can also help circulation and reduce emotional stress.

The fact that all metabolism forms acid end products focuses attention on the two major systems for acid-base control. These are the lungs and the kidneys. The lungs are a passive system in that they are limited to gaseous exchange and cannot make electrolyte corrections, are unable selectively to conserve or excrete, and are totally dependent for effective functioning upon an intact rib cage and musculature (and are thus related to posture). It is the nervous system that controls the respiratory muscles and causes breathing. The lungs themselves do not act as primary sensors for gaseous concentration, respiratory rate, or depth. If respiratory difficulties persist over a protracted period of time, the respiratory centers in the brain "reset" to cause breathing only at a higher concentration of acid and carbon dioxide in the blood. This will, of course, decrease the rate of respiration and materially lessen the amount of oxygen taken in. A backup receptor system then becomes the sole cause of breathing and unfortunately does so when the oxygen concentration in the blood drops to about 60 percent of normal. The individual breathes then only when the amount of available oxygen is low.

This phenomenon can become a special problem in hospitals or nursing homes, or even in private homes of the affluent where bottled oxygen is available. In such a circumstance, if the elderly individual is given nasal oxygen without being carefully observed he can drift off to sleep, stop breathing, and die of acidosis. A very simple test of function is to request the elderly person to blow out a match held six inches from the mouth with the mouth wide open. If he cannot manage to do that one may conclude that respiratory function is compromised and he needs close observation and help. There is also in that event a high probability that he will not be able to cough adequately, either.

The other system involved in acid-base management is the kidneys. Kidney function decreases in efficiency almost 50 percent with a steady decline in ability to concentrate urine between twenty and ninety years of age. Problems with dehydration as well as the possibility of bladder problems become potential threats to the physical well-being of elderly persons.

ENVIRONMENTAL STRESS AND DISABILITY

Within the large body of research on the effects of stress in general, there is a growing emphasis on those particular elements of stress in the environment that generate a specific impact on the aging process. Convincing evidence clearly demonstrates not only the psychological and emotional trauma but also the noxious physical consequences of environmental stress. Studies indicate an even closer linkage of physical and health factors in the overall well-being of the elderly to environmental determinants than to any other single disease-inducing variable.

Health profiles of the aged are typically developed on the basis of number of disease syndromes, pathological entities, and disabilities or "impairments." Gerontologists have begun to emphasize that in any such health evaluation what must also be taken into account is the equally important fact that disabilities do vary greatly in intensity and effect upon each individual. Disabilities also vary with respect to duration. Disabling conditions of mild intensity and brief duration may have little effect upon the older person. Other disabling conditions of high intensity and greater chronicity are presumed to have much greater impact. Also to be considered are the variations of these factors.

A counterpart or discontinuity hypothesis, proposed by Birren (1963), states that it is only when a physiological function becomes "abnormal" that the physical function affects behavior variables. Physical factors within a normal range not affecting the behavior of young persons may affect the behavior of older persons when the physical function reaches an abnormal level (in intensity and duration). Such a notion is not inconsistent with the findings that most elderly tend to underestimate the "seriousness" of certain health factors in overall subjective judgment.

NUTRITION

An optimal state of physical and emotional well-being is highly dependent upon adequate dietary or nutritional regimens. The familiar saying "we are what we eat" may indeed have special applicability to aging. Many different but related elements strongly influence customary dietary patterns among the elderly: social, motivational, financial, cultural, and physical factors; habit patterns; knowledge base; and the like. Adequate nutrition for an elderly person invariably becomes a problem when there is a breakdown in one or some combination of these elements.

One possible contributor to poor nutrition with advanced years is the incidence of periodontal disease, which increases with age to over 90 percent of those sixty-five to seventy-five years of age. Such difficulties include the failure to use dentures at all or the persistent use of ill-fitting dentures. Consequent pain or discomfort in biting down can tempt an elderly person to concentrate on nutritionally deficient junk foods or a bread-soaked-in-milk diet or its equivalent.

Other gastrointestinal changes with age can also spark dietary deficiencies and poor eating habits. For instance, delay in emptying by the esophagus, which may lead to difficulty or pain in swallowing, is not rare in late life. Digestive secretions diminish markedly after sixty years of age, although the amount of enzymes necessary for carbohydrate and protein digestion appears to remain adequate.

The overall conclusion of nutritionists and dietary experts familiar with the eating habits of the aged is that where nutritional deficiencies are found among older persons these deficiencies appear to be more closely linked to level of income, general health, feelings of well-being, and other factors that have been mentioned than to old age itself.

Thus when such cognitive dysfunctions as confusion, disorientation, and memory lapses occur, or when intellectual functioning is impaired, one must carefully examine those behaviors to determine to what extent the nutritional status of the aged individual may be implicated. Certain toxic states (which can also be caused by the interaction of certain drugs or by inappropriate dosages), inadequate supply of thiamine or nicotinic acid, avitaminosis, endocrine disorders, or anemia are all capable of producing the so-called signs of "senility" mentioned above. These are essentially transient conditions, and to the extent to which they are linked to eating habits, they can be practicably minimized or eliminated altogether by effective dietary modifications. The appropriate addition of vitamins and other nutritional supplements also helps. When these temporary conditions are removed, the related cognitive dysfunctions can be significantly improved or eliminated, too. Clearly factors associated with poor dietary patterns (solitary eating, lack of money, life-style habits, and so on) need to be assessed and taken into account in any effective intervention or service-delivery strategy.

EXERCISE

Along with nutrition, exercise plays a large role as one of the important elements in prevention of deterioration and maintenance of physical as well as psychological well-being in the later years (De Vries, 1975). The amount and kinds of exercise routines in which older persons participate serve not only as antidotes to certain kinds of physical change, stress, and the subjective experience of pain, but also have a direct (and often immediate) effect upon states of emotional stress, boredom, general morale, and outlook.

With aging, muscle cells decrease in number. Also the transmission rate of impulse in nervous tissue decreases approximately 15 percent in motor nerves and 30 percent in sensory neurons between twenty and ninety years of age. In addition, there is loss to some degree of vibra-

Appropriate exercise enables people to maintain their zest and a high level of well-being as they grow older.

tory sensation and a lessening of tendon reflex. Regularly performed exercise can increase the capacity for ventilation, the amount of oxygen used, cardiac output and blood flow, and not only slow the rate of muscle loss but cause the functioning cells to grow and react faster. Thus as long as nerve tissue is intact, impairment of function in aging muscles can be actively (and usually successfully) combated.

An important bonus to be had from regular, appropriate exercise in later life is its tranquilizing effect. Exercise has a significantly greater effect, without any undesirable side effects, than does meprobamate, one of the most frequently prescribed tranquilizers (De Vries & Adams, 1972). This should not be overlooked when a tranquilizer effect is desired. A fifteen-minute walk, for example, at a moderate rate is sufficient to have a tranquilizing effect for at least one hour afterward, according to De Vries.

Exercise appropriate for elderly persons has been found to decrease arterial blood pressure. A clear-cut case can also be made for the importance of habitual, lifelong, rigorous physical activity as a preventive measure against obesity and its accompanying ills.

De Vries also points out (1971) that only if exercise in late life is appropriate and carefully moderated will its benefits be maximized and its hazards minimized. Unless the intensity of exercise is vigorous enough to raise the heart rate more than 40 percent above the resting rate it is unlikely to produce significant benefits to the cardiorespiratory system, even though lower intensity exercise may benefit other muscles and the joints. De Vries and other physiologists point out that appropriate exercise means avoiding or minimizing high activation of small muscle masses and static (isometric) contractions. Much more desirable exercise regimens for the elderly should emphasize the rhythmic activity of large muscle masses. Natural activities such as walking, dancing, jogging, bike riding, running, and swimming are best suited for this purpose.

SUMMARY

A common denominator in the rapidly expanding gerontological literature is the notion of multiple loss. Physical and health factors, because they represent a major category of change and loss factors and also provide a large base for planners and practitioners, have received much attention by researchers.

Chronic conditions are more frequent in an older population than acute physical ailments. Yet most elderly are able to function quite adequately. Chronic disabilities may limit activities but need not identify such persons as sick.

Cosmetic signs of aging are highly visible and may elicit negative attitudes, especially toward women. Other losses associated with aging, such as the changes in the sense modalities, may penalize older persons in more subtle ways. These physiological changes interact in various ways to affect the health as well as mental competence and emotional well-being of the older individuals. Many of these factors are reversible and preventable. The major maintenance and prevention strategies in this regard have to do with nutrition and exercise.

REFERENCES

Abbey, J. "Physiology of the Aged" (mimeographed lecture delivered at Andrus Gerontology Center, University of Southern California, Los Angeles, 1975).

Birren, J. "Psychophysiological Relations." In J. Birren, R. Butler, S. Greenhouse, L. Sokoloff, and M. Yarrow (eds.), *Human Aging: A Biological and Behavioral Study.* Washington, D.C.: Government Printing Office, 1963.

Birren, J., and J. Renner. "Developments in Research on the Biological and Behavioral Aspects of Aging and Their Implications." In J. Birren and K. W. Schaie (eds.), *Handbook of the Psychology of Aging.* New York: Van Nostrand Reinhold, 1977.

Carlson, R. *The End of Medicine.* New York: Wiley, 1975.

Corso, J. "Auditory Perception and Communication." In J. Birren and K. W. Schaie (eds.), *Handbook of the Psychology of Aging.* New York: Van Nostrand Reinhold, 1977.

Cosin, L. Z. "The Philosophy, Strategy, and Practice of Care of the Elderly" (mimeographed paper, Tavistock House (South), Tavistock Square, London, W.C.1, 1975).

De Vries, H. "Exercise Intensity Threshold for Improvement of Cardiovascular-Respiratory Function in Older Men." *Geriatrics,* 1971, 26.

De Vries, H. "The Physiology of Exercise and Aging." In D. Woodruff and J. Birren (eds.), *Aging: Scientific Perspectives and Social Issues.* New York: D. Van Nostrand, 1975.

De Vries, H., and G. Adams. "Electromyographic Comparison of Single Doses of Exercise and Meprobamate as to Effects on Muscular Relaxation." *American Journal of Physical Medicine,* 1972, 51.

Engen, T. "Taste and Smell." In J. Birren and K. W. Schaie (eds.), *Handbook of the Psychology of Aging.* New York: Van Nostrand Reinhold, 1977.

Fozard, J., et al. "Visual Perception and Communication." In J. Birren and K. W. Schaie (eds.), *Handbook of the Psychology of Aging.* New York: Van Nostrand Reinhold, 1977.

Kenshalo, D. R. "Age Changes in Touch, Vibration, Temperature, Kinesthesis, and Pain Sensitivity." In J. Birren and K. W. Schaie (eds.), *Handbook of the Psychology of Aging.* New York: Van Nostrand Reinhold, 1977.

Maddox, G. L. "Self-assessment of Health Status: A Longitudinal Study of Selected Elderly Subjects." *Journal of Chronic Diseases,* 1964, 17.

National Center for Health Statistics. *Acute Conditions: Incidence and Associated Disability, United States, July, 1969–June, 1970.* Vital and Health Statistics, Series 10, No. 77. Washington, D. C.: Government Printing Office, 1972.

National Society for the Prevention of Blindness. "Estimate of Statistics on Blindness and Vision Problems." New York, 1966.

Rossman, I. "Anatomic and Body Composition Changes with Aging." In C. Finch and L. Hayflick (eds.), *Handbook of the Biology of Aging.* New York: Van Nostrand Reinhold, 1977.

Schwartz, A. "A Transactional View of the Aging Process." In A. Schwartz and I. Mensh (eds.), *Professional Obligations and Approaches to the Aged.* Springfield, Ill.: Charles C Thomas, 1974.

Schwartz, A. "Mental Health of the Aged and Long-Term Care." *Concern,* 1977, 111:4.

Snyder, L., J. Pyrek, and K. Smith. "Vision and Mental Function of the Elderly." *The Gerontologist,* 1976, 16:6.

Sontag, S. "The Double Standard of Aging." *Saturday Review*, September 23, 1972.

Tiberi, D., A. Schwartz, and W. Albert. "Envy versus Greed: Proposed Modifications of Medicare Policy." *Long Term Care and Health Services Administration Quarterly*, Fall 1977.

US Public Health Service. *Vital Statistics Report*, 1974, 22:13.

Wright, B. *Physical Disability: A Psychological Approach.* New York: Harper & Row, 1958.

FOR FURTHER READING

Fox, J., J. Topel, and M. Huckman. "Dementia in the Elderly—A Search for Treatable Illnesses." *Journal of Gerontology,* 1975, 30:5.

Holmes, J.H., and M. Masuda. "Psychosomatic Syndrome." *Psychology Today,* April 1972.

Illich, I. *Medical Nemesis.* London: Calder and Boyars, 1974.

Insel, P., and R. Moos (eds.). *Health and the Social Environment.* Lexington, Mass.: D.C. Heath, 1974.

Kaplan, J. "The Hospital Model: Curse or Blessing for Homes Serving the Aged." *The Gerontologist,* 1974, 14:4.

Loeb, M., and S. Howell (eds.). "Nutrition and Aging: A Monograph for Practitioners." *The Gerontologist,* 1969, 9:3.

Pastalan, A., and D. Carson. *Spatial Behavior of Older People.* Ann Arbor: Institute of Gerontology, The University of Michigan–Wayne State University, 1970.

Powles, J. "On the Limitations of Modern Medicine." *Science, Medicine and Man.* Oxford: Pergamon Press, 1973.

Proshansky, H., W. Ittelson, and L. Rivlin (eds.). *Environmental Psychology: Man and His Physical Setting.* New York: Holt, Rinehart and Winston, 1970.

Rahe, R. "Life Change and Subsequent Illness." In E.K. Gunderson and R. Rahe (eds.), *Life Stress and Illness.* Springfield, Ill.: Charles C Thomas, 1974.

Shanas, E. *The Health of Older People.* Cambridge, Mass.: Harvard University Press, 1962.

Tiberi, D., A. Schwartz, I. Hirschfield, and P. Kerschner. "Correlates of the Medical and Psychosocial Models of Long Term Care (paper delivered at 11th International Congress of Gerontology, Tokyo, 1978).

CHAPTER 9

Psychological Aspects of Behavior in Later Life

Enjoy your achievements as well as your plans. . . . Be
yourself . . . take kindly the counsel of the years, gracefully
surrendering the things of youth. . . . Beyond a wholesome
discipline, be gentle with yourself. . . .You are a child of the
universe no less than the trees and the stars; you have a
right to be here.

Allegedly found in Old St. Paul's
Church, Baltimore, Maryland, dated 1672

A lthough this chapter discusses the subject as a separate topic, the
student of gerontology should understand clearly how
psychological factors in aging are securely and intimately interwoven
with all other aspects of the aging process.

The old truism that the whole is more than the sum of its parts is
borne out by conclusions to be drawn from studies of psychological
behaviors in later life. Starting with the concept of the "whole" person,
the student can in this chapter examine many of the "parts" in terms of
psychological issues. Among these are issues related to learning,
performance, memory, intelligence, and motivation. The chapter
directs attention then to such factors as stress, environment, and
adaptation (coping), all of which are constituent elements in behavior
and personality. The student can relate this information to the
important concept of self-esteem, which constitutes a basic, guiding

201

understanding behavior of the aged. This chapter should also help the student gain an appreciation of the continuity of behavior and personality through the life cycle and at the same time see how it is that individuals become more psychologically unique with advancing years.

Gerontologists are as much interested in uncovering and specifying laws of behavior in the later years as psychologists are in discovering general laws that govern human behavior at every age. In addition, students of human behavior are interested in identifying the specific laws or principles that will account for individual styles and patterns of behavior. The degree of success in accomplishing this for the gerontologist determines the degree to which he can more fully understand and subsequently anticipate or predict behavior in late maturity. The state of the art at this time is such that gerontology can claim only partial understanding of the dynamics of behavior in old age. But while it must be said that many findings are not at all conclusive and much of our understanding is an approximation, there is much information available about the psychological aspects of aging which is relevant to theory building about aging and which can be put to practical use.

The following essay, reprinted from the *New York Times* (1977), gives as well as anything can the flavor of psychological uniqueness as to how one individual perceives and attempts to cope with events in the later years. From this portrayal the reader can sense the intense feelings associated with several problems occurring in later life with which many older persons can identify. The essay is reprinted in its entirety.

HOW OLD IS OLD?*

I have recently been retired. I use the passive voice deliberately. This retirement was no act of mine; it was forced upon me by a computer that simply threw up a name to be discarded. It was no act of an administrator who rationally considered the worker and her work. The worker with an excellent record of attendance, responsibility and reliability, whose vigor and willingness were in no way diminished, had to be dismissed. The years of experience were less than nothing.

For some time I had been uneasy, aware that however fit I might be, students, growing up in a society in which the emphasis is on youth, would think of me as diseased. After all, old age is a disease in America. The aged person becomes a leper, to be put away in an institution, or, if lucky, and affluent, in an expensive colony, separated from the rest of mankind.

I found myself beginning to feel apologetic for my continuing tenure. I felt that I should do as everyone said, go away and make room for a younger

*The writer, who requested anonymity, was assistant professor of English in the City University system.

person, someone with little or no experience, whose chief asset would be youth, and therefore with more right to the position.

Accordingly, when that dire notice arrived, my reaction was to disappear quietly, to let no one know that I had been struck down with that dread "disease." I was no longer an active, intelligent human being, but a supernumerary to be put out of the way. I wanted no testimonials to my condition. I was ashamed.

Walking about my own neighborhood in the light of day, I would not reveal the truth to inquiries about my idleness. I was on leave, I was writing a book, I was on sabbatical. I could not confess that I was now a relic. I edged away from organizations for the retired, shunning my own kind. I refused to take advantage of the privileges for "senior citizens," continuing to pay full fares, full charges.

But some things are unavoidable, and the whole apparatus of Social Security hit me: papers to be filled out, official ukases to be interpreted, the mimeographed word to be construed, the muddy language of the computer to be painfully transmitted to the understanding, figures to be added up again and again.

Just now, when this great change in my life is taking place, and I need a structured routine, the structure is cut down under my slipping feet. I get up in the morning, just as early, or even earlier, for now I cannot sleep, then go through the household chores, and have nothing further to do.

There is not the stimulation of a shared experience with colleagues, the preoccupation with the work. There is only the lonely house and the lonelier walk. Entertainment soon palls; the freedom of one's own time, the time that stretches endlessly, is not used. But there is also the prickling awareness that that very time is limited, that it must be used at once, or it will be gone. And then one thinks, "What the hell, let it go, it doesn't matter."

Everything seems to be coming to an end anyhow. With the cut in income there is also a cut in benefits, to which I am no longer entitled. So I begin to worry about money: Should I spend it all now—there's so little future left; or should I watch every penny, I may get sick and need private nurses; there will be no one to take care of me when I'm destitute. Should I move, can I afford it, is it worth the effort?

Then there is the question of relationships with former colleagues. I have the time, but they're working, taking on new loads; they're occupied. I must proceed carefully so as not to intrude into their precious time, careful not to injure the fragile bond, careful not to become an annoyance.

Some of these colleagues have expressed envy of my freedom. I used to bewail the fact that I had not enough free time; there were so many things I wanted to do. Now I have all that time, but not the will to do anything. I used to bake bread on those Sundays when I had five sets of papers to mark. I managed to find the time and the energy. Fatigue? It was well-earned fatigue, I had a right to pamper myself. Now I have no right, I have not earned it, I cannot go on that long trip.

The doctor tells me I am "in very good shape." My mind is teeming with ideas, but no one wants them. I don't want to fill in the time before I die. I want to use the time. I need to work, not make-work, not a hobby, not volunteer work. I need a job. I want my old job back. I was good at it.

To be considered unfit for the very job for which I was trained, in which I have many years of experience, is the cruelest kind of rejection.

Then I am truly unfit, no good at anything. There is no longer any incentive to work; there is only the overwhelming fear of further rejection. Nothing else matters, nothing else affords any kind of compensation.

We do not know many details of this anonymous writer's life and circumstances. Still, this brief autobiographical excerpt is enough to suggest some of the questions with which the psychology of aging is concerned.

1. How do we identify the "continuities" and the "discontinuities" between old age and the middle years?

2. In what ways is old age "connected" to earlier life experiences?

3. What kinds of factors are involved when the elderly try to cope with stress?

4. To what extent are issues like coping, competence, and creativity relevant to the study of the aging process?

5. Are cognitive factors in aging (changes in memory, learning) more or less important than affective (emotional) factors?

6. Are changes in some levels of competent thinking or behavior to be construed as senility?

7. Is senility (often called senile dementia) a useful label, and is it an inevitable result of old age?

8. Are there basic criteria for intervention in old age, or are we to believe that *any* kind of helping is "good"?

THE MIND-BODY PRINCIPLE

Probably the most venerated truism in psychology has been the principle that there can be no mental or emotional processes apart from the underlying physiological processes. In other words, the mind and body are inextricably woven together into a unitary, functioning whole. Events that affect the body will invariably have impact, too, upon cognitions and emotions, and vice versa.

This fundamental fact has given rise to the principles of psychosomatic medicine, which tell us, for example, that we are more likely to catch cold when under severe emotional stress than when not under such stress. Anyone who has ever witnessed a bad scene (like a bloody accident) and as a result experienced a feeling of nausea in the pit of the stomach and a pounding heart knows full well how universally applicable this principle is.

All the while examining various aspects of the psychology of aging, the student will do well to keep in mind that a host of interrelated circumstances—physical, genetic, social, religious, environmental, cultural, maintenance (dietary and exercise), economic, and other environmental factors—as discussed in other chapters of this text, converge in a multiplicity of uniquely patterned ways to influence and determine psychological events and outcomes.

At the same time, additional emphasis on the previous cautions made about generational versus age differences (see chapter 1) should be made here.

The traditional experimental models widely used in psychological studies of aging behavior are vulnerable to criticism on at least two counts: both the methods employed and the methods of selection of subjects for experimental studies (Birren & Renner, 1977). Earlier investigations have been almost without exception cross-sectional, and the measures used were validated on a population of youth through middle age. Also, as we shall see, when elderly subjects are tested, the control of extraneous factors (ones irrelevant to the concerns of the study) such as physical deficit have not always been stringently observed. The discontinuities between child, adult, and aged behavior changes, therefore, largely remain to be systematically explored.

Among the elements basic to psychological behavior in later life are learning and memory. These are given a great deal of research attention because they are considered fundamental in understanding also the nature of intellectual functioning.

LEARNING

The old adage "You can't teach an old dog new tricks" dies hard. In spite of the fact that little experimental evidence of learning in old dogs has been uncovered, recent research suggests, and experience confirms, the notion that the old adage is pure myth when referring to elderly humans.

This is not to suggest that we cannot distinguish between the performance of young and old learners. In most instances, comparison of learning performance of different age groups favors the young adult (Arenberg & Robertson-Tchabo, 1977). But considerable progress has been made in identifying conditions that impair or improve the learning performance of older individuals.

In studies of learning and aging, gerontologists ask three types of general questions:

1. Is the learning of older individuals affected by specific conditions?

2. Is the magnitude of the age differences affected by specific conditions?

3. Does the learning process change with age, and are age changes affected by specific conditions?

It is the task of gerontologists to identify the specific conditions referred to. As already mentioned, few studies have used the longitudinal approach to study learning in older adults, an approach that is most appropriate to answering particularly the third question.

A series of studies reported by Gilbert (1973) tested subjects in their twenties and thirties on verbal learning and then retested them thirty-five to forty years later. Other studies have compared learning in independent subsamples (different subjects born at the same time and subjects born at different times). The basic method used has been test-retest (over extended time), using lists of paired words. Serial learning tasks have also been used. Investigators measured the efficiency of learning and recalling words in such controlled tasks.

Such research has found a decline in learning performance among older participants. One question researchers raise is whether retesting the same individuals at a later time introduces a "retesting bias" practice effect in performance. Although initial learning and retention measures showed a decline with age, vocabulary scores on such testing remained high. Therefore Arenberg's caution regarding such studies is important, namely the need to control for retest effects and to control for effects of noncomparability of testing materials (Arenberg & Robertson-Tchabo, 1977).

What still remains unspecified is the efficiency of learning when other than rote learning tasks performed in the laboratory are at issue. Rote learning appears to represent a combination of registering, storage, and retrieval of information. The processing of information is an essential element in verbal learning performance. Will the same decline with age be evidenced in other than verbal learning tasks?

Of special importance in interpreting age differences is the distinction to be made between *learning* (acquisition of information or skills) and *performance*. It is still possible for an older individual to "know" an item on a list and yet fail to produce a response under certain conditions. Researchers in learning, therefore, refer to permanent (built-in processes) and modifiable (controllable) aspects of learning (Arenberg & Robertson-Tchabo, 1977). An example of the first is age-related central nervous system (CNS) changes; of the second, the nature of the instructions given or level of motivation or experience on the part of the learner.

In rote-learning tasks for the elderly, pacing is widely acknowledged to be a critical factor. Pacing refers to the input (of information) rate and the output (performance) rate. The interval between the two is the time the individual has available to take in information, make associations and "inspect" the information, make sense of it, encode it (perhaps by a mnemonic device), rehearse, select out, and then make an appropriate response.

One study reported that when the interval was relatively long (3 seconds), both young and old made fewer errors than when the time interval was shorter (1.5 seconds) (Canestrari, 1963). The older group benefited more than the young from the slower pace. When old and young groups are permitted to interrupt the course of experimental events so as to extend the length of any inspection or anticipation interval, both groups again make fewer errors, but the older group benefits most.

Researchers have also concluded from such studies that age-related declines in learning performance can be attributed to difficulty with retrieval rather than with storage of information. This reflects the older individual's need for additional time to search for, recover, and produce a stored response. This conclusion is supported by the fact that additional errors on the part of the old at a fast pace are mostly errors of omission—that is, failure to respond.

Additional studies also suggest that individuals must, indeed, learn how to search for and produce a required response. This finding, coupled with the evident need for increased time on the part of the older subject, has been interpreted to mean that the older person may be characteristically more reluctant to take a chance on giving a response about which he is uncertain. This means that the kind of presented learning material (meaningfulness or lack of it), the nature and clarity of the instructions, and the degree of emotional support involved are also important considerations directly related to the possible arousal of anxiety, the level of confidence, and the ultimate degree of success in learning on the part of elderly individuals.

MEMORY

Since the 1950s, a shift in emphasis from studies of learning to studies of memory has taken place, a shift that parallels the increasing emphasis on the study of information processing (Craik, 1977). Studies of memory usually focus on single (or one-trial) presentation of the task. In such memory research the concern is with registration, storage, and retrieval of information. "Learning" may, therefore, be thought of as the more global acquisition of general knowledge and rules, whereas "memory" is more narrowly viewed as the retention of specific events occurring at a given time and place.* These two aspects should be viewed as opposite sides of the same learning-memory coin.

Most widely accepted today according to Craik (1977), is a three-stage model of memory which works like this: first stage, information storage; second stage, transfer to short-term memory (assuming no interference or "decay"); third stage, transfer to a relatively permanent long-term memory bank. Some investigators prefer the terms "primary" and "secondary" memory as more precise indicators than the terms short- and long-term memory. The emphasis, Craik states, must be on *processes.* "It is no longer satisfactory to state that retention over 30 seconds, or recall of a 20-word list reflects short-term memory; even immediate retention can involve a long-term component. . . ." In this view, primary memory is thought to be a more temporary holding and organizing process than the more permanent memory storage bank. Many findings suggest that primary memory is unimpaired in older persons but that age-related deficiencies do occur in secondary memory.

The student of gerontology needs to keep in mind that the initial stage (of storage) is highly dependent upon the efficient operation of the various senses in any given individual. It is also vulnerable to the impact of many other relevant factors, as already indicated. The incredible number of variations that do occur account for the many differences between older individuals, a fact confirmed by careful observation. Dealing with aged persons in a clinical context or in any other one-to-one situation, therefore, requires that evaluation be individualized and must to the highest degree possible sensitively reflect these variations.

INTELLIGENCE

Learning and memory clearly are related to intelligence. The concept of intelligence, however, has come to occupy an especially important status simply because it has come to be so widely used as the basis for judgments and decisions affecting vocational and educational careers. Nevertheless, intelligence is an intangible, a concept, a construct. Psychologists have tried to make it more tangible by defining certain ways of measuring the concept. Selected (and presumably representative) behaviors are measured by devices called intelligence tests. The results of these tests are summarized in a statistic known as the intelligence quotient (IQ).

---

*For example, general information: Stockholm is the capital of Sweden; one's zip code is 10508; $7 \times 6 = 42$. This is in contrast to the recall of a specific incident like the names of persons who attended your last birthday party or what you had for breakfast last Tuesday morning.

A concise summary of the difficulties attendant on the study of intellectual functioning in old age is offered by Botwinick (1977):

1. What is meant by aging (how defined)
2. Types of tests used (are they valid and reliable for an older population)
3. Definitions of intelligence (capacity vs. ability, fluid vs. crystallized intelligence)
4. Sampling techniques (random vs. matched sampling)
5. Research methods (cross-sectional vs. longitudinal).

Given the problems of validity associated with the cross-sectional method of research in gerontology, it is important to distinguish between age changes and generational changes also with respect to intelligence. Cross-sectional measures of IQ have typically shown a decline for older cohorts beginning at mid-life. Such data contrast sharply with some longitudinal data reported (Schaie & Strother, 1968).

As can be seen from Figure 9–1, follow-up studies in the early 1960s by Schaie and Strother in effect converted their earlier cross-sectional studies into a longitudinal study. Schaie (1975) concluded that the relatively small declines in his longitudinal data reflected age differences rather than true age decrement. That is, he reported that different

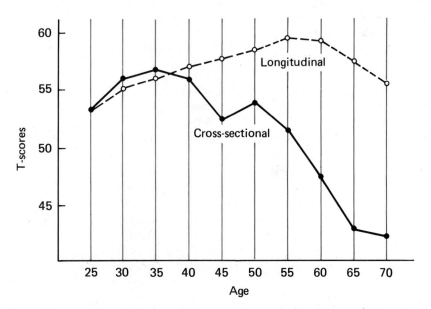

Figure 9–1. COMPARABLE CROSS-SECTIONAL AND LONGITUDINAL AGE GRADIENTS FOR THE VERBAL MEANING TEST

generations performed at different levels of ability. And measures on an aging sample also reflect instances within the sample where extraneous, intruding factors interfere with the ability of the individual to respond.

Figure 9–1 shows the results of a vocabulary recognition test when reported on the appropriate composite age gradient within generations. Schaie draws attention to the fact that the peak age in the longitudinal sequence is fifty-five (not thirty-five as in cross-sectional data). Even at age seventy, estimated performance is still at a higher level than it would have been at age twenty-five.

When, in another study, measures were taken over a fourteen-year period (from which three cross-sectional test gradients were derived),

Psychological and intelligence tests must be used with great caution with the elderly so that they are not penalized or stigmatized by inappropriate or invalid test procedures.

the shape of the gradient (curve) decline appeared identical for each age group (Schaie & Labouvie-Vief, 1974). That is, for each time period tested, later-born cohorts performed better than earlier-born ones. As a result the age of peak performance keeps increasing, which the investigators conclude points to generational (not age) differences, and which indicates, as the investigators put it, "we are smarter than our parents were and our children in turn are likely to be smarter than we are."

Obviously, longitudinal studies of intelligence in old age, too, have their problems. Many factors contribute to the behaviors (performance) measured on IQ tests. These include (but are not limited to) such changes as the amount and complexity of general information disseminated in society; the speed of dissemination (e.g., the differences between those who grew up before TV and those after); the experience of living through a severe economic depression and a series of worldwide conflicts; changes in nutritional values and habits; and many other environmental variations that occur from one era to another, thus providing a different set of experiences from one generation to the next.

Interpretation of longitudinal IQ data, therefore, must take into account all the circumstances that can substantially make a difference in responses to IQ tests. Investigators who have found declines in the intellectual performance of aged based on cross-sectional data may be right. But those who, on the basis of longitudinal data, deny such declines in performance are also right. The observed decline may not be a decline in IQ at all but rather a reflection of age differences. What is being measured is not capacity so much as the fact that different age groups perform at different levels of ability to respond correctly and efficiently (Schaie & Labouvie-Vief, 1974).

Obviously the older groups tested are likely to show a higher incidence of disability of one kind or another. They are also much closer to death. Such factors can inhibit the ability to respond well on IQ tests. It has been pointed out, for example, that because elderly subjects are more likely to tire during extended testing, the fatigue factor would impair performance. If so, then any conclusions regarding intellectual capacity would be inaccurate unless the fatigue factor is taken into account.

Furry and Baltes (1973) compared the performance of individuals in three age groups eleven to fourteen, thirty to fifty, and fifty-one to eighty on the Primary Mental Abilities (PMA) test. One procedure was a twenty-minute pretest in order to induce fatigue. Half the participants in each age group were given this test, half were not.

A statistically significant interaction between age and fatigue was found on three of the PMA subtests. On the subtests called Reasoning and Verbal Meaning, the two younger groups were unaffected while

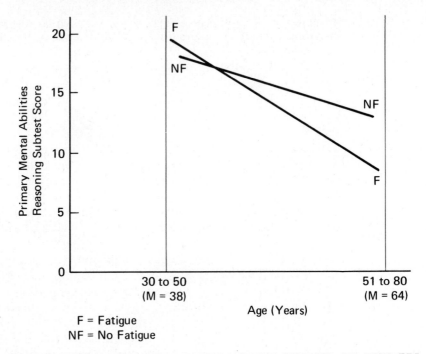

F = Fatigue
NF = No Fatigue

Figure 9-2. THE RESULTS OF TWO ADULT GROUPS ON THE PRI-MARY MENTAL ABILITIES SUBTEST FOR REASONING

the oldest group was adversely affected. On another subtest (Word Fluency), both adult groups were adversely affected by fatigue but the adolescents were not; they actually performed better. The results of the two adult groups on the Reasoning subtest are shown in Figure 9–2, which clearly shows how an intruding factor like fatigue (F) can easily lower the performance of an older group.

The main point here is that when the performance aspect of intelligence is to be measured, then "fatigability" is a relevant dimension of that performance. On the other hand, when intellectual capacity (or potential) is at issue, such factors as fatigue (as well as education, social or economic status, and the like) become extraneous to the issue. Insofar as these extraneous factors are implicated without suitable controls when testing for intellectual capacity of the old, to that extent any final conclusions about the decline of IQ in later life are inaccurate and unwarranted.

The Wechsler Adult Intelligence Scale (WAIS) is likely the most widely used clinical instrument for measuring adult IQ. Two decades ago, David Wechsler observed that "nearly all studies dealing with the age factor in adult performance have shown that most human abilities

. . . decline progressively after reaching a peak somewhere between ages eighteen and twenty-five" (Wechsler, 1958). Although the test has been available since 1939, it was not until 1955 that WAIS norms beyond age sixty-four became available. Repeated testing of older adults has produced what is now called "a classic aging pattern": namely, elderly subjects consistently perform much better on the Verbal Scale (first half) than on the Performance Scale (second half) of the WAIS. This holds true for men, women, blacks, whites, institutionalized and community-based, and for older persons with differing socioeconomic status.

INDIVIDUAL VERSUS GROUP DIFFERENCES

All of the findings touched on so far refer, of course, to studies of groups. What about individual variations? Some elderly individuals may show intellectual decline, but so have some young individuals. By the same token, some individuals have shown a gain in performance between seventy and eighty years, while others have shown a decline between twenty and thirty years of age. What accounts for such variations?

We have already touched on the rich complexity of events and conditions (both internal and external to the individual) that can either enhance or inhibit successful performance on tests of various kinds, including intelligence tests. Most often older persons who continue to be active in a richly stimulating environment confirm the "use it or lose it" principle.

A question that gerontological researchers ask in this connection is, how important, pragmatically, are differences in intellectual performance between young and old? Without question, behavioral scientists pay a great deal of attention to differences that are "statistically significant." All that really means is that the differences found are reliable differences. That is, they are highly likely to occur again if the same testing is repeated under the same conditions. It does not mean that the differences are necessarily large. In practical terms, some "statistically significant" differences turn out to be so small as to have no practical meaning for the activities of daily living (Schaie, 1975). Some differences do have practical consequences; some differences make little difference. The fact that an older person can recall four nonsense syllables fewer per three-minute interval than a younger person is likely to have little direct impact upon the life of anyone. On the other hand, demonstrated age differences in spatial visualization may in fact require revisions in the criteria for employment of older tool-and-die makers or airline pilots.

There are marked differences in performance, not capacity, between successive generations. Often these differences are attributable to the slowing-down process associated with advanced years. That is why elderly subjects perform much better on the Verbal Scale of the WAIS than on the Performance Scale. Most of the subtests of the latter are timed tests and, because they put a premium on speed, do not allow for pacing. Thus they penalize the slower-performing older person.

MOTIVATION

Implicit in the assessment of intelligence in older persons is the factor of motivation. Every beginning student of psychological testing soon learns how important it is to the outcome of testing to make sure the individual being tested has some good reason to apply his best efforts. One cannot talk about motivation, then, without a careful consideration of such motivational forces as drives and incentives. In some contexts the word "need" has been used synonymously with drive.

In general, theorists in the field of motivation have generated two major formulations. One source of motivation is described as coming from prior events or conditions in a person's life, a "push from behind." In varying degrees this can be true of any single event or series of events earlier in an individual's life. Another major source of motivation is characterized as being drawn toward some goal, that is, a "pull from in front." Ordinarily incentives are associated with the latter, and may be either positive or negative incentives. Both sources of motivation may be operating in an individual at the same time, sometimes in concert, at other times in conflict.

It should be obvious that identifying motivational factors is just as important to a fuller understanding of personality and general functioning in an older individual as it is to assessing intelligence or learning behavior. It cannot be overemphasized that the student of gerontology cannot begin to understand the behavior of the elderly fully until the circumstances of life and the motivations that influence such behaviors are understood fully.

PERSONALITY

Psychologists define personality in terms of the probabilities of certain responses and the patterns of characteristic behaviors that flow from the way in which a given individual is dynamically organized. This is in contrast to the more common parlance pop-definition of personality as "social impact," that is, the effect or impact an individual has upon others in social situations (warm, outgoing, "lots of fun," "wet blanket," and so on). The study of aging, too, follows on the premise that the behavior of the elderly is ordinarily not random behavior but is consistent with certain general laws of behavior, common to all humans, (nomothetic), and consistent with specific laws unique to one given individual (idiographic). It is a curious fact that only in recent years has gerontology come to recognize that many problems associated with old age are not "aging problems" at all but clearly are human problems, common to all. We do not have the same fine-tuned, developmental norms for late life as we have for the neonate, the child, and the preadolescent, to be found in any book on child rearing. Pervasive in society, however, are implicit norms for the elderly. Most of these norms are negative ("he did pretty well for an eighty-year-old"), just as males have developed negative norms about the performance of women in certain areas, or whites vis-à-vis blacks.*

The student of gerontology must learn, then, that there are indeed solid connections between what one's personality is at sixty-five or seventy and what it was at twenty-five or thirty years of age. If a woman or man wants to be a sweet, kindly, generous eighty-year-old, those qualities need to be developed very early in life. For there is a consistency in personality throughout most of the life span. This is not to imply that personality (or behavior) is immutable or irreversible. People do learn and do change, given appropriate incentives, in significant ways even in late maturity. Because many and varied social, physical, cultural, and environmental factors do directly and indirectly affect the individual, personality is subject to and, in varying degrees, can and does change throughout the course of life.

Still, we come back to the fact of the consistency of personality and behavior patterns. To cite one instance, Masters and Johnson have pointed out that those who have established a low, moderate, or high level of sexual activity in their early or middle years are most likely to follow the same pattern of sexual activity in their later years. When the level of such activity diminishes significantly, it is invariably caused by extraneous factors such as ill health or lack of an available, willing partner, boredom, fear of "failure," or related anxieties (Masters & Johnson, 1966; Peterson, 1968). When disturbance in the level of sexual activity in the later years does occur for psychological/emotional reasons (the vast majority of instances), counseling, retraining, or some other form of therapeutic intervention has proved to be highly effective (Sviland, 1975).

---

*Such negative expectations, which produce discriminatory effects, are what Robert Butler and others have called "ageism."

CHANGES IN PERSONALITY

Middle-aged sons and daughters sometimes notice what appear to be sudden, even "dramatic" changes in behavior in aging parents. An elderly mother, for instance, who was always seen by her children to be a conscientious, even compulsively neat housekeeper, is described as having "suddenly" lost all interest in keeping her house orderly and clean. She is observed to have become not only slovenly, but unwilling to invest time and energy in cooking. Not infrequently such changes are attributed to "senility."

But a careful examination and fuller understanding of that woman's life patterns and motivations may reveal that she has never liked either cooking or household chores. With advanced years, her children grown and away from home, living alone with a husband whose appetite has diminished (or living by herself or with a daughter who subtly discourages her attempts at housework), her earlier distaste for such chores surfaces. In effect, what has occurred is not a sudden change in personality. Rather, the underlying behavior pattern of long standing is unmasked by changed life circumstances and motivation (Goldfarb, 1976).

A similar explanation can be advanced for the case of an elderly woman who was always known to her family as a quiet, compliant, self-effacing person in her younger and middle years. Now living alone with her retired husband, her children gone, she exhibits unusual behavior for her: "suddenly" she has become loudly assertive, demanding, controlling. Again, a careful reading of her earlier history may reveal a person who has consistently shown demanding, controlling characteristics over a period of many years. Much of this behavior in the past, however, was displayed in the context of child rearing, which took place in a home where her husband was a virtual stranger. Now he is continuously at home with her, and her controlling behavior is no longer siphoned off in child rearing. What appears to be a sudden shift in personality is merely, by dint of changed circumstances, the unmasking of a long-standing behavior characteristic.

Clinical geropsychologists can cite many variations on the same basic theme. One task of the gerontological clinical researcher is to test the validity of the assumptions raised by observations of the clinician and other service providers. Typical of the research questions raised by clinical practice are:

1. What kinds of coping strategies do older persons use?

2. Which factors contribute positively and negatively to competent behavior and maintenance of self-esteem?

3. To what extent is senile-like behavior a result of brain damage and to what extent are behaviors associated with brain trauma reversible?

4. What kinds of intervention strategies are relevant, appropriate, and therapeutic for the aged person?

The difficulties associated with systematic study of these issues based on cross-sectional data have been emphasized already. Testing and evaluation of very old adults who may, in fact, be very close to death and, therefore, already experiencing a "terminal decline," is likely to bias the results in a significant way (Kleemeier, 1962, Jarvik & Blum, 1971). On the other hand, initiating therapeutic interventions designed to help the elderly adult cope more effectively with daily living is quite another matter.

MENTAL HEALTH

The term "mental health" is at best a very imprecise one. Yet because it is so widely used it is repeated here in spite of the fact that the authors much prefer the more descriptive term "emotional well-being." Such terms as mental health, mental illness, senility, dementia, and psychiatric impairment tend to be used rather loosely and often have different connotations for different persons and different disciplines. Some connotations are of dubious validity.

Senility

The word senility is not, strictly speaking, a medical diagnosis, although it is often used synonymously for dementia and often loosely applied to any eccentric or unaccountable behavior of the old.

Organic brain syndrome (OBS), subdivided into acute and chronic brain syndromes (CBS), is a vague descriptive term used to denote disease entities implicated when cognitive and other behavioral deficits or deviations are observed. The commonest characteristics of senile-like behaviors include disorientation as to time, place, or person; impairment of memory; and deficits of comprehension (states of confusion). Some clinicians have added to this descriptive triad such conditions as emotional instability and poor judgment. Peth, a clinical geropsychologist, for instance, has originated the mnemonic device JAMCO, which stands for judgment, affect, memory, confusion, and orientation (Peth, 1976).

When the onset of such behaviors as indicated above is fairly rapid and recent, then acute brain syndrome is diagnosed, a condition believed to be reversible. Brain damage that occurs more gradually over greater duration of time, and which is caused by Alzheimer's or Pick's disease or from other causes (e.g., arteriosclerosis), is referred to as chronic brain syndrome (CBS). This latter condition is usually believed to be degenerative in nature and therefore less amenable to reversal. CBS is believed to be a function of the death of brain cells, which do not regenerate. Acute brain syndrome is believed to result from brain cell malfunction due to a wide variety of transient conditions (Pfeiffer, 1977). Two short "portable" diagnostic instruments are available that the practitioner/clinician can easily learn to administer. They are the Mental Status Questionnaire (consisting of ten questions) and the Face-Hand Test (Pfeiffer, 1975).

Given the present state of knowledge, a number of problems as well as hazards are attendant on any precise characterization of senile-like behavior. In part this is due to the paucity of research in this area. One of the major and more obvious dangers is erroneous evaluation or misdiagnosis. Great harm can be done when an acute syndrome is incorrectly assessed and the elderly individual is written off as untreatable, or when depression is mistaken for "senility" (Reichel, 1976; Geschwind, 1975).

Goldfarb (1974), Pfeiffer (1977), and others have pointed out that a number of transient (and therefore treatable) physical conditions can and do produce behaviors in the old that cause them to be labeled "senile." Among these conditions, to cite a few, are a variety of toxic conditions resulting from drugs, electrolyte imbalances, diabetes, vitamin deficiencies, hypothyroid states, hypoglycemia, tumors, dietary deficiencies, and fever. When such physical conditions are appropriately treated, the senile-like behavior is eliminated.

Senile behavior can also be produced under conditions of an exceedingly stressful environment. A number of social-behavior-oriented researchers, including design specialists, have contributed elegant studies that clearly show how the designed environment itself can induce senile behavior apart from the presence of brain damage, or how such environments can exaggerate the effects of OBS. Researchers like Kiritz and Moos (1974) at Stanford University have gathered convincing documentation on how physical health and psychological well-being can be severely compromised or even damaged by a poor or ambiguous social environment. These kinds of studies deepen our understanding of the findings of Neugarten and her associates (1974). These gerontologists have described a change in later life from an active to a more passive orientation in terms of mastery of the environment and control of one's life. The implications of other corollary data (Schwartz & Proppe, 1969) strongly indicate that this change may in large measure be coerced by environments that do not at all "fit" the aging adult suffering from multiple losses.

Severe emotional crises are also to be included among temporary conditions that can produce behaviors so maladaptive as to be labeled pathological. In certain respects, elderly persons are especially vulnerable to such stresses. In mid-1963, for example, approximately 292,000 persons with "mental disorders" were residing either in long-term-stay psychiatric facilities, nursing homes, psychiatric hospitals, homes for the aged, or related facilities. Of the 23,480 who suicided in the United States in 1970, almost 7,400 (31.5 percent) were sixty-five years or older. Yet they represent only 10 percent of the total population. There is also a relatively high incidence of alcoholism among older persons. Obviously none of this happens in a vacuum; it is indicative of the severe emotional stress to which many elderly are exposed.

Even in instances where irreversible damage to portions of the brain has occurred, experience has demonstrated that *behavior* associated with such damage (as in the case of strokes) can very often be reversed. Victims of strokes can incur paralysis on one side of the body or the other (or both) or can suffer a receptive aphasia (inability to understand messages) or an expressive aphasia (inability to speak coherently or to "name" objects). When appropriate exercise regimes or speech therapy is instituted very soon after the stroke, success in rehabilitating the stroke victim to an adequate level of function is not uncommon. What is true of intervention with physical traumas is applicable with respect to intervention in instances of emotional disruption and trauma. Great caution must be observed about leaping to the conclusion, therefore, that senile-like behavior, when observed in older persons, is irreversible and that "nothing much" can be done beyond mere custodial care taking.

Statistics paint a rather grim picture in this respect. A recent report to the Gerontological Society (Birren & Sloane, 1977) for use by the Department of Health, Education and Welfare relative to assessing manpower and training needs in mental health and illness of the aging points up the dramatic need. Table 9–1 shows in some detail the mental health needs of the population at large, including those over sixty-five, based on certain assumptions of need.

Assuming that 10 percent of the population sixty-five and over required certain mental health services, then, as can be seen from the estimates, 220,354 actually received such care (column 3). But 1,-996,646 persons sixty-five and older did not receive such services (column 8). In other words, 90.1 percent of those who were estimated to need such help did not receive it. Equivalent estimates for 1980 are 234,018 receiving care, 2,171,282 not receiving care, again based on a 10 percent estimate of need.

The dimensions of the need for elderly with respect to emotional stress is further dramatized by one of the conclusions of the report. It

TABLE 9–1.   EXTENT TO WHICH NEEDS FOR PSYCHIATRIC SERVICES WOULD BE MET IN RELATION TO VARIOUS ASSUMPTIONS OF NEED: ASSUMING 1971 USE RATES ONLY, BY AGE, UNITED STATES, 1975 AND 1980

	Estimated general population (in 000's)	Estimated patient care episodes	Estimated persons receiving care	ESTIMATED NUMBER OF PERSONS NEEDING CARE, ASSUMING			NUMBER IN NEED NOT RECEIVING CARE, ASSUMING			% UNMET NEED, ASSUMING		
				2% in need	10% in need	20% in need	2% in need	10% in need	20% in need	2% in need	10% in need	20% in need
	(1)	(2)	(3)	(4)	(5)	(6)	(7)	(8)	(9)	(10)	(11)	(12)
1975												
Total, all ages	215324	4237576	3390061	4306480	21532400	43064800	1060510	18142339	39674739	24.6	84.3	92.1
Under 18	68109	809377	647502	1362180	6810900	13621800	714678	6163398	12974298	52.5	90.5	95.2
18–24	27780	716150	572920	555600	2778000	5556000	0	2205080	4983080	0.0	79.4	89.7
25–44	53835	1504340	1203471	1076700	5383500	10767000	0	4180029	9563529	0.0	77.6	88.8
45–64	43430	932267	745814	868600	4343000	8686000	122786	3597186	7940186	14.1	82.8	91.4
65+	22170	275442	220354	443400	2217000	4434000	223046	1996646	4213646	50.3	90.1	95.0
1980												
Total, all ages	228676	4500344	3600275	4573520	22867600	45735200	1030028	19267325	42134925	22.5	84.3	92.1
Under 18	69646	859566	687653	1392920	6964600	13929200	705267	6276947	13241547	50.6	90.1	95.1
18–24	29156	760558	608446	583120	2915600	5831200	0	2307154	5222754	0.0	79.1	89.6
25–44	62332	1597622	1278097	1246640	6233200	12466400	0	4955103	11188303	0.0	79.5	89.7
45–64	43489	990076	792061	869780	4348900	8697800	77719	3556839	7905739	8.9	81.8	90.9
65+	24053	292522	234018	481060	2405300	4810600	247042	2171282	4576582	51.4	90.3	95.1

*US Bureau of the Census, Series D projection of the US population (Current Population Reports—Series P-25, No. 493)

Derivation of columns 2–12

Col. 2. Total patient care episodes obtained by applying 1971 patient episode rate per 100000 population (1968 per 100000) to the projected 1975 and 1980 total US population. Age distributions of patient care episodes obtained by applying 1971 percentage distribution of patient care episodes by age to the 1975 and 1980 estimated total patient care episodes.

Col. 3. Represents a conversion of patient care episodes into number of persons accounting for these episodes by multiplying patient care episodes by a factor of 0.80. This factor was derived from findings of the Maryland Psychiatric Case Register that every person in that register had an average of 1.2 episodes of care per year.

Col. 4 = Col. 1 × 0.02.
Col. 5 = Col. 1 × 0.10
Col. 6 = Col. 1 × 0.20
Col. 7 = Col. 4 – Col. 3. (*Note: For this column negative values were assumed to be zero, i.e. the need for services would be met. Also the total is the sum of the parts.*)

Col. 8 = Col. 5 – Col. 3.
Col. 9 = Col. 6 – Col. 3.
Col. 10 = Col. 7 ÷ Col. 4.
Col. 11 = Col. 8 ÷ Col. 5.
Col. 12 = Col. 9 ÷ Col. 6.

recommends to HEW the training of the following numbers within the next ten years to work with the aged: 1,000 psychiatrists, 2,000 clinical psychologists, 4,000 psychiatric social workers, 4,000 psychiatric nurses, 8,000 nurses' aides and related personnel, and 10,000 paraprofessional personnel.

Surveys of the concerns as well as life satisfactions of older persons repeatedly demonstrate the high incidence of loneliness and depression. It is quite evident that such emotional reactions are closely related to a variety of stressful life circumstances. These include, but are not limited to, the psychological consequences of unrelieved multiple losses (social, physical, and vocational); inadequate and inappropriate physical environments, which penalize the old and thus further impair competence; inadequate or inaccessible transportation, which creates obstacles to mobility and discourages social contact; crimes (muggings, purse snatchings, rapes) that are attendant on the special vulnerabilities of the elderly and which, by increasing anxiety and fear, tend to isolate the elderly; mandatory unemployment (retirement), which arbitrarily separates the old from a major source of satisfaction and self-worth; demeaning and patronizing attitudes on the part of others (frequently middle-aged persons), as is evident from much of the humor about aging (Davies 1977; Richman 1977).

Stress and Adaptation

Because the effects of undue stress are such common, day-by-day dangers to emotional well-being with which the aged and those who serve them must cope, additional elaboration on these issues is warranted. Hans Selye has defined stress as "the non-specific response of the body to any unusual demand made upon it" (Selye, 1977). That is, stress is the state one is in, not the agent that produces it. The stimulus may be a physical, psychological, or social one, and may originate within the individual or from an outside source. To be stressful the event must be perceived in some fashion as being threatening, unpleasant, or overwhelming (that is, beyond one's ability to cope). Selye has described three stages (1956): alarm; a stage during which the individual increases capacity to respond; exhaustion, the loss (temporarily) of functional capacity to respond.

The concept may be illustrated by the following example: "Love at first sight" is popularly thought to be signaled by the experience of a pounding heart, sweaty palms, uneasiness in the pit of the stomach, a bit of faintness, and similar physical signs. In terms of Selye's definition of stress, practically identical symptoms are likely to be experienced when you open a closet door and come face to face with a large, snarling, hungry rat. In one sense, then, the physical apparatus of the body may be said to be rather stupid. It does not distinguish between what is obviously a pleasant and what is an unpleasant experience. It responds in a nonspecific way.

This is not to say that all stress in every circumstance is necessarily "bad." Certain levels of stress, in fact, serve as an activating, alerting mechanism. But stress beyond a given level of tolerance (allowing for individual differences) can become disorganizing and even disruptive to physical and emotional well-being. This means that human beings are enormously adaptable in many respects, but they are not infinitely adaptable. Beyond a given threshold (which can vary at times even within one individual), the older person who can no longer cope (adapt) effectively will begin to behave in a maladaptive way. Clinical gerontologists have just begun to scratch the surface of the hypothesis that much of what has customarily and sometimes casually been called senility may simply represent such maladaption to overwhelming stress or trauma of one kind or another.

Stress for the older person, therefore, may consist not merely in migrain-producing noise or an unbearably stuffy room or odors so foul as to induce nausea. Understimulation can be just as stressful: a room or environment filtered and devoid of interesting things to taste, smell, feel, and hear; lack of meaningful things to do; and the loss of a sense of variety and adventure in daily living (Schwartz, 1975b).

Effects of undue stress show themselves in a large variety of ways in older persons. The experienced practitioner will become sensitive to the nuances as well as the gross indicators of stress by careful observation and by thoughtful analysis of individual history and behavior. Among the varied symptoms of stress are memory lapses and/or difficulty in concentrating; undue fatigue, loss of zest; general irritability, "nervousness," restlessness, uneasiness; emotional instability; feelings of worthlessness; dizziness; sleep disturbances or marked changes in eating or sleeping patterns; and headaches and other physical complaints.

Depression is one of the major manifestations of undue stress. It occupies a continuum of time (from a brief to extended duration) and a continuum of degree (from a mild state of pessimism to a deep, pervasive, black gloom and even despair). Along these dimensions one may see in an older person a general withdrawal of interest, a slowing down of activity, sometimes to the point of complete immobility when the depression is very pronounced. A not uncommon indicator of depression is the marked inclination to spend much time dozing in chairs or sleeping in bed, an inclination which is associated in older persons, too, with a high degree of boredom. The common physical signs of depression in older persons are appetite disturbances, weight loss, an unusual degree of fatigue or feeling of malaise, and constipation

(Pfeiffer, 1977). Also associated with depression is crying, of course, although on occasion individuals will report that they *feel* like crying but cannot actually do so. It is also important to recognize that a depressed older person may deny being depressed yet may develop physical ailments. This is where the perceptive observer or interviewer will look for the relevant instances of stress.

A major source of stress and thus a contributor to depression (and one frequently overlooked) is the feeling of helplessness—that is, the feeling of having lost direction and control over one's own life. Most notably the research by Seligman (1973) has dramatically illuminated this issue. Frail elderly particularly are vulnerable to this feeling, often as a result of particular environments, which we shall discuss shortly. Most gerontologists will acknowledge that many older persons die simply because they have come to feel useless, helpless, and that they have no good reason to go on. We know that certain life changes can induce physical sickness and even death (Rahe, 1974). Indeed, Perlmuter and Monty (1977) have found that even the *illusion* of control over one's actions or destiny can significantly improve performance in a variety of situations, and the converse, of course, is true, too.

In some instances the response to undue stress is exhibited through an almost morbid preoccupation with aches, pains, illness, and disease (hypochondriasis). Sometimes the response follows a pattern of suspiciousness (in its milder forms), which can develop into a full-blown paranoia (where elaborate systems of persecution and hatred are generated). Yet here, too, an assessment of the behavior of aged persons must follow a cautious course: Even so-called paranoids can have real enemies and those who complain excessively of ill-health can have real aches, pains, and disease.

Drugs

Still another potential contributor to disrupted behavior in the elderly is the misuse or abuse of drugs, not an uncommon phenomenon. An investigation of drug usage by older persons was done by faculty researchers at the USC School of Pharmacy (Kayne & Cheung, 1975). They studied the utilization of drugs within randomly selected long-term-care facilities located in Los Angeles County. They found that their sample of older persons ingested an average of 8.9 drugs per day. The investigators also found an average medication error rate of 21.8 percent. Medication errors were defined as wrong drugs, wrong dose, wrong patient, missed dose, or inappropriate dosing interval. The most frequent type of medication error was missed dose (52 percent).

What also worries physicians and other providers of service to the elderly is repeatedly uncovering drugs that have been hoarded over extended periods of time. The effects are magnified by those aged who tend to be "physician shoppers"—that is, those who go from one physician to another and in the course of time accumulate a substantial stockpile of unused drugs prescribed for a variety of purposes. Outdated medications can be useless or worse, and exchange of drugs among friends can increase the potential hazards of toxicity through inappropriate usage.

Of even greater clinical significance is the fact that many commonly used drugs have a substantially different effect upon the older than they do upon the younger person. This occurs because of the changes in renal and hepatic efficiency with advanced years. Such changes make the older person more prone to side effects and adverse reactions (Eisdorfer & Stotsky, 1977). Increased sensitivity may require a lower dosage of psychoactive drugs in elderly persons (over 50 percent less in many cases). For example, a given dosage appropriate for a thirty-year-old can produce overwhelming or even lethal effects in the eighty-year-old. Also the interaction of certain medications (e.g., diuretics, corticosteroids, barbiturates, and even multivitamin preparations containing vitamin K) can decrease drug sensitivity. Antidepressants, sedatives, and tranquilizers (such as Mellaril, Valium, and Librium) as well as analgesics and vasodilators (all of which are frequently prescribed for older persons) are capable of generating toxic effects in certain elderly individuals and thus produce senile-like behaviors (Eisdorfer & Faun, 1973). There are some physicians, not accustomed to working with the elderly, who are not familiar with these differential effects in the aged.

Competence and Coping

Within the past decade increasing attention has been paid to the design of so-called prosthetic environments for older persons, especially institutionalized elderly. Such environments are called prosthetic because they are intended to eliminate elements that penalize impaired or frail elderly, and thus literally compensate for their losses. Many professionals who provide services to institutionalized aged recognize the necessity of such environments as basic to the maintenance of competent functioning. Indeed, the matter of competent functioning may well be of more practical social significance for the aged than intelligence. Even so eminent a psychologist as David McClelland (1973) of Harvard University has suggested that we ought to test for competence rather than intelligence, an argument further elaborated and documented in aging by Jerome Fisher (1973).

Gerontologists are able to define competence very well: ". . . competence is characterized by a flexible, adaptable, and personally reward-

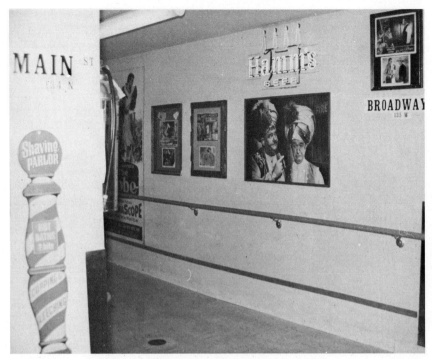

An "intersection" in a nursing home which uses street signs, old posters, and advertising signs to "normalize" life to provide environmental cues and the visual stimulation so necessary to competent functioning.

ing response to environmental demands, whatever they may be" (Kuypers & Bengston, 1960). Adaptation of the individual to life situations is the focus of such definitions. This is an appropriate point of view. Nevertheless, we raise the question as to why the entire burden must be placed on the older person as responder. A much stronger case can be made for the reverse situation, that is, designing the environment to fit the older individual (Lawton, 1974).

The application of this principle is particularly congruent with respect to any congregate living, especially to long-term-care facilities for the aged. It is equally applicable to all environments in which elderly persons find themselves. A compelling rationale for this is provided by such research as that of Rudolph Moos and his associates (Kiritz & Moos, 1974) and (Moos, 1976) at Stanford University. In their perceptive and creative analysis of social environments they have developed an elaborate scheme for categorizing elements of the environment that contribute to competent functioning and emotional and physical well-being. They have refined their observations of the environment into three major components:

1. *Relationship dimensions:* These refer to the degree to which individuals are involved in their environment and the extent to which each helps and assists the other. This dimension focuses on the sense of belongingness. Other descriptive words relevant to this environmental dimension are affiliation, peer cohesion, and staff support.

2. *Personal development dimension:* These refer to self-enhancement and self-actualization possibilities within a given environment. Independence, practical orientation, and responsibility are three of the subcategories within this dimension cited by the researchers. Privacy options, suggested by some researchers as a necessary environmental component for the maintenance of the oldster's self-esteem (Aloia, 1973; Meier, 1976), might also be included in this dimension.

3. *System maintenance and system change dimensions:* The primary categories here are order and organization, clarity, control, and change. The implication is that individuals cope much more effectively in unambiguous environments where it is easy to negotiate space, where there is sufficient self-direction and self-initiated modification.

There appears to be little question about the applicability and relevance of these dimensions in serving basic environmental needs of older persons. These dimensions should be able to be translated directly into adequate environmental support, environmental cues, and environmental stimulation as prerequisites for continued competent functioning in daily living for the aged.

Figure 9–3 shows a schematic suggested by Kiritz and Moos which can guide the gerontologist who wishes to help develop increased competence in an older population, especially those elderly who have accumulated a substantial number of disabilities. The model shows that social environmental stimuli are to be judged in terms of their impact upon the individual, not as they "are," but how they are perceived by the individual. Adaptation as exhibited in behavior is the outcome of a complex process strongly influenced by the individual's personality

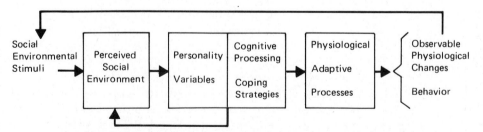

FIGURE 9–3.   CONCEPTUAL MODEL FOR THE RELATIONSHIP BETWEEN SOCIAL ENVIRONMENT AND OBSERVABLE PHYSIOLOGICAL CHANGES

TABLE 9–2. PSYCHOSOCIAL NEEDS BY LEVEL OF CARE FREQUENCY AND PERCENTAGE DISTRIBUTION

Needs	TOTAL				SKILLED NURSING FACILITY				INTERMEDIATE CARE FACILITY I				INTERMEDIATE CARE FACILITY II			
	N	Freq.	%	Rank	N	Freq.	%	Rank	N	Freq.	%	Rank	N	Freq.	%	Rank
1. Need to enrich daily life	421	246	58.4	1	210	162	77.1	1	125	56	44.8	1	86	28	32.6	2
2. Compensation for poor vision	415	196	47.2	2	205	106	51.7	6	124	48	38.7	3	86	42	48.8	1
3. Interaction with residents	405	174	43.0	3	205	151	73.6	2	114	21	18.4	14	86	23	26.7	4
4. Recent memory	396	161	40.7	4	185	97	52.4	5	125	49	39.2	2	86	15	17.4	5
5. More self-reliance	419	148	35.3	5	208	120	57.7	3	125	27	21.6	11	86	1	1.2	21
6. Compensation for hearing	417	136	32.6	6	206	71	34.5	12	125	38	30.4	6	86	27	31.4	3
7. Other	418	136	32.5	7	207	115	55.6	4	125	13	10.4	20	86	8	9.3	9
8. Orientation to time	399	118	29.6	8	188	97	51.5	7	125	39	31.2	5	86	12	14.0	6
9. Orientation to place	398	115	28.9	9	187	81	43.3	8	125	28	22.4	10	86	6	7.0	14
10. Remote memory	394	113	28.7	10	183	73	39.9	9	125	30	24.0	9	86	10	11.6	7
11. Overall communication	416	109	26.2	11	205	80	39.0	10	125	27	21.6	11	86	2	2.3	19
12. Tendency to stay in own room	419	109	26.0	12	208	57	27.4	17	125	45	36.0	4	86	7	8.1	10
13. Satisfaction with life in facility	382	99	25.9	13	172	58	33.7	13	126	32	25.4	8	84	9	10.7	8
14. Interaction with family	408	101	24.8	14	200	78	39.0	10	125	14	11.2	19	83	9	10.8	25
15. Self-concept	391	87	22.3	15	183	47	25.7	18	123	34	27.6	7	85	6	7.1	13
16. Concern with death and dying	261	55	21.1	16	108	36	33.3	14	73	13	17.8	15	80	6	7.5	12
17. Interaction with staff	419	75	17.9	17	209	64	30.6	16	124	10	8.1	21	86	1	1.2	21
18. Tendency to be restricted-movement	418	64	15.3	18	207	64	30.9	15	125	0	0	27	86	0	0	26
19. Personal decision-making ability	403	60	14.9	19	194	28	14.4	23	123	25	20.3	13	86	7	8.1	10
20. Personal appearance	407	55	13.5	20	205	43	21.0	19	116	8	6.9	23	86	4	4.7	17
21. Ability to accept change in schedule	408	53	13.0	21	202	28	13.9	24	123	21	17.1	16	83	4	4.8	16
22. Ability to target communication	392	50	12.8	22	202	41	20.3	20	104	8	7.7	22	86	1	1.2	21
23. Adjustment to present residence	409	51	12.5	23	200	31	15.5	22	123	15	12.2	18	86	5	5.8	15
24. Ability to name objects	232*	27	11.6	24	146	27	18.5	21	–	–	–	–	86	0	0	26
25. Life review	360	39	10.8	25	162	19	11.7	25	113	17	15.1	17	85	3	3.5	18
26. Tendency to wander	417	28	6.7	26	206	21	10.2	26	125	5	4.0	24	86	2	2.3	19
27. Ability to recognize objects	400	22	5.5	27	190	19	10.0	27	124	3	2.4	26	86	0	0	26
28. Smell, touch, taste	405	11	2.7	28	198	7	3.5	28	121	3	2.5	25	86	1	1.2	21

*Data were not collected for this item in ICF I; total represents only ICF II and SNF.

SOURCE: From an NIMH project report on the human development program of the Ebenezer Society, 2626 Park Ave., Minneapolis, Minn., 1975. NIMH Grant R12-MH 2392402.

makeup, his intellectual and emotional capabilities, and his available repertory of coping strategies. Increased longevity allows for greater differentiation based on the individual's history of experience. Thus older individuals become more and more psychologically unique, a fact reflected in individual coping strategies.

The implications of this concept of "prosthetic," compensating environments, which are adaptive to the special needs of older persons, are fairly obvious. Environments that are appropriate, nonthreatening, and non-anxiety-arousing (and perceived to be so) and which literally assist the aged are calculated to make such common activities as shopping in a supermarket, transacting business in a bank, using the public library or a shopping center, or getting to theaters, lectures, or social events via public transportation, a continuing measure of success in activities of daily living, rather than a source of apprehension.

A further implication of the notion of the prosthetic environment for aged persons is that priorities assigned to the design of space for institutionalized aged must emphasize meeting the psychosocial needs of those aged. Studies by researchers at the Ebenezer Society (Rupprecht et al., 1976) have produced the rank order listing of such needs as they were articulated by elderly long-term-care residents (see Table 9–2).

This listing suggests that physical care is an important need, but for most elderly people it does not have highest priority. This observation is supported by the data of a survey done for the National Council on the Aging (Harris, 1976). When persons sixty-five and older were asked what constitute "serious problems" in their lives, only 26 percent with incomes under $7,000 annually replied that poor health is such a problem. Those with greater income were even less inclined to identify poor health as a very serious problem: 9 percent affirmative for those with income of $7–14,000, 11 percent for those with income of $15,-000. This does not mean that older people are not concerned about health. It does mean that those things that make life worthwhile take precedence for the elderly over things that make continuation of life possible.

SELF-ESTEEM

No discussion of the psychology of aging would be complete without some attention to the matter of self-esteem in the later years. Indeed, this aspect of personality dynamics constitutes the linchpin* of all programs and services for the aged. It would be virtually impossible

---

*Webster defines linchpin as: "something that serves to hold together the elements of a complex."

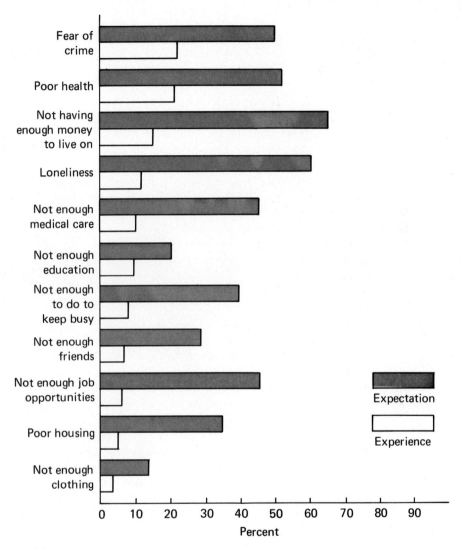

Figure 9–4. "SERIOUS" PROBLEMS OF OLDER PEOPLE (PUBLIC EX-
PECTATIONS VERSUS PERSONAL EXPERIENCE)

to define any properties of quality of life for the aged that do not in
some fashion impinge upon their sense of self-worth (Schwartz,
1975b). By the same token, this very same criterion is reflected in the
statements of older persons who describe what makes life worthwhile
for them.

Basically, self-esteem is developed in the individual via those innu-
merable events, large and small, that provide emotional support and

Many older persons are able to function very well, even creatively, in their later years. Many factors in the early and middle years contribute to psychological well-being in old age.

psychological reward. Such events range from the cuddling and stroking of the newborn to the public recognition of certificates and other awards of adult life. All such events mirror back to the individual an image of self that says, "You belong, you count, you have an impact, you are important." Along with this go the internal signals that derive from a growing sense of mastery and control over oneself and the environment which tells the individual, "You are effective."

With the increasing accumulation of multiple losses (physical, social, vocational) in the middle and later years, the positive reflections that form the basis of self-esteem become blurred in some instances quite negative.

There are many ways this can occur. Perhaps the most prevalent way, and one that is usually masked because done in the name of "helping," is infantilizing the aged person. This is a trap into which professionals too easily fall. It consists merely in taking over, doing much more for older persons than they actually require or ask for. It is often done in the interest of safety (as if all hazards in life could be eliminated), efficiency (as if dressing quickly and the like were essential to life satisfaction), and cleanliness (as if not spilling food from a tremorous hand were to be avoided at all costs). The trade-off for getting things done for the elderly in a brisk, efficient, neat manner and in a less time-consuming way—things they could do for themselves—infantilizes the old and thus tends to reduce their sense of competence, self-worth, and self-esteem. If self-esteem is thus consistently eroded, it can be substantially diminished and even destroyed. The consequences of that have already been discussed. The antidote to diminished function or support is by way of direct or indirect interventions that can provide compensations for loss and other supports in an appropriate way.

INTERVENTION STRATEGIES

Interventions often take the form of physical, social, and psychological compensations and supports. Intervention strategies with respect to physical losses are much better understood in our society because of the many precedents and models we have. Compensations for physical loss have become almost a matter of routine planning: a prosthetic limb for the amputee, eyeglasses for defective visions, hearing aids, heart pacers, false teeth, canes, "walkers," and the like. All these attachments to the body constitute compensatory devices. Their relevance to certain needs of an older population is beyond debate.

We have only begun to study and learn more about other compensating strategies and techniques (e.g., via the prosthetic environment) and the need for compensating other than physical losses. The appalling neglect on the part of the professional communities in the past of the emotional well-being (loosely and perhaps inappropriately called "mental health") of those in later life has been so well documented as to have now become a cliché. Earlier comment in this chapter has touched on this. Much of this neglect has been attributed to the disinterest and uncertainty about the usefulness of sustained specialized services to the aged on the part of many professional groups (psychologists, physicians, clergy, psychiatrists, attorneys, dentists, to name a few), to say nothing of legislators and other policymakers. This is changing through the efforts of gerontologists and organized groups of elderly, but it is changing, unfortunately, at a slow rate.

Given the current state of the art, much of what we learn from the psychology of aging and from clinical work in particular teaches us the following:

1. The elderly, as a group, need considerable assistance of a relevant, appropriate nature; they need also to learn how to cope with aging (Kalish, 1969).

2. The limits of "helping" must be recognized so that it does not become infantilizing, "taking over," or patronizing in manner.

3. When properly motivated, older persons are very responsive to therapeutic and compensatory interventions.

4. The focus on strategies that include appropriate environmental designs aimed at competent functioning is much more productive than mere descriptions and diagnoses of pathologies in old age.

Prosthetic devices attached to the body have already been mentioned as a class of intervention strategies for physical losses. To such a list might be added the careful dissemination of information about differential effects of common drugs and a more conscientious monitoring of drug usage. Vasodilators and hyperbaric oxygenation (oxygen administered under high pressure) have also been found to increase the oxygen supply to the brain and thus increase alertness, cognitive acuity, and a feeling of well-being. In the case of drug and mood-changing agents where the effort and cost are not prohibitive, permanent therapeutic effects have appeared to be quite unremarkable and often outweighed by the hazards involved.

How effective are psychological therapies and social interventions? An increasing interest in and design of prosthetic (compensatory) environments reflects the general notion of its appropriateness and usefulness. Although much work needs to be done to specify and describe variables in such research, studies of the effects of therapeutic intervention via the environment have shown positive results. One study of wandering behavior among older people in a nursing home (Rupprecht et al., 1976), one of the first such investigations, indicated that wandering behavior occurred (in the most active) only about 50.1 percent of the time and was not simply a function of brain damage; it was not significantly associated with sex, marital status, age, stroke, or heart disease. Wandering was not necessarily random behavior; it was influenced by environmental circumstances. Further, lifelong habits and social experiences might be important determinants of such wandering behavior. Applied research such as this, carried out in the living laboratory, is much needed by service providers and practitioners in all professions.

Psychological therapies during the early part of this century were dominated by psychoanalytic theory, which was neither attuned to nor available to people of advanced age. With the rise of the existential, reality, transactional, and "here-and-now" schools of thought (derived in large measure from Sullivan's and Rogers' interpersonal formulations), individual and group counseling of the aged and their families has begun to achieve legitimacy.

This is not to say that counseling of older persons did not exist.

Much of it was done informally by professionals (most notably by social workers) as an incidental service and by volunteer helpers. Generally such efforts were viewed as a supportive, kind gesture. Until recently, no serious effort was made to train counselor/therapists in a regular and systematic way.

Within the past half decade the picture has begun to change dramatically. Strong voices are being heard throughout the country ("Special Issue on Counseling," 1976) arguing for the validity and efficacy of counseling and therapy for the aged. More than that, a strong case is made for the utilization of para- and non-professionals in counseling (Oden, 1974). Carkhuff and Truax (1965) have written extensively on the need to develop empathy, warmth, and genuineness as necessary characteristics for effective counseling. Such traits, these investigators contend along with Oden, open the door wide to nonprofessional counselors and peer counselors of older adults.

Although the training of the indigenous nonprofessional is not new, training older persons to be counselors of their peers has proved to be an effective strategy. This is evident from the pilot work in this area being done by such groups as the Andrus Gerontology Center at the University of Southern California, which has been training older volunteers to be peer counselors in one-to-one and group counseling of elderly persons (including minority elderly) and their families and is evaluating the effectiveness of such training. Another pioneer in peer counselor training is the four-year-old program at Oakland University in Michigan, which has specialized in "growth group" counseling of the elderly. Currently, training of nonprofessionals and, in more limited fashion, professionals for counseling older adults has sprouted all across the country.

The amazing proliferation of varied programs of therapeutic intervention in recent years may be viewed in terms of what businessmen call "growth industries." Older volunteer outreach groups (RSVP), nutritional programs (Meals-on-Wheels), legal counseling, Foster Grandparent programs, widow-to-widow counseling, day activities programs and multiservice centers, ombudsman programs, hospices (centers that provide familial and emotional support to the terminally ill), adult education reentry and special interest educational programs: All these fall within a widening matrix of intervention strategies for older persons.

Among the many intervention strategies is the increasing attention of and input by gerontologists to TV and other media as influencers of public attitudes toward the aged. One of the foremost pioneers in the use of TV for use by and in behalf of the aged is Richard Davis at the University of Southern California's Gerontology Center. His research in this area and strong advocacy have been instrumental in developing public broadcasts, special films, and TV documentaries on the aged which have stimulated much interest and activity in this area (see chapter 12).

SUMMARY

Studies in the learning, memory, and intelligence of the aging indicate that when cross-sectional data are used older persons perform less well than do younger individuals. On a longitudinal basis this finding is reversed, especially when such "outside" variables as time constraints, fatigue, and poor motivation are removed. Research indicates that the intellectual capacity of the older individual does not decline as a function of age; the information of the old may simply become obsolete.

Many of the differences between groups may have little practical significance when applied to individuals. Where dealing with the aged on an individual basis, competence in daily living should then be the primary factor. The consistency of personality must be taken into account in understanding behavior. But, in addition, the characteristics of the environment and its interaction with the individual are important in understanding the behavior of older individuals. As a consequence, maladaptive (senile) behavior may be seen as often induced by transient physical, stress, and environmental causes. Help and assistance, if appropriately designed, are called for, and many such intervention strategies are now unfolding. Assistance to the elderly must be compensatory in nature and must always be so presented as to contribute to the maintenance of self-esteem in the elderly.

REFERENCES

Aloia, A. J. "Relations between Perceived Privacy Options, Self-esteem, and Internal Control among Aged People" (doctoral dissertation, California School of Professional Psychology, Los Angeles, 1973).

Anonymous. "How Old Is Old?" *The New York Times,* August 8, 1977.

Arenberg, D., and E. Robertson-Tchabo. "Learning and Aging." In J. Birren and K. W. Schaie (eds.), *Handbook of the Psychology of Aging.* New York: Van Nostrand Reinhold, 1977.

Birren, J., and J. Renner. "Research on the Psychology of Aging." In J. Birren and K. W. Schaie (eds.), *Handbook of the Psychology of Aging.* New York: Van Nostrand Reinhold, 1977.

Birren, J., and B. Sloane. "Manpower and Training Needs in Mental Health and Illness of the Aging." A Report to the Gerontological Society for the Committee to Study Mental Health and Illness of the Aging, for the Secretary of the Department of Health, Education and Welfare, 1977.

Botwinick, J. "Intellectual Abilities." In J. Birren and K. W. Schaie (eds.), *Handbook of the Psychology of Aging.* New York: Van Nostrand Reinhold, 1977.

Canestrari, R. E., Jr. "Paced and Self-paced Learning in Young and Elderly Adults." *Journal of Gerontology,* 1963, 18:2.

Carkhuff, R., and C. Truax. "Training in Counseling and Psychotherapy." *Journal of Consulting Psychology,* 1965, 29.

Craik, F. I. M. "Age Differences in Human Memory." In J. Birren and K. W. Schaie (eds.), *Handbook of the Psychology of Aging.* New York: Van Nostrand Reinhold, 1977.

Davies, L. J. "Attitudes toward Old Age and Aging as Shown by Humor." *The Gerontologist,* 1977, 17:3.

Eisdorfer, C., and W. E. Faun (eds.). *Psychopharmacology and Aging.* New York: Plenum Press, 1973.

Eisdorfer, C., and B. Stotsky. "Intervention Treatment, and Rehabilitation of Psychiatric Disorders." In J. Birren and K. W. Schaie (eds.), *Handbook of the Psychology of Aging.* New York: Van Nostrand Reinhold, 1977.

Fisher, J. "Competence, Effectiveness, Intellectual Functioning, and Aging." *The Gerontologist,* 1973, 13:1.

Furry, C., and P. Baltes. "The Effect of Age Differences in Ability-Extraneous Performance Variables on the Assessment of Intelligence in Children, Adults, and the Elderly." *Journal of Gerontology,* 1973, 28:1.

Geschwind, N. "Clinical Pathology Conference." *New England Journal of Medicine,* April 1975.

Gilbert, J. G. "Thirty-five-Year Follow-up Study of Intellectual Functioning." *Journal of Gerontology,* 1973, 28:1.

Goldfarb, A. *Aging and Organic Brain Syndrome.* Health Learning Systems, Inc. Bloomfield, N.J., 1974.

Goldfarb, A. Personal communication, 1976.

Harris, Louis, and Associates, Inc. "The Myth and Reality of Aging in America." A survey for the National Council on the Aging, Washington, D.C., 1976.

Jarvik, L., and J. Blum. "Cognitive Declines as Predictors of Mortality in Twin Pairs: A 20-year Longitudinal Study of Aging." In E. Palmore and F. Jeffers (eds.), *Prediction of Life Span.* Boston: D.C. Heath, 1971.

Kalish, R. *The Dependencies of Old People.* Ann Arbor: Institute of Gerontology, University of Michigan—Wayne State, 1969.

Kayne, R., and A. Cheung. "An Application of Clinical Pharmacy in Extended Care Facilities." In R. Davis (ed.), *Drugs and the Elderly.* Andrus Gerontology Center, University of Southern California, Los Angeles, 1975.

Kiritz, S., and R. Moos. "Physiological Effects of Social Environments." *Psychosomatic Medicine,* 1974, 36:2.

Kleemeier, R. "Terminal Drop-Intellectual Changes." Proceedings of the Social Statistics Section of the American Statistics Society, 1962.

Kramer, M. "Issues in the Development of Statistical and Epidemiological Data for Mental Health Services Research." *Psychological Medicine,* 1976,6.

Kuypers, J., and V. Bengston. "Competence, Social Breakdown, and Humanism." In A. Feldman (ed.), *Community Mental Health and Aging: An Overview.* Los Angeles: University of Southern California Press, 1960.

Lawton, M. P. "Coping Behavior and the Environment of Older People." In A. Schwartz and I. Mensh (eds.), *Professional Obligations and Approaches to the Aged.* Springfield, Ill.: Charles C Thomas, 1974.

McClelland, D. "Testing for Competence Rather Than for 'Intelligence.'" *American Psychologist,* January 1973.

Masters, W., and V. Johnson. *Human Sexual Response.* Boston: Little, Brown, 1966.

Meier, L. "Modes of Privacy and Self-esteem among Institutionalized Aged." Master's thesis, Leonard Davis School of Gerontology, University of Southern California, Los Angeles, 1976.

Moos, R. *The Human Context: Environmental Determinants of Behavior.* New York: Wiley-Interscience, 1976.

Neugarten, B., and Associates. *Personality in Middle and Later Life.* New York: Atherton Press, 1974.

Oden, T. "A Populist's View of Psychotherapeutic Deprofessionalization." *Humanistic Psychology,* 1974, 14:2.

Perlmuter, L., and R. Monty. "The Importance of Perceived Control: Fact or Fantasy?" *American Scientist,* 1977, 65: November–December.

Peterson, J. *Married Love in the Middle Years.* New York: Association Press, 1968.

Peth, P. "Personal Communication." In I. Burnside (ed.), *Nursing and the Aged.* New York: McGraw-Hill, 1976.

Pfeiffer, E. "Functional Assessment: The OARS Multidimensional Function Assessment Questionnaire." Duke University Center, Durham, N.C., 1975.

Pfeiffer, E. "Psychopathology and Social Pathology." In J. Birren and K. W. Schaie (eds.), *Handbook of the Psychology of Aging.* New York: Van Nostrand Reinhold, 1977.

Rahe, R. "Life Change and Subsequent Illness." In E. Gunderson and R. Rahe (eds.), *Life Stress and Illness.* Springfield, Ill.: Charles C Thomas, 1974.

Reichel, W. "Organic Brain Syndromes in the Elderly." *Hospital Practice,* May 1976.

Richman, J. "The Foolishness and Wisdom of Age: Attitudes toward the Elderly as Reflected in Jokes." *The Gerontologist,* 1977, 17:3.

Rupprecht, P., J. Pyrek, and L. Snyder. "A Study of Wandering among Older People in a Skilled Nursing Facility." Research Report to NIMH, Grant 23924, Ebenezer Society, 2626 Park Ave., Minneapolis, Minn., 1976.

Schaie, K. W. "Age Changes in Adult Intelligence." In D. Woodruff and J.

Birren (eds.), *Aging: Scientific Perspectives and Social Issues.* New York: D. Van Nostrand, 1975.

Schaie, K. W., and G. Labouvie-Vief. "Generational vs. Ontogenetic Components of Change in Adult Cognitive Functioning." *Developmental Psychology,* 1974, 10.

Schaie, K. W., and C. R. Strother. "A Cross-sequential Study of Age Changes in Cognitive Behavior." *Psychological Bulletin,* 1968,70.

Schwartz, A. "An Observation on Self-esteem as the Linchpin of Quality of Life for the Aged." *The Gerontologist,* 1975a, 15:5.

Schwartz, A. "Planning Micro-environments for the Aged." In D. Woodruff and J. Birren (eds.), *Aging: Scientific Perspectives and Social Issues.* New York: D. Van Nostrand, 1975b.

Schwartz, A., and H. Proppe. "Perceptions of Privacy among Institutionalized Aged." Proceedings, American Psychological Association, 1969.

Seligman, M. "Fall into Helplessness." *Psychology Today,* June 1973.

Selye, H. "Secret of Coping with Stress." *U.S. News and World Report,* March 21, 1977.

Selye, H. *The Stress of Life.* New York: McGraw-Hill, 1956.

"Special Issue on Counseling Over the Life Span." Washington, D.C.: *Personnel and Guidance Journal,* American Personnel and Guidance Association, 1976.

Sviland, M. "Helping Elderly Couples Become Sexually Liberated." *The Counseling Psychologist,* 1975, 5:1.

Wechsler, D. *The Measurement and Appraisal of Adult Intelligence.* 4th ed. Baltimore: Williams and Wilkins, 1958.

FOR FURTHER READING

Baltes, P., and K. Schaie. "Aging and I.Q.: The Myth of the Twilight Years." *Psychology Today,* July 1974.

Birren, J. "Toward an Experimental Psychology of Aging." *American Psychologist,* 1970, 25:2.

Bourestom, N. "Evaluation of Mental Health Programs for the Elderly." *Aging and Human Development,* 1970, 1:3.

Davies, L. J. "Attitudes toward Old Age and Aging as Shown by Humor." *The Gerontologist,* 1977, 17:3.

Downey, G. "The Next Patient Right: Sex in the Nursing Home." *Modern Health Care,* June 1974.

Gaitz, C. M., and P. Baer. "Diagnostic Assessment of the Elderly: A Multifunctional Model." *The Gerontologist,* 1970, 10:1.

Lawton, M. P., and L. Gottesman. "Psychological Services to the Elderly." *American Psychologist,* 1974, 29:9.

Lieberman, M. "Adaptive Processes in Late Life." In N. Datan and

L. Ginsburg (eds.), *Life Span Developmental Psychology: Normative Life Crises.* New York: Academic Press, 1975.

Ornstein, R. *The Psychology of Consciousness.* 2d ed. New York: Harcourt Brace Jovanovich, 1976.

Rosenhans, D. "On Being Sane in Insane Places." *Science,* 1973, 19:1.

Simon, A., M. Lowenthal, and L. Epstein. *Crisis and Intervention: The Fate of the Elderly Mental Patient.* San Francisco: Jossey-Bass, 1970.

Solnick, R. (ed.). *Sexuality and Aging,* rev. ed. University of Southern California, Los Angeles, 1976.

CHAPTER 10 | Death, Dying, and Grieving

I cannot tell how I shall behave when aches and
decrepitude come, or that illness which will thrust me,
roughly or not so roughly, out of this world . . . it does not
seem to me sensible to dwell upon unpleasant things
before they have even happened. I only beg that I may,
without weakening, remain true to the oaths that I have
inwardly sworn; honor the life dwelling within me to its
very last, and even if only a spark remains to me, treat it
still as a holy flame.

MAURICE GOUDEKET, *The Delights of Growing Old* (1966)

*There is much resistance to dealing with death and the dying. This
chapter can be used to help each student begin to come to terms with
his or her own apprehensions about dying, in whatever manner it may
seem most appropriate to do so.*

*In this chapter the student is led to examine the process of dying
(nonphysiological) and the issues associated with this universal event.
Within the same context the role of religion is also considered. Included
is a very necessary discussion of the conspiracy of silence and its
effects upon the dying person.*

*Further discussion in the chapter deals with rituals associated with
dying and death, ways in which society handles the dying process, and
who some of the major actors are in this life drama.*

A well-known radio newscaster a generation ago customarily concluded his newscast by referring to the death of some famous person-

age with the words, "Death came today, as it must for all men, to . . . ." This is just one of the many events that tend to remind us of human mortality and the inevitability of death. A constant litany throughout the Old Testament is the poetic phrase, "he was gathered unto his fathers." In spite of Freud's insistence upon the importance of mourning, the reaction to grief and bereavement has been little studied by psychologists and psychiatrists until recent years. As gerontology has broadened its data base in the study of the aging process, the characteristics of each succeeding generation, and the differences between generations, it has also focused increasing attention upon the process of dying and death (Parkes, 1972).

This discussion ought to start with a simple definition of death. We ought to have a clear construct that we can use in further discussions in the chapter. But the student will soon discover that a precise definition of death has not surfaced; in fact the question of what death means is currently a topic that troubles both the courts and physicians.

Medical signs of death are fairly standard. They are cessation of respiration and heartbeat, changes in the eye, insensibility to electrical stimuli, rigor mortis, pallor, hypostasis, and relaxation of the sphincters (Mant, 1976). A further dimension involves cellular death. Transplantation is dependent upon organ removal before cellular death occurs. Mant raises the issue this way: ". . . when is the person from whom the organ is to be removed in a state which is incompatible with the persistence of life?" The more quickly the organs are removed, the greater are the chances for the grafted organ to survive.

A third aspect of the modern definition of death has to do with "brain death." "Brain death" is marked by a flat EEG (electroencephalogram), which shows a lack of brain function. If some vital brain cells are deprived of oxygen for even a few seconds, they die and can never be restored. But other parts of the brain are hardier and may survive temporary trauma. So an individual may lose his personality, thought processes, and voluntary movement and still have a heartbeat (Mant, 1976).

In the Western world a final judgment regarding death is recorded on a death certificate that specifies time and cause of death. Shneidman (1976) estimates that 10 to 15 percent of all coroners' cases are "equivocal" as to cause of death. Shneidman thinks that the death certificate is anachronistic because it is based on the premise that a person is only a "biological machine" to which "things happen." He would introduce the dimension of intentionality under a new category on the death certificate: "imputed lethality," with four designations— "high," "medium," "low," "absent." He describes each of these dimensions carefully. For instance, the low imputed lethality "would indicate that the decedent played some small but insignificant role in effecting or hastening his own demise" (Shneidman, 1976). The value of adding this dimension would provide basic research data about the mental status of any individual and give a much fairer summary of the death episode.

HOW IT IS TO DIE

No one has returned to describe what it is like to be dead—not to think, or laugh, or love. But we do know something about the feelings and reactions of persons about death. Kalish (1976) lists three reasons why the meaning of death is different for older persons:

1. The anticipated life span is normally foreshortened. . . .

2. Older persons . . . often perceive themselves as not having sufficient futurity to deserve a major investment of the resources of others. . . .

3. Older persons receive more reminders of impending death from within their bodies. . . .

Kalish reasons that these factors encourage disengagement psychologically and socially to provide a detachment that would make the last days meaningful. One can then ". . . turn inward, contemplate the meaning of the past in reminiscence, concern for past and the future, and pull back from the emotional pain that occurs when attachments are lost or broken" (Kalish, 1976).

The same writer suggests three meanings of death for older persons. The first has to do with the way a sense of finitude organizes our time. Table 10–1 contrasts the answers of 434 Los Angeles County residents to a question of what they would do if they knew they were to die in thirty days.

The second meaning is *death as loss*. There is a devastating sense of loss of self, with all the self's meaningful relationships. Shneidman's book (1976) ends with a poem by a very sensitive young man who is dying. The last lines are:

Step lightly, we're walking home now.
The clouds take every shape.
We climb up the boulders, there is no plateau.
We cross the stream and walk up the slope.
See, the hawk is diving.
The plain stretches out ahead.
Then the hills, the valleys, the meadows
Keep moving people. How could I not be among you?

TABLE 10–1.   ROLE CHOICES WITH LIMITED LIFE EXPECTANCY

	AGE (BY PERCENT)		
	20–39	*40–59*	*60+*
Marked change in life-style, self-related (travel, sex, experiences, etc.)	24	15	9
Inner-life centered (read, contemplate, pray)	14	14	37
Focus concern on others, be with loved ones	29	25	12
Attempt to complete projects, tie up loose ends	11	10	3
No change in life-style	17	29	31
Other	5	6	8

SOURCE: Kalish (1976).

"How Could I Not Be Among You?" is an anguished cry of loss so great as to reflect all of our own abhorrence of losing the clouds, the stream, the birds, the people—life. There are other losses. For men, an inability to care for dependents and for women, the grief caused for friends and family (Kalish, 1976).

A third reaction for others is that death is punishment for sin. Kalish tested this in his study and found this attitude directed more to the death of a young person than an older one. Furthermore, if an older person has suffered a long and painful disease, death may be viewed as a relief or blessing.

Gerontologists also have recognized that the study of dying and death is not done without some reluctance. It does generate some resistance. Humans cherish life so highly that they find it difficult to contemplate its end. While the harvesting hand of time cannot be stayed, the reality of death is often denied in many subtle ways: by the elaborate cosmetology of the undertaker, by the vocabulary of the mourners, by the conspiracy of silence on the part of family, even on the part of professional helpers like physicians. In his early investigations of attitudes toward death, Feifel (1959) found that many physicians were not able to deal realistically with death. Physicians' distorted notions about the awareness of either patients or their families regarding impending death made it difficult, if not impossible, for them to help patients cope with the reality of death. In doing interviews for his study of death and death role expectations, Mathieu found in interview after interview that older persons said: "I'm glad to talk with you about death. My doctor and my minister won't discuss it and I'm tired of talking with my undertaker" (Mathieu, 1972). But not only physicians; such professionals as nurses, clergy, and psychiatrists deny death by shunning both the topic and the dying person. Feifel had reported much the same experience.

Such denial forecloses opportunities for those approaching death to cope psychologically or spiritually with all of the emotions that contemplation of their end might arouse as opportunity to complete unfinished business of their personal histories. Intimates of those dying are thus denied honest and meaningful interactions with the dying person. The growth and spread of study in gerontology has begun to reverse this situation; a great many colleges and universities are giving their students the opportunity to face the reality of death, to study research about dying, and to modify their attitudes toward the dying process. The issues that need to be investigated in terms of the process of dying and death are:

1. Is there some consistent process in the dying trajectory?

2. What valid kinds of supports during this process prevent loneliness and pain?

3. What are the current rituals with which we cope with death? Are they changing?

4. How do we constructively cope with bereavement, grief, and mourning?

THE PROCESS OF DYING

Kübler-Ross has given us the most explicit analysis of psychological stages of dying. She calls these "coping mechanisms at the time of terminal illness" (Kübler-Ross, 1969). Her stages are:

1. Denial and isolation ("No, not me, it can't be true")

2. Anger-rage, envy, resentment ("Why me?")

3. Bargaining ("If You'll let me . . . then I'll . . . .")

4. Depression ("What's the use?")

5. Acceptance

These stages were first identified in a seminar at the University of Chicago in which dying patients were interviewed as to their feelings. One pervasive theme important to Kübler-Ross is the observation that *hope* persists through all of these stages.

Another experienced investigator of the phenomenon of suicide has questioned these stages of dying (Shneidman, 1973):

> My own limited work has not led me to conclusions identical with those of Kübler-Ross. Indeed, while I have seen in dying persons isolation, envy, bargaining, depression, and acceptance, I do not believe that these are necessarily "stages" of the dying process, and I am not at all convinced that they are lived through in that order, or for that matter, in any universal order. What I see is a complicated clustering of intellectual and affective states, some fleeting, lasting for a moment, a day, a week, set, not unexpectedly, against the backdrop of that person's total personality, his "philosophy of life."

Shneidman rejects the notion of a unidimensional pathway to death, feeling that there is a constant alternation between acceptance and denial. Likewise, he detects among his interviewees many who exhibit on one level of consciousness a need to be aware of death and on another a need not to know.

In contrast, Weisman, a Harvard psychiatrist, has studied the myths that preclude effective interaction with the dying person (Weisman, 1972). Such myths about dying include the following:

1. Only suicidal and psychotic people are willing to die. Even when death is inevitable, no one wants to die.

2. Fear of death is the most natural and basic fear of man. The closer he comes to death, the more intense the fear becomes.

3. Reconciliation with death and preparation for death are impossible. Therefore, say as little as possible to dying people, turn their questions aside, and use any means to deny, dissimulate, and avoid open confrontation.

4. Dying people do not really want to know what the future holds. Otherwise, they would ask more questions. To force a discussion or to insist upon unwelcome information is risky. The patient might lose all hope. He might commit suicide, become very depressed, or even die more quickly.

5. After speaking with family members, the doctor should treat the patient as long as possible. Then, when further benefit seems unlikely, the patient should be left alone, except for relieving pain. He will then withdraw, die in peace, without further disturbance and anguish.

6. It is reckless, if not downright cruel, to inflict unnecessary suffering upon the patient or his family. The patient is doomed; nothing can really make any difference. Survivors should accept the futility, but realize that they will get over the loss.

7. Physicians can deal with all phases of the dying process because of their scientific training and clinical experience. The emotional and psychol-

ogical sides of dying are vastly overemphasized. Consultation with psychiatrists and social workers is unnecessary. The clergy might be called upon, but only because death is near. The doctor has no further obligation after the patient's death.

Weisman goes on to point out that these fallacies do all kinds of mischief. They lead physicians into inconsistencies and justify the physician's penchant for avoiding death issues himself. They help him feel somewhat more easy about his own withdrawal from the dying patient. The fourth fallacy, which says the patient doesn't want to know, absolves the physician from talking about it. This investigator asserts that the most dangerous fallacy of all is oversimplification through stereotyping patients when each person ought to be treated as a special case.

We may conclude from these studies that while we are learning more about the process of dying, the research is still in its early stages. Service providers who work with dying persons, however, will achieve additional understanding from Kübler-Ross, Shneidman, Weisman, Feifel, Mathieu, and others whose observations have given us additional insights into the dying process.

SUPPORTS FOR THE DYING PERSON

If one moves from the question of what constitutes the dying process to an analysis of what supports are available for the dying person, there are some concrete examples of help and some research studies that have specific insights.

In his study of rural Montana, suburban Pasadena, and retirement home (Laguna Hills) samples Mathieu asked about supports when "thinking about death" (Mathieu, 1972). Table 10–2 summarizes his findings.

TABLE 10–2. RELIGION AS A COMFORT WHEN THINKING OF DEATH

Which of the following comforts you most as you think of death?	PASADENA (N=189)		LAGUNA HILLS (N=183)		MOUNTAIN STATE (N=115)	
	N	%	N	%	N	%
My religion	62	32.8	58	31.7	43	37.4
Love from those around me	49	25.9	51	27.9	29	25.2
Memories of a full life	78	41.3	74	40.4	43	37.4

SOURCE: Mathieu (1972).

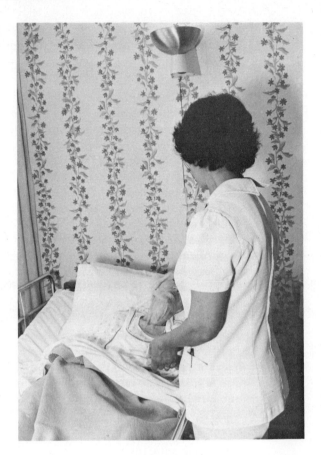

The introduction of the hospice in the United States from England humanizes the dying process and enables the old to share their feelings, to be with family and understanding staff, and to die with dignity.

Several implications of this study are significant. There is a rather remarkable consistency of response from these three diverse samples. A second observation is that even from a rural sample only about one-third of the sample depend upon religious sources as their support in thinking about death. On the other hand, "remembrance of things past" (the life review) turns out to have much power in giving support.

All of our research sources speak about the value of allowing dying persons to talk about their death trajectory. Weisman (1972), in particular, emphasizes the need for a most sensitive response pattern on the part of the helper. While sensitivity is essential, the positive effect that openness and responsiveness can have is well illustrated in case studies presented by all of the researchers. Accessibility for intimate sharing is obviously the opposite of the withdrawal tendencies implied in the seven fallacies Weisman indicates as typical beliefs on the part of physicians.

Because of the general denial of death by Western society and because of rejecting and withdrawing tendencies on the part of doctors, nurses, clergy, and other service providers, it became apparent that some new form of institutional caring would be required to overcome these inhibitions. One such change came to the University of Chicago Medical Hospital due to the experience and teaching of Kübler-Ross. In many cities her influence has encouraged the medical staff to modify its approach to the dying.

A second and even more unique response to this need has been the innovative St. Christopher's Hospice developed in London. Dr. Cicely Saunders is the medical director there and most of the reports on this creative approach to death came from him (Saunders, 1971–72). The Hospice is modeled after the hospices of the Middle Ages which were located in towns "for the sick and poor." The basic aim of St. Christopher's is to build a new type of institutional community involving doctors, nurses, staff, patients, and their families where the last weeks of life can be humanized, full of joy, and relatively painless. Analgesics are given freely but no heroic, technological methods for prolonging life are ever used. All staff and members of families are trained to have a new attitude toward death so that the dying person is surrounded by positive supports through the terminal illness. Thus, through compassion, a good deal of training, and continuing contact with family and friends, patients are helped to have a decent and "appropriate" death.

St. Christopher's also has a research and teaching function. It does research on aspects of care for terminally ill patients to try to help those in charge better understand conditions for ultimate help to patients and it trains other doctors and nurses in its techniques. Saunders has visited America many times. A number of institutions similar to the original hospice in England are now opening in the United States. A critical issue is whether it is sound public policy to try to build hospices all over the United States or whether it might not be possible so to educate our medical and nursing staffs, nursing home and hospital administrators, that the spirit, attitudes, and processes that uniquely characterize St. Christopher's effectiveness could be adopted by existing hospitals and nursing homes.

THE COMMEMORATIVE RITUALS

The commemorative process begins when a person dies. If he has died in a nursing home or a hospital, the physician remains the chief actor. Although he is a "symbol of life rather than death," he must shift from that role to one where he acts, if only for a moment, as the one who tells the family about the death and the circumstances surrounding it, and offers what comfort he can (Warner, 1965). In doing so, he still must protect his essential identity as a healer. He must also preserve his own self-image and convince himself that he used all of his skill to prevent that death.

The family must now call in a second professional to handle the body, prepare it for burial, make arrangements for burial, and perhaps for the funeral itself. This is the undertaker. He plays several roles. In one sense he stands beside the minister as a counselor to help the family through its crisis of grief. He does this both with words and with actions. His preparation of the corpse so that the dead person looks good or at least peaceful during final viewing is of first importance. Warner observes that he must "take the ritually unclean, usually diseased, corpse with its unpleasant appearance and transform it from a lifeless object to the sculptured image of a living human being who is resting in sleep." The social defense mechanisms are nowhere better displayed than in this ability to make the dead look as if still alive but only "sleeping."

The undertaker has also taken the role of manager of the commemorative ritual. He arranges the casket, flowers, family, friends of the family, and other mourners. Warner says of him: "In one sense he is the producer who fashions the whole enterprise so that other performers, including the minister, the eulogist, the organist, the vocalist, family, and mourners can act becomingly and get the approval and praise for the funeral's success and receive the sensuous satisfaction that the funeral's symbolism evokes."

The undertaker has developed a series of public relations maneuvers that add to the alacrity with which mourning family members subscribe to all of his charges. It is widely heralded by mortuaries that viewing the body in the "slumber room" is a significant form of grief therapy. To see the person who was devastated by illness "transfigured with peace and happiness" is the justification for the enormous amount of energy expended by morticians (Baird, 1972). But Jessica Mitford examined this ritual in great detail and found it wanting as grief therapy (Baird, 1972).

A second contention by funeral directors is that embalming and the purchase of a tightly sealed casket prevent decomposition. In one famous case, *Chelini v. Silvio Nieri*, Chelini sued Nieri, the undertaker, because upon interment he found his mother in an advanced state of decomposition. Out of the trial emerged the fact that embalming in no way slows down decomposition and a "seal-type" casket only hastens decay. Chelini won the case (Baird, 1972).

A common myth is that cemeteries are nonprofit. Cemetery land is tax-free, based on the supposition that the operation is nonprofit, which probably stems back to the days when a church or city maintained the plots. But more recently the promoters have begun to take a large amount of the fees as well as levying additional charges for "perpetual care" (Baird, 1972). The mausoleum in which crypts are piled on top of each other simply saves land and maintenance for the cemetery proprietor.

There has been some concerted action taken in response to the high costs of dying. In almost every large city funeral societies have sprung up. One pays a very modest fee to belong to these organizations. The society contracts with a funeral director who agrees to work with it for minimum amounts of money depending on the type of casket and disposition that an individual selects. These funeral societies are really cooperatives because they are run by elected boards of directors (Nora, 1962).

Another alternative response to the high cost of dying is the growing practice of cremation. The general practice is to cremate the body, scatter the ashes, and hold a memorial service later. No coffin or urn is present at the memorial service. In some cases the urn or container of the ashes, sometimes a miniature casket, may be placed in a mausoleum, which serves then as a focus for visits by family or friends. The cost of cremation is a fraction of what it costs to embalm, purchase a casket, and inter a body. Some of the environmentalists are making strong pleas for the use of cremation as urban land becomes increasingly scarce.

A congressional committee held hearings on the funeral industry across the country during the summer and fall of 1976. Included in the testimony were many examples of gouging prices and unfair business practices. On the other hand, a great many morticians have served their communities for a great many years, which has earned them the respect of the community. It is probable that the pressure of memorial societies, crematoriums, and an enlightened public may force the funeral industry to moderate many of its policies and become more realistic in its claims. Yet the vast majority of Americans still choose an old-fashioned funeral complete with casket and burial rituals. This is traditional in America and these customs will not soon be abandoned.

BEREAVEMENT AND GRIEF

Much of the data about dying reminds us that psychological factors have a profound effect upon even healthy people. For years it has been known that widows and widowers have a higher mortality rate than married men and women of the same age. This still would not necessarily account for a peaking of mortality rate in widowers during the first year of bereavement. Young and his colleagues (1963) found an increase in the death rate among 4,486 widowers over the age of fifty-four of almost 40 percent during the first six months of bereavement. What must be added to the equation is the psychological impact of bereavement. Rahe and Holmes (1967), for example, have developed a schedule of life-change events that have been rank-ordered on the basis of increasing impact. Such recent life changes are good predictors of physical breakdown and illness. At the top of the rank-ordered list—that is, the recent life change with the greatest psychological impact—stands "death of spouse." This may account substantially for the findings of Young and his associates.

Parkes has done a great deal of systematic review of the literature on grief as well as much research of his own in developing what he calls a "biological theory of grief." Yet he reports that the data do not provide consistent support for this view. This theory views grief as a stressor that elicits the sympathetic part of the autonomic nervous system while inhibiting the parasympathetic system. Thus bereavement causes alarm, much akin to fear.

Acute and episodic pangs of grief are expressed, according to Parkes, through a series of phases of behavior. These include:

1. Searching ("I can't help looking for him everywhere . . . ", "I walk around searching for her.")

2. Illusions ("I keep thinking I see him in a crowd . . .", "I imagine I hear her moving about in another room.")

3. Withdrawal (avoidance of close friends or familiar places; disbelief that the loss has really occurred; developing emotional numbness; attempts to rationalize the loss or "make sense of it")

4. Guilt and anger (self-reproach over some act or omission that might have harmed the dying person; anger or protest over the pain of grief caused by the "desertion" of the dead one)

5. Attempts to gain a new identity (developing new expectations about one's life or self and new roles)

The classical study of grief reactions is that of Eric Lindemann (1944). He studied the responses of 101 persons who lost close relatives in the nightclub fire in Boston. He gives a somewhat different series of responses than Parkes:

1. *The syndrome of physical distress:* The survivor experiences sighing, choking, shortness of breath, digestive troubles, and exhaustion.

2. *Preoccupation with the image of the deceased:* Other persons fade away while the survivor is obsessed by remembrances of the lost person.

3. *Feelings of guilt:* The bereft feel responsible for the death.

Bereavement and grief are as difficult for the elderly as they are for middle-aged persons. The elderly are especially vulnerable to the effects of the loss incurred at the death of a spouse, a relative, or a life-long friend.

4. *Hostile reactions:* The survivor feels irritability, anger, and some concern that the present state of instability may lead to insanity.

5. *Loss of pattern:* Old roles are disrupted, life is out of joint.

A third study is significant. Schoenberg, Carp, Peretz, and Kutscher (1970) asked 133 professional consultants (ministers, psychologists, and psychiatrists) to list significant aspects of grief. They found the following:

1. Ninety-nine percent of the respondents thought that the death of a mate would result in depression, loss of weight, sleeplessness, and despair.

2. Ninety percent thought that the bereaved would have dreams about the deceased.

3. Seventy-five percent thought that a widower would experience impotence and diminished sexual desires.

4. Seventy-four percent expected the widowed to fantasize or have illusions about the presence of the dead person (compare Lindemann on "images").

5. Seventy-three percent thought the bereaved would seek advice.

Schoenberg et al. also asked for a suggestion of behaviors that would be helpful. Ninety-one percent thought that talking with someone who had the same experience would be very useful. Ninety percent thought that continuation of a work role was helpful and 85 percent recommended a future remarriage. The emphasis on sharing with others who have been in the same loss situation has been actualized by the CRUSE Widow-to-Widow groups in England and by the spontaneous growth of innovative experimental groups in this country.

In looking at ways in which groups can be used to facilitate the grief process, Barett (1974) organized three different kinds of groups of widows. Half of her sample said they had never thought about the death of their husband before it occurred, and two-thirds had never considered what it would be like to be a widow. Their average income, even though half of them worked, was about one-half of what it had been at the time of their husband's death.

The first group was called a *self-help* group because the leader was only a facilitator and not a teacher. She helped members of the group help each other. This type conformed to what is generally referred to as a widow-to-widow group in England and in some cities in this country. The second group was called the *confidante group*. She used intimate techniques and group activities where individuals were paired and participated as couples. In this group the leader tried to facilitate a "helping relationship" for each pair.

The third group was labeled a *woman's consciousness-raising group*. In discussions, the focus of this group was on ways in which sex roles were viewed by widows in the group. Such topics as "Sexuality among Widows: Are You Still A Wife?" characterized the interaction. Each of the groups gathered for two hours a week for some eight weeks. These three groups were then matched with a control group.

Several measures were used to determine whether the groups had any impact on the attitudes and values of participants. One measure was "predicted future health." This is a measure of the sense of well-being and of optimism. Subjects in all groups showed growth in self-esteem and all were appreciative of being women. Those who participated in the experimental groups showed higher hopes for future health in contrast with the control group. All groups were less depressed as the result of their participation, but the control group stressed health problems and loneliness more than the other three. The confidante group became more active in social roles and showed greater positive change in self-esteem than the others. Significantly, all three treatment groups decided to continue meeting even when the experiment was over. Barett concluded that each of these groups had much to offer in assisting widows toward adjustment and in growth of emotional well-being. In England almost all communities now have a chapter of CRUSE, which is a widow-to-widow program. There are few such programs in the United States, although the American Association of Retired Persons is actively engaged in promoting such a program now.

After the immediate psychological interventions in dealing with grief, many critical issues still face a widow or widower when the mate dies. Some of these involve federal and state income taxes, probate, inheritance and estate taxes, state inheritance taxes, the federal gift tax, the implementation of the wishes expressed in a will, analyzing financial resources and one's financial future, the possibility of employment or training for employment. Loss of a mate involves not only a shift in social roles but the need to establish new roles. All of these tasks may require expert guidance by an accountant, an attorney, or a counselor. In any case life does *not* go on as it did before. Death changes many things.

SUMMARY

This chapter has reviewed the most significant research findings regarding dying, death, and coping with grief. The student must assess his own attitudes about death if he is to work with older persons. It is one thing to review the kind of cognitive material that is discussed in this chapter, but it is another to feel comfortable in discussing death with peers or elders. This review may introduce some basic considerations to help the student evaluate his own denial or acceptance of the total life span . . . from birth through death.

REFERENCES

Baird, J. "The Funeral Industry in Boston." In E. Shneidman (ed.), *Death and the College Student.* New York: Behavioral Publications, 1972.

Barett, C.J. "The Development and Evaluation of Three-Group Therapeutic Intervention for Widows" (doctoral dissertation, University of Southern California Libraries, Los Angeles, 1974.)

Feifel, H. (ed.). *The Meaning of Death.* New York: McGraw-Hill, 1959.

Kalish, R. "Death and Dying in a Social Context." In R. Binstock and E. Shanas (eds.), *Handbook of Aging and the Social Sciences.* New York: Van Nostrand Reinhold, 1976.

Kubler-Ross, E. *On Death and Dying.* New York: Macmillan, 1969.

Lindemann, E. "Symptomatology and Management of Acute Grief." *American Journal of Psychiatry,* September 1944.

Mant, A. K. "The Medical Definition of Death." In E. Shneidman (ed.), *Death: Current Perspectives.* New York: Mayfield, 1976.

Mathieu, J. T. "Dying and Death Role-Expectation: A Comparative Analysis" (doctoral dissertation, Department of Sociology, University of Southern California, Los Angeles, 1972).

Nora, F. *Memorial Associations: What They Are—How They Are Organized.* New York: Cooperative League of America, 1962.

Parkes, C. M. *Bereavement: Studies of Grief in Adult Life.* New York: International Universities Press, 1972.

Saunders, C. *Annual Report,* St. Christopher's Hospice, 1971–72.

Schoenberg, B., A. Carp, D. Peretz, and A. Kutscher (eds.). *Loss and Grief: Psychological Management of Medical Practice.* New York: Columbia University Press, 1970.

Shneidman, E. *Deaths of Man.* New York: Quadrangle, 1973.

Shneidman, E. "The Death Certificate." In E. Shneidman (ed.), *Death: Current Perspectives.* New York: Mayfield, 1976.

Warner, W. L. "The City of the Dead." In R. Fulton (ed.), *Death and Identity.* New York: Wiley, 1965.

Weisman, A. D. *On Death and Dying: A Psychiatric Study of Terminality.* New York: Behavioral Publications, 1972.

Young, M., B. Benjamin, and C. Wallis. "Mortality of Widowers." *Lancet,* 1963, No. 2.

FOR FURTHER READING

Bowman, M., et al. *Counseling the Dying.* New York: Thomas Nelson, 1964.

Brim, O.G. (ed.). *The Dying Patient.* New York: Russell Sage Foundation, 1970.

Freese, A. *Help for Your Grief.* New York: Schocken Books, 1977.

Fulton, R.L. (ed.). *Death and Identity.* New York: Wiley, 1965.

Glaser, B.G., and A. L. Strauss. *Awareness of Dying.* Chicago: Aldine, 1965.

Gorer, G. *Death, Grief, and Mourning.* Garden City, N.Y.: Anchor Books, 1967.

Hinton, J. *Dying.* Baltimore: Penguin Books, 1967.

Jury, M., and D. Jury. *GRAMP.* New York: Grossman Publishers, 1976.

Kastenbaum, R., and R. Aisenberg, *The Psychology of Death.* New York: Springer, 1978.

Peterson, J., and M. Briley. *Widows and Widowhood: A Creative Approach to Being Alone.* New York: Association Press, 1977.

Shneidman, E. *Death: Current Perspectives.* New York: Mayfield, 1976.

Toynbee, A., et al. *Man's Concern with Death.* New York: McGraw-Hill, 1969.

IV | The Discipline of Gerontology

CHAPTER 11

Gerontology: A New Science?

While you and I have lips and voices which
are for kissing and to sing with
who cares if some oneeyed son of a bitch
invents an instrument to measure Spring with?

E.E. CUMMINGS

Anyone beyond the casually curious entering the field of gerontology for the first time may feel a bit overwhelmed by the complexity of the subject matter. The wide range and diversity of topics and issues with which gerontology deals may seem somewhat intimidating. It is understandable that the student will be tempted to identify one single common, underlying theme in the study of aging or else single out one aspect or dimension of this complex field to pursue as that most consonant with an individual interest.

By recapping and highlighting here some of the major areas of interest and activity in the field of gerontology, this chapter will help the student begin to synthesize in his thinking the many bits of information in this text. Through the process of developing a "cognitive map" of gerontology, the student can begin to see where his or her special interest or concern fits into the larger picture of the study of aging. Obviously, this chapter cannot complete the process. It can only stimulate and foster it.

257

DID YOU KNOW . . .

At 100, Grandma Moses was painting?
At 94, Bertrand Russell was active in international peace drives?
At 93, George Bernard Shaw wrote the play *Farfetched Fables?*
At 91, Eamon de Valera served as president of Ireland?
At 91, Adolph Zukor was chairman of Paramount Pictures?
At 90, Pablo Picasso was producing drawings and engravings?
At 89, Mary Baker Eddy was director of the Christian Science Church?
At 89, Albert Schweitzer headed a hospital in Africa?
At 89, Artur Rubinstein gave one of his greatest recitals in New York's
    Carnegie Hall?
At 88, Michelangelo did architectural plans for the Church of Santa Maria
    degli Angeli?
At 88, Pablo Casals was giving cello concerts?
At 88, Konrad Adenauer was chancellor of Germany?
At 85, Coco Chanel was the head of a fashion design firm?
At 84, W. Somerset Maugham wrote *Points of View?*
At 83, Alexander Kerensky wrote *Russia and History's Turning Point?*
At 82, Winston Churchill wrote *A History of the English-Speaking Peoples?*
At 82, Leo Tolstoy wrote *I Cannot Be Silent?*
At 81, Benjamin Franklin effected the compromise that led to the adoption
    of the U.S. Constitution?
At 81, Johann Wolfgang von Goethe finished *Faust?*
At 80, George Burns won an Academy Award for his performance in *The
    Sunshine Boys?* (Wallechinsky, Wallace, & Wallace, 1977)

Such a list represents only a tiny, select sample of the varied activities and accomplishments, widely known or not, associated with persons in the later years of life. How, then, does gerontology relate to such achievements as well as other aspects of old age?

1. Is the study of aging to be viewed essentially as a consciousness-raising phenomenon, or is it truly a new science?

2. Does it make a difference which questions we ask in the study of aging?

3. How do we determine what is truly relevant to the study and our understanding of the aging process?

4. If gerontology is, indeed, a new science, what place has direct service and practice in this field?

As more and more professionals and paraprofessionals from many differing backgrounds become attracted to and involved in gerontology, it seems evident that much of what is "new" in gerontology consists in large measure of traditional scientific concepts and methods applied to a new segment of the population. The same can be said about direct service and practice. Therefore, the issue of whether gerontology is on its way to becoming a recognized discipline in its own right or should be considered another specialty within existing disciplines and professions remains moot. It is a question of some significance to those considering a career in gerontology although one that may raise certain dilemmas for educational institutions.

CHARACTERIZING GERONTOLOGY

To approach the study of gerontology with the question "What causes aging?", which appears from time to time in scientific as well as popular literature, is misleading in the same sense as it would be to ask what "causes" adolescence. What is confounding is the dimension of time and chronology. Implied in such a question are the references to the losses and dysfunctions often associated with the normal processes of aging. Gerontologists have made an excellent beginning in uncovering many salient facts about normal aging. Even so, we are still not entirely clear to what extent normal aging involves losses and dysfunctions as a function of passage of time and to what extent multiple loss or malfunction is the consequence of causal factors distinct from merely added years.

In an earlier era attitudes toward long-lived individuals were imbued with much mysticism, magic, and superstition. Views of aging were highly speculative. This is not to say that such speculations were necessarily in every instance invalid or incorrect. Nonetheless, many such perceptions and opinions have been shown to be inaccurate or very limited in scope and have led to myths and stereotypes about aging which continue to exist today. Later a marked shift took place with the advent of the scientific method (in the 1600s); systematic observation of naturally occurring events led to the discovery of underlying laws governing these events. This basic scientific mode of thought has come to be used in the study of the underlying processes of aging, especially within the last half dozen decades.

In this regard the relatively brief "career" of gerontology parallels the more extensive history of medicine. Early medicine can be characterized essentially as a practitioner's art, only later on adding scientific methodology and the resources of a growing technology. Throughout the recent history of medicine we can trace the consistent interplay between scientific/technological methodology and the concerns and requirements of the direct-service practitioner/clinician. The field of gerontology has been developing in much the same fashion: The early mystical speculations and superstitious responses to the aged were followed in due course by application of scientific/technological methods generating information utilized in services to the aged. This, in turn, extended the base of systematic observations and organized information about the aging process.

The newcomer to gerontology needs to know that at present a substantial amount of information about aging is available to our society, probably more than we effectively use. Much of these data are derived from systematic research, much from service to and rich experience in working with the elderly. An urgent task for gerontologists, therefore, is to synthesize these data for maximum utility. At the same time the student needs to appreciate that the present state of the art is such that we appear to have just scratched the surface in our studies of the underlying processes of aging. In other words, there are still far too many gaps in our knowledge and understanding of aging. Because multiple causation (Birren & Clayton, 1975) enjoys the preferred explanatory role in the study of aging, cross-disciplinary cooperation between scientific inquiry and direct service professionalism serves an obvious and useful purpose in providing the richest context for the study of aging. The fact that the full potential of this interaction between research and service has not always been fully realized in no way diminishes its merit as an ideal toward which gerontology can and should strive (Carp, 1974).

The scientific mode of thought has come to be widely applied to the study of aging on the international as well as national scene. The nature and content of worldwide gerontological research varies greatly. Although it has become conventional to distinguish between basic and applied research in principle, it is sometimes very difficult to make such a distinction in practice. That is, scientific studies that might be characterized as basic or "pure" research often turn out to have very practical applicability.

INTERNATIONAL GERONTOLOGY

Although scientific gerontological research has proliferated and flourished rather dramatically in America, with its principal base in universities, increasingly the scientific study of aging has become international in scope. A review, for example, of scientific reports appearing in the journal *Mechanisms of Aging and Development* (published in the Netherlands) between 1973 and 1977 indicates that out of 177 scientific articles, 84 report work done in twenty-two foreign countries, including Denmark, Czechoslovakia, France, Hungary, Rumania, Italy, Japan, Israel, India, Sweden, Great Britain, and the USSR. For additional research studies on the international scene, see the international issue of *The Gerontologist* (1975, 15:3). Another indication of gerontological interest on the international scene is shown by the kind of participation at the International Congress of Gerontology which convenes every three years. The most recent congress held in Tokyo (1978) reported some 2120 participants representing gerontological research and practice in 38 countries.

SCIENTIFIC FOCI

What kinds of scientific inquiry related to gerontology are being carried out? The following is not a detailed survey but rather highlights of some of the major areas of study and a sample of some research strategies being used.

Heredity Factors

Research in genetic factors is pursued as fundamental to the study of aging because the genetic component at the minimum is implicated in the determination of life span of any given species. Even though, as is now thought, many humans do not attain the full measure of their hereditary limits, genetic factors are understood to establish the outside limits of longevity and functional capacities, whatever they may be. Thus genetic researchers, as exemplified by the now classic work of Kallman and Jarvik (1959), typically examine life-span developmental themes of one-egg and two-egg twins. Analyses of behaviors and other developmental variables of twins and siblings raised in similar and dissimilar settings lead to differential conclusions about the varying effects of environmental and hereditary factors upon the individual.

Many of the conclusions about the role of heredity with respect to aging are necessarily tentative. The best longitudinal studies of twins and siblings are complicated by many external intervening variables, such as marital status, rural or urban living, dietary and nutritional patterns, exercise or the lack of it, smoking, presence or absence of diseases, even levels of radiation to which individuals are exposed over a lifetime. Such external factors may directly affect genetic material or may affect the efficiency of individual cells comprising body tissue.

Biomedical Factors

Much research is producing important data on the nature and extent of cell changes associated with aging. These studies constitute important basic research simply because cells are the fundamental units of

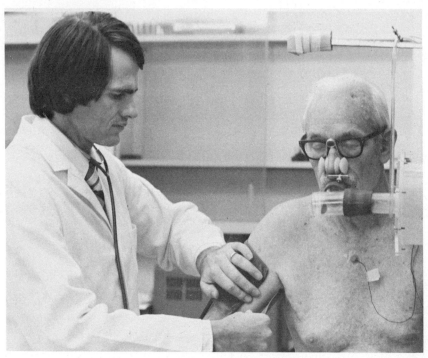

Investigations into various aspects of the physiology of aging have become very complex and sophisticated. Such research has contributed to the growing identification of gerontology with basic science.

structure and functioning in living organisms. Such changes thus offer important clues as to the nature and role of physiological changes in the aging process. Basic cellular research in aging is related to genetic research as its field of inquiry includes the study of the genetic material DNA, which contains the blueprint for the organization and development of the entire organism. It is also the source of most information about the everyday maintenance and function of cells in the body. A basic research strategy is to examine closely changes in cell size and color with age. Changes in cell integrity, permeability, function, and replication across time are also studied. One perspective in such study is not so much to eliminate the aging process as to modify it in some useful way or to slow it down.

Metabolic and chemical elements (endocrine control system) are also studied in conjunction with a variety of experimental conditions, as, for example, stress and nutritional variations. As might be expected, a substantial amount of this work is done with animals, where study of living cells can be accomplished under relatively well-defined conditions and where proper controls can effectively be maintained. For the most part, a variety of subhuman species (typically rats, mice, fruit flies, and larvae) are utilized in such studies. This is done for three reasons: Such species are readily available to research laboratories; they are relatively short-lived and so age effects are more easily tested; and their cellular responses to experimental conditions are judged, within defined limits, to be applicable to human physiology.

Biomedical strategies of research also include studies of homeostatic (state of equilibrium) imbalance as it relates to other aspects of the aging process. Disease and stress factors become critical considerations in such investigations. Biomedical research in aging also turns the scientific spotlight on the efficiency of various organs and organ systems (e.g., the liver, kidney, circulatory system) with respect to maintenance of body temperature, blood sugar regulation, processing of drugs, waste disposal, and the like, all of which are studied in great detail.

Basic gerontological research is also being done on vision, hearing, taste, touch, and smell, and at the neurological level. These studies, in turn, are closely linked to the following.

Psychological Factors

All psychological functioning has a physical substrate (base). Researchers in the psychological aspects of aging (cognition, memory, learning, visual-motor performance, perception) must, therefore, have sufficient familiarity with the mechanisms and functions of the central nervous system (CNS), the brain, and related processes. Typical basic research strategies in this area employ a variety of discrimination, memory/learning, and visual-motor skill tasks under highly specified, controlled conditions. These experiments allow (on cross-sectional as well as longitudinal bases) comparison of behavioral responses on the part of an individual with himself, one individual with another, and across groups. The intent is to discover what kinds of changes (if any) associated with age or with other, nonaging factors do occur in these functions.

Sociological Aging

Another major area of basic gerontological scientific research consists in studies of the ways in which social structure and social experience influence attitudes, life satisfaction, and behavior in the later years of life. A substantial proportion of such inquiry focuses on the essential structure and mechanisms of such social institutions as marriage, the family, organizations, and the like.

Because practically all data with which social scientists ordinarily deal are not derived from direct but rather from indirect measures, research strategies typically lean heavily on the use of self-reports, systematic repeated observations, analyses of surveys, role descriptions, socioeconomic indices, and systems analysis. The purpose of such basic research is to study social forces in later life as well as sociological (attitudinal) differences and similarities between generations. There is a high degree of congruence between basic sociological and psychological research in this regard.

Politics and Aging

One of the most rapidly growing dimensions in gerontology is the attention given to politics and governmental processes insofar as they affect the needs and interests of the elderly. Groups rather than individuals most affect the development and carrying out of public policy. The voting patterns, tendencies, and habits of the aged are of great interest to gerontological specialists in this area. In addition, the organization and working of such special interest groups as AARP/NRTA, the National Council on the Aging, and similar groups organized in the interest of the aged provide useful models of organized impact on the political process.

Of more recent origin is the research in progress in many areas on the decision-making process in government. Gerontologists who are studying these aspects of political life are interested in who gets involved in the decision-making process, who the decision makers are, what information about aging is available to the process, what is used, and what kinds of data are not available and not used.

Economics and Aging

During and following the Colonial period of our history, in an agricultural society, economic power remained vested in the landholder. Children were an important source of economic strength because they helped the father work his land. He maintained his authority and economic power in large measure because he held title to the land as long as he was alive. With the urbanization and particularly the industrialization of our society, this source of economic power for the elderly gradually drained away.

Of special concern to the gerontologist, beyond the financial needs of the aged, is the sources of income for persons in later life, especially for those in retirement. Social Security and Old Age Assistance have been the principal sources. The myth of pension systems as a principal source of economic support after retirement has been unmasked by James Schulz, a gerontological economist, who has concluded that private pensions grew largely out of a need to supplement Social Security (Schulz, 1970). One truly innovative plan grew out of work done by UCLA economist Yung-Ping Chen (1974), who has proposed a "reverse annuity." Under this plan, homeowners would deed their property to a cooperating financial institution prior to retirement with the guarantee that the homeowners maintain the right to live in their home until their deaths. Extensive repairs, taxes, and other large maintenance costs would be borne by the financial institutions during the lifetime of the residents, the home going to the institution for sale upon the death of the residents. Research on the economics of aging has so far turned up far too little of such imaginative and innovative approaches to the economic problems of the aged.

APPLIED RESEARCH

As already indicated, the differentiation between basic and applied research comes down to a very fine line at times. A large amount of the scientific study of problems related to the aging process and elderly persons generates information and techniques of practical use to providers of direct services. This broad dimension of scientific gerontology complements the basic research in aging, some of which was indicated above. Notwithstanding the fact that characterizing certain kinds of research as "applied" in contrast to "basic" is a debatable proposition, the following brief descriptions will provide at least a sketch of applied research relevant to the needs of practitioners, policy planners, and other direct service providers.

Nutrition

Increasing attention is being paid to the role of proper nutrition and dietary patterns in alleviating the effects of degenerative diseases in the old and maintaining a high quality of life (Mayer, 1974). Such studies are aimed at the relationship of diet to coronary heart disease and to management of diabetes, hypertension, and anemia.

Exercise

A number of physiologists are studying gross losses of functional capacity which the aged individual himself experiences as loss of vigor. The seedwork of De Vries (1975), for example, has persuasively demonstrated the trainability of elderly individuals to increase the efficiency of the cardiovascular and respiratory systems, improve muscle function, enhance physical work capacity, and improve overall health factors. This is accomplished via appropriate types and regimens of exercise determined by means of systematic study.

Environment

Although person/environmental transactions have long been recognized as a fundamental principle in understanding human behavior, only within the last decade or so has substantial scientific attention been given to differential effects of environmental factors upon the aging process. Increasingly designers like Joseph Koncelick, Novere Musson, and Thomas Byerts and social scientists like M. Powell Lawton, Robert Sommer, Rudolph Moos, Kermit Schooler, Arthur Schwartz, Harold Proshansky, William Ittleson, Victor Regnier, and many others have been studying environmental issues ranging from broadly conceived urban planning to microenvironment design components. Some have been doing this within the context of aging; others are now beginning to apply their work to older populations.

The essential research strategies are designed to identify elements of prosthetic (compensating) environments for the elderly and how these elements contribute to the aged's satisfaction and health (Carp, 1974). A major task is to translate specific environmental components into measurable variables, in terms of both their character as features of the designed environment and their influence or impact upon users of the environment. Lindsley (1964), for example, has made a strong case for developing prosthetic environments for older persons as a free-operant conditioning mode, and Hoyer (1973) has reviewed the applicability of operant techniques to behavior modification in the elderly.

Emotional Well-being

The appalling neglect of the mental health, so-called, of our society's aged has been so well documented and is now so widely acknowledged as to need little elaboration on that point here. There are still many problems associated with research on the psychological and social contributors to emotional well-being of the aged (Larson, 1978). Much of what has been available in the scientific literature has described the use of drugs as a major therapeutic intervention or has described what are very primitive, limited techniques.* One major contributor to this state of affairs is the tendency to focus attention on elderly people with continuing disabilities as persons who are chroni-

---

*For example, the widely cited use of "reality orientation" (RO), a technique for use with disoriented, "senile" elderly, first developed by Dr. James Folsom at the Veterans Administration in Alabama.

cally "ill." The consequence of such labeling is a limiting factor in the range of intervention utilized (Schwartz, 1975). Medical rather than psychological interventions are frequently brought to bear. We can expect that these issues will get the research they deserve in the future.

A second contributor to the historical neglect of emotional well-being of the elderly is the lack of extensive scientific study of "senility." The conventional argument continues to be raised (Wershow, 1977) that because brain damage is irreversible, senile behavior (itself a very imprecise, often loosely used term) resulting from damage is by definition also irreversible. Therefore, the argument goes on, psychosocial therapies in many cases are worse than useless. In contrast to this argument can be placed the work done at such treatment centers as the Philadelphia Geriatric Center in Philadelphia, and the rehabilitative successes with aphasic and paralyzed victims of strokes (also irreversible brain damage). What is clearly needed, then, is intensive research on these questions: What criteria are to be used to establish "senility"? Are behaviors *associated* with brain damage modifiable or reversible? Which are and which are not effective therapies and when and how should these be applied?

Mixed classes of young and old are a growing phenomenon in education in recent years, as more and more elderly are taking classes to seek new knowledge or to up-grade their education. Some even earn advanced degrees in late life.

Research to date has indicated that more than a little of what is taken for senility is in fact misdiagnosis (depression, for instance, can easily be mistaken for "senility"). The authors envision increased research effort being devoted in the future to this phenomenon, suspecting as we do that more careful and extensive applied study may demonstrate much of what we now call senility to be an artifact rather than a fact. Research strategies to identify responses to environmental demands such as those employed by the Ebenezer Society Center for Aging and Human Development (Rupprecht et al., 1976) may provide a useful model for such study. The identification of psychosocial needs embedded in their Human Development Inventory as a guide for therapeutic intervention is an example of needed applied research.

Research on Intervention

Group and individual counseling continues to be widely used, especially by nonprofessionals, with the elderly. Within the past several years some interest among professionals has been stimulated. They are beginning to regard counseling and similar relationships and self-help modalities as appropriate vehicles for reestablishing and enhancing emotional well-being of the elderly. This is in part evidenced by the growth in numbers of university-based programs to train counselors of older people. Much more applied research is needed, however, to establish useful criteria for selecting effective counselors. In addition, there is urgent need for effective impact (outcome) evaluation of counseling, self-help, and community programs for the aged (O'Brien & Streib, 1977).

An important applied research thrust related to emotional well-being is the study of drug usage and drug interaction effects upon the elderly. Such investigations hold great promise for familiarizing professionals and laymen alike with the special hazards of drug usage by the elderly, not least because of differential effects of "normal" dosages in older bodies. This work potentially can pay off in reducing the alarming rise of drug abuse observed in our society in general, particularly among the vulnerable aged.

Clinical Assessment

With the graying of America, we have been observing an increasing demand for clinical evaluation in gerontology. This stimulates applied research to develop more effective clinical diagnostic and evaluation tools and skills, particularly in medicine, psychology, psychiatry, and social work. Decisions affecting elderly persons relative to housing, therapeutic interventions, conservatorship, services in mental health, retirement and work policies and programs, and the like require appropriate, relevant, and valid assessment techniques and skills. It is now clearly understood by gerontologists that most problems experienced by the aged are multidimensional in nature. Thus they require multidisciplinary evaluation and attention. Three current research thrusts illustrate the manner in which applied research relates to clinical practice.

1. The first is research in testing out methods for screening cognitive and functional capacity. Work is being done along this line with such devices as the Face-Hand Test, the Graham-Kendall "Memory for Designs," the Mental-Status Questionnaire (of which there are several versions: Kaplan, Goldfarb, Pfeiffer), and the Bender Motor Gestalt Test. The purpose of such studies (Haglund & Schuckit, 1976) is to refine instruments and procedures so as to distinguish more accurately the impaired from normal group of elderly and to differentiate brain-damage-generated dysfunction from maladaptive behaviors that are psychogenic (caused by emotional disturbances). This work is carefully coordinated with family/social histories, with physical/health status evaluations, and with environmental inventories, all potential contributors to the determination of clinical judgments. For example, the effects on behavior and mental functioning of impaired vision in the elderly is another instance of what is meant by applied research in the clinical area (Snyder et al., 1976).

2. A second aspect of clinical assessment is the reevaluation of traditional constructs and measurements and their validity with respect to gerontological applications. This is demonstrated in the seedwork of Warner Schaie and his associates on IQ and aging, complementary assessment of the Wechsler Adult Intelligence Scale (WAIS) by Martha Storandt (1977), as well as much needed recapitulation of MMPI test "profiles" in examining personality changes with age (McCreary & Mensh, 1977), which are examples of such clinically related applied research.

3. A third, relatively new dimension useful for establishing clinical referents has recently been suggested. This new dimension in gerontology is a "social indicators" index. Kaplan and Ontell (1974) have proposed the developing of age-related social indicators that will furnish interpreted information about social conditions (are they getting better or worse?) and social goals (future compared to past). Thus, a statistic like the mortality rate for those over seventy-five would not be a social indicator. This statistic becomes a social indicator when, for instance, it is compared to the past and when cross-geographical, cross-cultural, and cross-age comparisons are made. If the aged were regarded as a distinctive social entity, a social-indicators report would

include a description of how the aged population fares in each social domain (e.g., health, housing, education, economics, and so on). At the same time it should be noted that social indicators are more than descriptive statistics. In spite of some problems connected with such proposals (for example, the problem of making value judgments about social conditions), it is clear that research along these conceptual lines would have considerable relevance not only to the concerns of clinicians but also to current applied research in the arena of public policy and the aged.

Patterns of Aging

Another useful ongoing area of gerontological research is to be noted in the observation of a variety of configurations of aging patterns. Such studies range from essentially basic research as that of the Bonn Longitudinal Study of Aging (Thomae, 1976) to the anthropological work by Margaret Clark and her associates at Langley Porter Institute on ethnicity and aging. Such studies show not only the diversity of aging patterns but also common themes within a number of such dimensions as ethnic, socioeconomic, health status, and survival patterns. The development of tools to assess continuity and change in coping strategies of the aged is evidenced in the work, for example, of David Chiriboga, Mary Quayhagen, Lorraine Cutler (Langley Porter Institute), Eva Kahana and A. Kiyak (Wayne State), Barbara Felton (NYU), and Boaz Kahana (Oakland University). Research such as this provides a very nice model of applied research with special relevance and utility for the clinician as well as other providers of direct services to the aged.

Terminal States

A special applied research concern related to gerontology involves issues of death and dying. C.M. Parks in England has done much careful, well-organized research on the grieving and bereavement process. In this country the applied work of Frances Scott at the University of Oregon, the well known work of Elisabeth Kübler-Ross, the clinical interviews of dying persons done by Leon Epstein and Lawrence White in San Francisco and Carl Eisdorfer and associates at the University of Washington, and programs like J. Peterson's and Rose Marie Smith's "Journey's End" foundation (JEFF), all serve to extend such basic studies on death and dying as that of J. Mathieu (discussed in chapter 10). In this connection the extensive analyses of patient responses to terminal illness done at M. D. Anderson Hospital in Houston, Texas, should also be noted. Glaser and Strauss's descriptions of the so-called conspiracy of silence with respect to dying persons have generated further interest and continuing study of this phenomenon.

Sexual Behavior

Sexuality of the aged has been for so long a taboo subject, heavily encrusted with mythology, that it has received only nominal attention in the past. Not until the now landmark studies of Masters and Johnson and the studies at Duke University has sexuality in the aged begun to receive serious, in-depth study. We must also acknowledge that basic scientific research on this subject has been so limited as to have had relatively little impact on society at large. An excellent scientific study comparing levels of sexual responses in older and younger adult males, completed as recently as 1977 (Solnick & Birren), was at the time the only such piece of research in the country. The continued demythologizing of sexual need and activity in later life will depend upon further careful scientific study of this subject.

These highlights of a number of aspects of gerontological endeavor provide some basis for answering the question that appears as the title of this chapter. Without doubt gerontology is a scientific endeavor. Whether it should or will be characterized as a "new science" in its own right or will continue to be an adjunct to other well-established scientific endeavors remains to be seen.

While the roots of gerontology as we know it today grow from seeds buried deeply in rich scientific soil, much of the richness of gerontology is fed by a vast and complex network of direct as well as indirect services provided the elderly. The practitioner, the planner, the administrator, the policymaker, the philosopher, the poet, the artist, too, take their stand right alongside the scientist within the domain of gerontology. And rightly understood, these constitute necessary elements and a source of strength for the study of aging in general. In order to understand what aging is all about for human beings, we need more than mere facts about aging. We need to remember the dictum of the gestaltists that the whole (of aging) is more than the mere sum of its parts. Victor Weisskopf, former head of the Department of Physics at MIT, has put the matter cogently and eloquently (1977):

A Beethoven sonata is a natural phenomenon that can be analyzed physically by studying the vibrations in the air; it can also be analyzed chemically, physiologically, and psychologically by studying the processes at work in the brain of the listener. However, even if these processes are completely understood in scientific terms, this kind of analysis does not touch what we consider relevant and essential in a Beethoven sonata—the immediate and direct impression of the music. In the same way, we can understand a sunset or the stars in the night sky in a scientific way, but there is something about experiencing these phenomena that lies outside science . . . There cannot be a scientific definition of . . . concepts like the quality of life or happiness. While it is certainly possible to analyze the nervous and psychological reactions that occur during the process of experiencing such ideas, there remains an important part of the experience that is not touched by this analysis . . . scientific results may not be the most relevant ones for human social problems and may even be counterproductive for the solution of these problems.

So while gerontology is scientific both in its conceptualizations and methodological approaches, the intrinsic value of its science will be considerably enhanced if its scientists, professional service providers, and nonscientists become more aware of the other ways of dealing with and understanding the aging process, such as through art, poetry, literature, and other forms of expression and impression, including the research strategy known as participant observation. The newcomer to gerontology needs to be assured that there are many roads to the understanding of aging and that the scientific mode should not be considered the only "serious" way of dealing with aging.

SUMMARY

Whether or not gerontology is to be considered a "new science" or traditional scientific methods applied to that growing segment of populations called the aged remains an open question. There is no question about the fact that the scientific method is making a major contribution to gerontology. This is an honor it shares with the gerontological clinician, planner, administrator, policymaker, and provider of direct services, professional and nonprofessional alike.

There is room in gerontology for the expressive arts as additional vehicles for deepening our understanding of the experience of aging, just as there is room in gerontology for developing new and less traditional research strategies, such as social indicators and studies of wisdom and creativity and autobiographical material. The increasing sensitivity of many others to the aging process and their growing collaboration in this field can only contribute materially to the depth and breadth of the science of gerontology.

REFERENCES

Birren, J., and V. Clayton. "History of Gerontology." In D. Woodruff and J. Birren (eds.), *Aging: Scientific Perspectives and Social Issues.* New York: D. Van Nostrand, 1975.

Carp, F. "The Realities of the Interdisciplinary Approach: Can the Disciplines Work Together to Help the Aged?." In A. Schwartz and I. Mensh (eds.), *Professional Obligations and Approaches to the Aged.* Springfield, Ill.: Charles C Thomas, 1974.

De Vries, H. "The Physiology of Exercise and Aging." In D. Woodruff and J. Birren (eds.), *Aging: Scientific Perspectives and Social Issues.* New York: D. Van Nostrand, 1975.

Haglund, R., and M. Schuckit. "A Clinical Comparison of Tests of Organicity in Elderly Patients." *Journal of Gerontology,* 1976, 31: 6.

Hoyer, W. J. "Application of Operant Techniques to the Modification of Elderly Behavior." *The Gerontologist,* 1973, 13:1.

Kallman, F., and L. Jarvik. "Individual Differences in Constitution and Genetic Background." In J. Birren (ed.), *Handbook of Aging and the Individual.* Chicago: The University of Chicago Press, 1959.

Kaplan, O., and R. Ontell. "Social Indicators and the Aging." In A. Schwartz and I. Mensh (eds.), *Professional Obligations and Approaches to the Aged.* Springfield, Ill.: Charles C Thomas, 1974.

Larson, R. "Thirty Years of Research on the Subjective Well-Being of Older Americans." *Journal of Gerontology,* 1978, 33:1.

Lindsley, O. R. "Geriatric Behavioral Prosthetics." In R. Kastenbaum (ed.), *New Thoughts on Old Age.* New York: Springer, 1964.

McCreary, C., and I. Mensh. "Personality Differences Associated with Age in Law Offenders." *Journal of Gerontology,* 1977, 32:2.

Mayer, J. "Aging and Nutrition." In S. Dreizen (ed.), "Symposium on Nutrition." *Geriatrics,* 1974, 29:5.

O'Brien, J., and G. Streib. *Evaluative Research on Social Programs for the Elderly.* AoA, DHEW Publication No. (OHD) 77-20120, Washington, D. C., 1977.

Rupprecht, P., J. Pyrek, and L. Snyder. "A Study of Wandering Among Old People in a Skilled Nursing Facility." Research report to NIMH, Grant 23924, Ebenezer Society, 2626 Park Ave., Minneapolis, Minn., 1976.

Schulz, J. "Pension Aspects of the Economics Aging: Present and Future Roles of Private Pensions." Special Report to Special Committee on Aging, US Senate, Washington, D.C., 1970.

Schwartz, A. "Designing Micro-environments for the Aged." In D. Woodruff and J. Birren (eds.), *Aging: Scientific Perspectives and Social Issues.* New York: D. Van Nostrand, 1975.

Synder, L., J. Pyrek, and C. Smith. "Vision and Mental Functioning of the Elderly." *The Gerontologist,* 1976, 16:6.

Solnick, R., and J. Birren. "Age and Male Erectile Responsiveness." *Archives of Sexual Behavior,* 1977, 6:1.

Storandt, M. "Age, Ability Level, and Method of Administering and Scoring the WAIS." *Journal of Gerontology*, 1977, 32:2.

Thomae, H. (ed.). *Patterns of Aging*. Vol. 3 of the Contributions to Human Development series, K. Riegel and H. Thomae (eds.). Basel, Switzerland: S. Karger, 1976.

Weisskopf, V. F. "The Frontiers and Limits of Science." *American Scientist,* 1977, vol. 65.

Wershow, H. "Reality Orientation for Gerontologists: Some Thoughts about Senility." *The Gerontologist*, 1977, 17:4.

Yung-Ping Chen. "Retirement Income Adequacy." In A. Schwartz and I. Mensh (eds.), *Professional Obligations and Approaches to the Aged*. Springfield, Ill.: Charles C Thomas, 1974.

FOR FURTHER READING

Eisdorfer, C., and M. Taves (eds.). "International Research and Education in Social Gerontology: Goals and Strategies." *The Gerontologist,* 1972,12:2.

Hendricks, J., and C. D. Hendricks. *Aging in Mass Society*. Cambridge, Mass.: Winthrop, 1977.

International Issue, *The Gerontologist*, 1975, 15:3.

Storandt, M., I. Siegler, and M. Elias, *The Clinical Psychology of Aging*. New York: Plenum, 1978.

Wallechinsky, D., I. Wallace, and A. Wallace. *The Book of Lists*. New York: William Morrow, 1977.

CHAPTER 12

Gerontology: Its Contributions and Prospects

By making imaginative use of change to channel change,
we can not only spare ourselves the trauma of future shock,
we can reach out and humanize distant tomorrows.

ALVIN TOFFLER, *Future Shock* (1971)

Some balance in understanding the "place" of gerontology in our society is useful. After studying the facts and conclusions that make up the bulk of the text, the student can use this chapter to consider where gerontology has gotten to and where it is going. The chapter can only summarily indicate at this introductory level the dimensions of gerontology's place and to what extent it represents a cutting edge in our society. If a career decision about gerontology is to be made, this chapter, along with the previous one, can help direct that decision-making process.

Not very long ago, an intriguing human interest story appeared in a major metropolitan newspaper—the Los Angeles *Times* (Rucker, 1978) —under this catchy headline: OFFICE SWEETHEART IS GOING STRONG AT 91.

275

Bessie Lyons, the person the story was about, was described as a diminutive, energetic woman who had been regularly employed since the age of sixteen, mostly in secretarial work. She had also been an insurance agent at one time and was once (during a World War II stint with Douglas Aircraft) even a member of the International Machinists' Union.

"When you work," Bessie was quoted as saying, "you don't have time for aches and pains."

Long after most people have retired, Bessie hired on as a secretary for a Los Angeles property management firm, and hadn't missed a day of work since. She first came to public attention on Valentine's Day 1974 (her 87th birthday), when she enjoyed the honor of being chosen the office valentine for her tireless efforts and persistent cheerfulness.

Her employer, himself seventy-five years old, is very proud of Bessie. He has boasted that she can type as fast as anyone and takes dictation about as fast as he can speak.

"She keeps this place rolling and has fun at the same time," her employer likes to say.

Bessie herself admits to gulping down vitamins every day, enjoys a drink now and then, and goes out at least three evenings a week. Bessie quite obviously continues to enjoy life. She firmly believes, and will tell anyone who asks, that keeping busy is the key factor.

By most standards, Bessie Lyons seems to be a prime example of that large group known as "successful agers"; they have also been referred to as "elite aged." These elderly are usually characterized as individuals who, beyond merely surviving, are able to maintain social contacts, pursue personal goals, and direct their own lives while achieving need satisfaction and enjoying life. Does gerontology contribute to successful aging? Does it go beyond theorizing, abstractions, data gathering, and statistical reports? In other words, does gerontology really produce practical benefits for the aged in our society? Furthermore, what are the prospects and portents for gerontology in its search for greater understanding of the aging process?

Admittedly, much of what follows in answer to these questions represents the authors' personal opinions. Yet they are based upon perceptions and perspectives influenced by a considered assessment of the materials gathered for this volume. They also reflect a total accumulation of over fifty years' personal experience in teaching, research, and writing about aging, as well as extensive clinical work with the aged.

Having reviewed the major substantive issues in gerontology, the student should now ask where gerontology has gotten to, look at its strengths and weaknesses, and inquire where it is likely to be going. One weakness in gerontology is inherent in every activity that strives to learn about the human condition: Much of the research and practice methodology remains at a primitive level. Researchers as well as practitioners still struggle with such basics as learning to ask the right questions. Indeed, the large amount of data already gathered about aging also serves to teach us how relatively little we do know. The field of gerontology as we know it today is still relatively young and the old cliché applies here: There is a long way to go. Most especially is this true for gerontologists and the larger society by way of translating accumulated knowledge and understanding into effective practice and relevant, appropriate service. What, then, are some of gerontology's contributions?

MULTIDISCIPLINARY EMPHASIS

Probably more than any other aspect, its focus on a multidisciplinary requirement may be said to be one of gerontology's major contributions to research and practice. As the material of the prior chapter clearly indicates, gerontology cuts across all areas of life. Gerontology's continuing holistic approach serves the "generalists" very well and helps the specialists in the field avoid undue fragmentation within research and service specialities. Both the generalist and the specialist, of course, have their appropriate place in gerontology as they do in other disciplines. Gerontology keeps insisting on the need to integrate a wide variety of interdisciplinary concerns and has achieved notable success in keeping the whole aged person firmly fixed at the center of a multidisciplinary emphasis.

Even a cursory review of any recent gerontological society program with its rich mixture of professionals and disciplines supports this argument. A partial listing of one such gerontological conference program is illustrative:

Programming in senior centers
Update on biological research on aging
Pre- and postretirement planning
Advocacy and the institutional church
Cultural differences among the aged
Practice of contemporary funeral services
Aging programs in rural areas
Crime and the elderly
Aging, fine arts, and the humanities
Dental services for the aged
Hospice programs
Preserving the past through oral history
Cognitive changes in old age
Media and attitude change

Evaluation research in gerontological programs
Issues in family help for the elderly
Environmental design for the aged
In-home support care

The inclusion of persons representing a wide variety of skills, expertise, knowledge, and experience in aging, as well as the efforts to interrelate on a broad spectrum of gerontological issues and concerns, points up the holistic approach now being discussed in medicine and yet generally championed by gerontologists. This multidisciplinary emphasis has served as an additional inducement for researchers, practitioners, policymakers, and funding agencies alike to identify those necessary linkages and interactions between many diverse factors involved in the aging process. This is a major contribution because the multidisciplinary emphasis best promises to serve the aged individual very well.

ATTENTION TO "SUCCESSFUL AGING"

The history of gerontology has been burdened with a preoccupation with the pathologies, deficits, and ills of a biased sample of elderly. During an earlier period most attention was given to sick aged, to those in hospitals, and to severely impaired institutionalized aged. The negative impressions of old age thus gained were further compounded by the use of inappropriate research and measurement methods.

Many of those negative impressions are now being successfully challenged. Gerontology can take substantial credit for its efforts in recent years to focus considerable attention on more positive aspects of aging: the capacities, strengths, skills, and potentials of persons in late maturity. It has uncovered systematic empirical data as well as many individual examples to demonstrate that Pablo Casals, Grandma Moses, George Burns, Bessie Lyons, and their like are not simply "exceptions to the rule." Aging remains a uniquely individual experience and successful aging equally so. Gerontologists can derive great satisfaction from the fact that they are in the vanguard of those leading our society to a more positive view of old age.

Such sentiments are very much encouraged by the unequivocal assertions of older individuals themselves: Ollie Randall, postoctogenarian founding member of the National Council on the Aging, has said, "If I have only one more day of life remaining, I still have a future." This is echoed by the eighty-year-old actress/model Judith Lowery.

"Age," she said, "is my greatest asset. My wrinkles are what get me my jobs. . . .I never sit in a rocking chair unless I am well paid for it." (*Modern Maturity,* 1971)

This shifting emphasis of attention from the pathologies of aging to successful aging is a most appropriate response to Abraham Heschel's unsettling comment made over two decades ago: "Enabling us to reach old age, medical science may think it gave us a blessing; however, we continue to act as if it were a disease" (Heschel, 1971). Based on a personal study of seventy-nine individuals between 87 and 103 years of age, a physician by the name of Jewett reported certain personality characteristics, traits, habit patterns, and heredity factors that he described as common to those long-living, successful agers (Jewett, 1973). These factors included moderate body size, relative freedom from accidents, investment in interesting activities, opportunity to be one's own "boss," good capacity to adapt to changing circumstances, having an appreciation for religious values, and having the capacity to enjoy life.

Pursuit of the notion of successful aging has enabled gerontologists to encourage others to open new doors of inquiry and to explore alternative ways of understanding and preparing for old age. Clues to successful aging, for example, are to be discovered in careful evaluation of the middle years, according to gerontologists (Greenleigh, 1974). Enriching the dialogue between the elderly and their middle-aged children is also strongly recommended by gerontologists as a useful stratagem for successful aging (Weinberg, 1974; Schwartz, 1977).

Attention to the ingredients of successful aging has also stimulated a renewed interest in the processes of creativity in the later years. Autobiographical journals and programmed reminiscing as approaches to the study of successful aging have uncovered procedures that are also showing indication of having potential therapeutic value for depressed elderly and those who have lost zest for living.

CONSCIOUSNESS RAISING

Although not part and parcel of gerontology's scientific and service activity, the sensitizing of the larger society to aging issues, facts, and concerns has turned out to be a contribution of major proportions and consequence. At the turn of this century the aged comprised a small percentage of the population. Societal interest in the aged, in terms of public policy or the provision of special services or even the recognition of the special needs of the old, was even smaller. There is no question but that that picture has radically changed.

No doubt that the lessons learned from the rise of certain social movements (including minority groups, women's liberation, civil rights) have contributed to the growing prominence of aging issues in our country. Nevertheless, the growth of research and practice in ger-

The findings of gerontology are helping to bring together the old and the young. A major contribution of gerontology is the demythologizing of the old for the young.

ontology and its own increasingly aggressive advocacy for the aged have focused national attention on this expanding segment of the population. Research in aging has provided substantial amounts of "ammunition" for such strong advocacy groups as AARP/NRTA, the National Council of Senior Citizens, the National Council on the Aging, and the Gray Panthers. Legislative bodies at all levels of government give not only increasing evidence of their sensitivity to the elderly as a special interest group but also somewhat more appreciation of the special needs of older persons. Governmental funding sources for training and demonstration projects have begun to show this.* None of this has occurred in a vacuum. Gerontologists from academia and from public and private organizations and agencies have played key roles in this growing tide of public awareness of aging.

*When Social Security and Medicare/Medicaid programs are taken into account, expenditures for the aged now constitute about one-third of the federal budget.

Again, gerontology has proved to be the major influence in encouraging (and sometimes demanding!) the communications media to avoid stereotypes, myths, and negative images of aging and to pay more attention to fact and to positive images. Much stereotyping still appears in newspapers, but gerontology's continued efforts do pay off. All the public communications media—newspapers, radio, and television —are also slowly but surely beginning to recognize gerontology as an important source of information. Articles on special issues concerned with aging appear with greater frequency in metropolitan dailies, such as the *New York Times* and Los Angeles *Times.* Many of these go well beyond mere listing of "senior citizens" activities and attempt to explore in some depth (or at least highlight) such substantive issues as the economic well-being of the elderly, housing, health, and pre- and post-retirement. Radio stations are airing discussions by experts in the field and carrying public service announcements of particular services for the aged.

Television continues to provide less than adequate programming for the elderly and most often presents the elderly in an inaccurate and demeaning manner. Gerontologists have provided the major stimulus for more acceptable programming for the aged and for those TV shows that have done justice to the old. One such pioneer in the field of TV gerontology is Richard Davis at the University of Southern California. Through negotiations with the Sears Foundation, through collaboration and production consultation with major networks and individual producers of movies and television programs, he has been instrumental in the successful production of such exemplary films and TV specials as "Peege," "Portrait of Grandpa Doc," and the *Use It Or Lose It* educational series.

Intensive efforts via formal and informal gerontology programs to increase public awareness and sensitivity have begun to affect major societal institutions and industry. Educational institutions have begun to design curricula to attract elderly students. Methods of instruction, grading criteria, and the accessibility and physical location of instructional offerings are beginning to take the special needs of older persons into account. The same can be said of religious organizations.

Medical schools and other professional training schools are giving some evidence of responsiveness to the need for specialized training in gerontology. Corporations are taking much more seriously their responsibility for assisting older workers to plan and prepare for their later years. A growing body of research literature in the field of architecture and environmental design dealing with barrier-free, prosthetic environments for the elderly is testimony to the growing sensitivity to the special environmental needs of the elderly. Environmental design is now understood to be not merely the background "scenery" of daily living. Environmental characteristics rather are recognized as often making the difference between competence and incompetence, growth and decline, for older persons.

While such designs are widely applicable for the aged across many settings (in many instances, relevant to all ages), the gerontological focus has begun to have important and encouraging effects upon long-term-care institutions, and particularly on nursing homes. In spite of the good sense that special design concepts make (strong use of environmental cues, stimulation, and support), in spite of the evident necessity for such designs, it is unfortunate that the nature of public funding for institutions strongly inhibits its more widespread utilization (Tiberi et al., 1978).

Nonetheless, gerontology continues to be the soil in which new and more appropriate environmental design concepts for the elderly flourish. The national Gerontological Society over the past several years has served as a clearinghouse for architectural design and urban environmental planning. This project, under the direction of Thomas Byerts and a steering committee made up of professionals in the field, has developed agenda and workshops for environmental designers and planners, has collected research data, developed curricula intended for introduction at colleges and universities, and produced a number of monographs and books on the subject. These efforts represent a major step forward and are a credit to those gerontologists who have tried to integrate gerontological research and practice.

GERONTOLOGY AND SPECIAL PROGRAMS

Many of the well-established programs in America that directly involve the aged and provide significant benefits for them are directly attributable to or associated with the growth of the science and practice of gerontology. The Foster Grandparents Program (only an older person can, by definition, be a foster grandparent), the Meals-on-Wheels and other nutrition/social programs, day activities centers and multi-service centers for seniors, Retired Senior Volunteer Program (enlisting a corps of elderly who contact the homebound, so-called invisible aged), "40-Plus" and "50-Plus" programs (which seek to place older persons in second and third careers), the DOVE program (older volunteers dedicated to encouraging educational opportunities for oldsters), as well as the Gray Panthers, headed by Maggie Kuhn, the various "helpline" and telephone reassurance programs, counseling programs for the elderly and their families, and the SAGE project in San Francisco, which emphasizes a combination of good nutrition, exercise, yoga and meditation, and other free-form activities to en-

The use of television to provide information, as a motivational tool, and as a method of assessment is another "frontier" that gerontologists are beginning to explore.

hance well-being for the aged, are examples of the pragmatic outcomes to which gerontology has contributed consistently and creatively.

If it appears to even the most casual reader that many additional contributions of gerontology could be specified and much more could be said about them, it should be acknowledged that what has been presented is only the tip of the iceberg. Additional familiarity with gerontology will inevitably reveal the rich complexity of the contributions gerontology has made and is making to the aged and to the broad spectrum of society along many lines. Gerontology cuts across every dimension of life and in so doing leaves its imprint. Gerontologists find themselves within traditional, even ancient, streams of human concern. Yet because they are in a very real sense pioneering in a "new" field of endeavor, they experience all the provocative sense of high drama and excitement in being on the "cutting edge."

In this manner gerontology's persistent efforts to enlarge public perspectives and raise public sensitivity to aging issues and needs have generated a major positive impact. Not every conclusion about aging presented by gerontology has been widely accepted without debate. But the process has introduced a strong element of advocacy into gerontology. And this, we believe, is an important contribution.

PROSPECTS AND PORTENTS

Although no claim to special insights is made by the authors, we think it is useful to describe for the newcomer to gerontology what we believe gerontology's future directions and prospects may be.

An introduction to gerontology, as to any discipline or body of knowledge, requires a reasonably comprehensive representation as well as accurate portrayal of the field. At the same time, it is necessary to avoid getting bogged down in details and technicalities so specific as to be of interest primarily to the more advanced student or experienced specialist. Any person fairly new to this field, having gone through the contents of this text, will surely appreciate that our excursion into gerontology can very well be likened to that of the novice traveler who visits as many foreign countries as possible on the first time-limited journey. First impressions no doubt reveal that there is much to be seen and heard, much to be learned, and much to be savored and understood. If the novice traveler has an adequate guide he will likely come away with some new perspectives, some sense of the size, shape, boundaries, "climate," and flavor of the places visited. But as a first-time visitor he cannot yet have the fullest sense of the nuances or familiarity with the nooks and crannies of those places in the same way as the longtime resident or experienced traveler.

The analogy is appropriate to this introductory text. Just as with most professions or disciplines, the study of gerontology encompasses much more than digging up bits of information about aging, even though that, too, has its own rewards. The study of gerontology, like the study of law, social work, medicine, engineering, or psychology, has essentially very pragmatic goals. Built into it is the assumption that what we learn about aging through research and practice will be translated into further research on the frontiers of aging. What we come to learn and understand about aging will also be applied to practice which serves the needs of society and betters the lives of those in their middle and later years. The assumption is also that what we learn will directly and indirectly improve the prospects for life satisfaction of the growing number of those who will survive into late maturity.

TASKS FACING GERONTOLOGY

Minorities

We can expect gerontology to give increased attention in the years ahead to the varied groups of ethnic aged, those "invisible" elderly who are a minority within a minority. Samoan, Philippine, Korean,

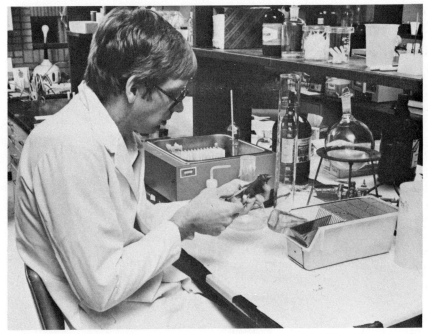

Much of the basic scientific research on aging is done with laboratory animals. Endocrinological research is one of the important directions that aging research will be taking in the future.

Japanese, Puerto Rican, and American Indian elderly are among those who fit within this group. One can expect gerontology, especially social gerontologists, to help us learn more about and understand better whatever variations in the aging process exist within such minority groups. We can also expect increased funding and more sophisticated and effective programs of service to such aged.

Clinical Activities

Just as with clinical psychology during the years following World War II, the increasing public demand for clinical services for the aged is already in evidence. A movement is gaining momentum in gerontology to interest and train clinical psychologists in clinical assessments of the aged and to provide individual and group counseling, therapeutic and behavior modification programs, and consultation. It seems very likely, too, that the growth of such activities will stimulate a comparable professional investment on the part of the legal profession, nurse practitioners, and the training of even greater numbers of paraprofessional peer counselors of the elderly and their families.

Training/Education

Along with this we can certainly expect to see a much stronger commitment to training at all levels. Whereas only a few years ago a mere handful of schools of any kind offered courses related to aging, over 1,240 colleges and universities across the country now offer some kind of training in gerontological subjects. We expect that the greatest growth in training programs in gerontology will occur in certain pre-professional schools such as schools of nursing and psychology and in religious seminaries. Undoubtedly a substantial increase in gerontological coursework will be seen in community college systems and specialized training for staff of a great many existing agencies and organizations.

Coordination and Prevention

We can expect gerontologists to join hands with other service providers and administrators who now insist that the proliferation of aging-oriented programs requires more careful comprehensive planning, better integration and coordination of a wide variety of services, more casework supervision and stronger advocacy. Information and referral has been a necessary element in the provision of services across the board to the elderly. But it has also pointed up much overlapping, redundancy, and far too many gaps in the actual delivery of services.

Along with this, we can certainly expect a greater focus of attention on prevention. Prevention of disabilities in old age, whether by emphasis on good nutrition, exercise, and more congenial environments to forestall physical decline or by reduction of undue stress factors to prevent emotional crippling, will surely be given the primary attention it deserves. Even now, gerontology clearly recognizes that the proper emphasis on individual attention and caring will serve to provide the balance to technology where at least the aged are concerned.

Public Policy

We can anticipate that gerontology will move steadily into an increasingly influential role in public policy and legislation affecting the aged. In many arenas public policy vis-à-vis the aged remains at best uncertain, ambiguous, and even problematic. Many legislative decisions affecting the aged appear to ignore basic research and available information on aging. Public policy and legislation governing the conduct and evaluation of long-term care (nursing homes) is a case in point. Much of the legislation affecting the lives of institutionalized aged is inappropriate and in some instances irrelevant. Gerontology will undoubtedly address itself to these issues with increasing candor and vigor.

It is our hope as well as our view, then, that gerontology can be seen as having a bright future and challenging prospects. For the next couple of decades, at the very least, gerontology will be in a period of internal growth and external expansion.

As the newcomer to gerontology catches some of the excitement in this relatively new and pioneering enterprise, as he increases knowledge and enhances skills, he will develop familiarity with the many aspects and "faces" of aging. Surely he will also come to appreciate more fully how closely intertwined scientific perspectives and social issues in aging really are.

REFERENCES

Greenleigh, L. "Facing the Challenge of Change in Middle Age." *Geriatrics,* November 1974.

Heschel, A. J. *To Grow in Wisdom.* New York: Synagogue Council of America, 1971.

Jewett, S. P. "Longevity and the Longevity Syndrome." *The Gerontologist,* 1973, 13:1.

Modern Maturity, June–July 1971.

Rucker, S. "Office Sweetheart Is Going Strong at 91." *Los Angeles Times,* February 13, 1978.

Schwartz, A. *Survival Handbook for Children of Aging Parents.* Chicago: Follett, 1977.

Tiberi, D., A. Schwartz, I. Hirschfield, and P. Kerschner. "Correlates of the Medical and Psychosocial Models of Long-Term Care." Presented at the XI International Congress of Gerontology, Tokyo, Japan, 1978.

Weinberg, J. "What Do I Say to My Mother When I Have Nothing to Say?" *Geriatrics,* November 1974.

FOR FURTHER READING

Kaplan, J. "Social Planning: A Continuing Challenge." *The Gerontologist,* 1970, 10:4.

Kirtin, H., and R. Morris. "Alternatives to Institutional Care of the Elderly and Disabled." *The Gerontologist,* 1972, 12:2.

Knopf, O. *Successful Aging.* New York: Viking Press, 1975.

Linn, M., and L. Carmichael. "Introducing Pre-professionals to Gerontology." *The Gerontologist,* 1974, 14:6.

Mensh, I. "Community Mental Health and Other Health Services for the Aged." In C. Eisdorfer and M. P. Lawton (eds.), *The Psychology of Adult Development and Aging.* Washington, D.C.: American Psychological Association, 1973.

Pressey, S., and A. Pressey. "Genius at 80 and Other Oldsters." *The Gerontologist,* 1967, 7:3.

Weg, R. "Concepts in Education and Training for Gerontology: New Career Patterns." *The Gerontologist,* 1973, 13:4.

Indexes

Name Index

Subject Index